MW01618423

RIGHT BRAIN PHOTOGRAPHY

BE AN ARTIST FIRST

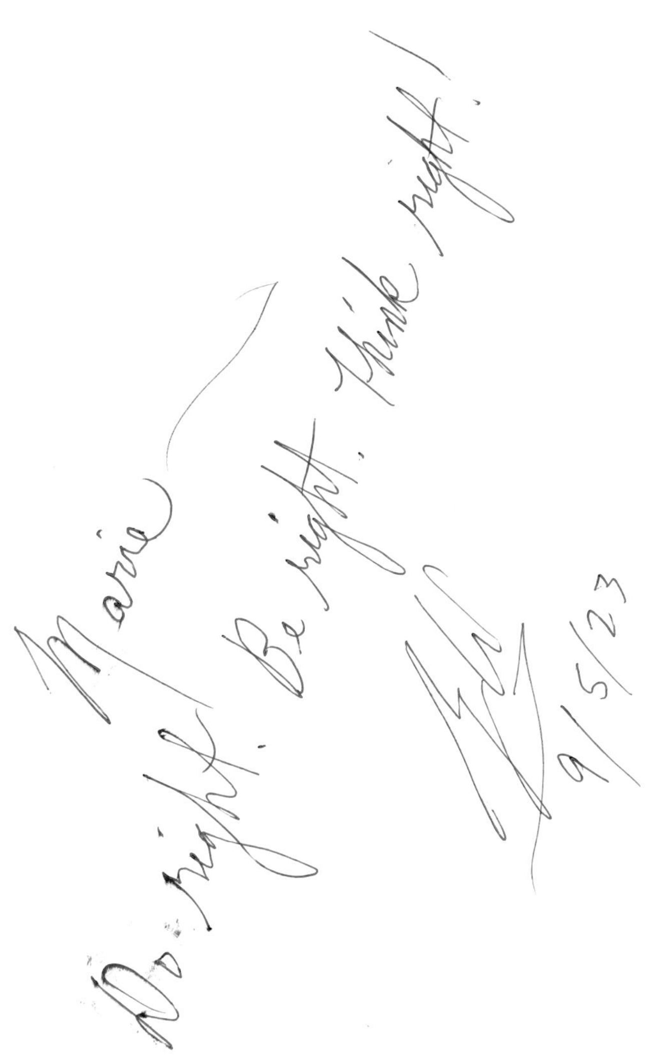

The best photography is found where technical know-how and creative aesthetics meet.

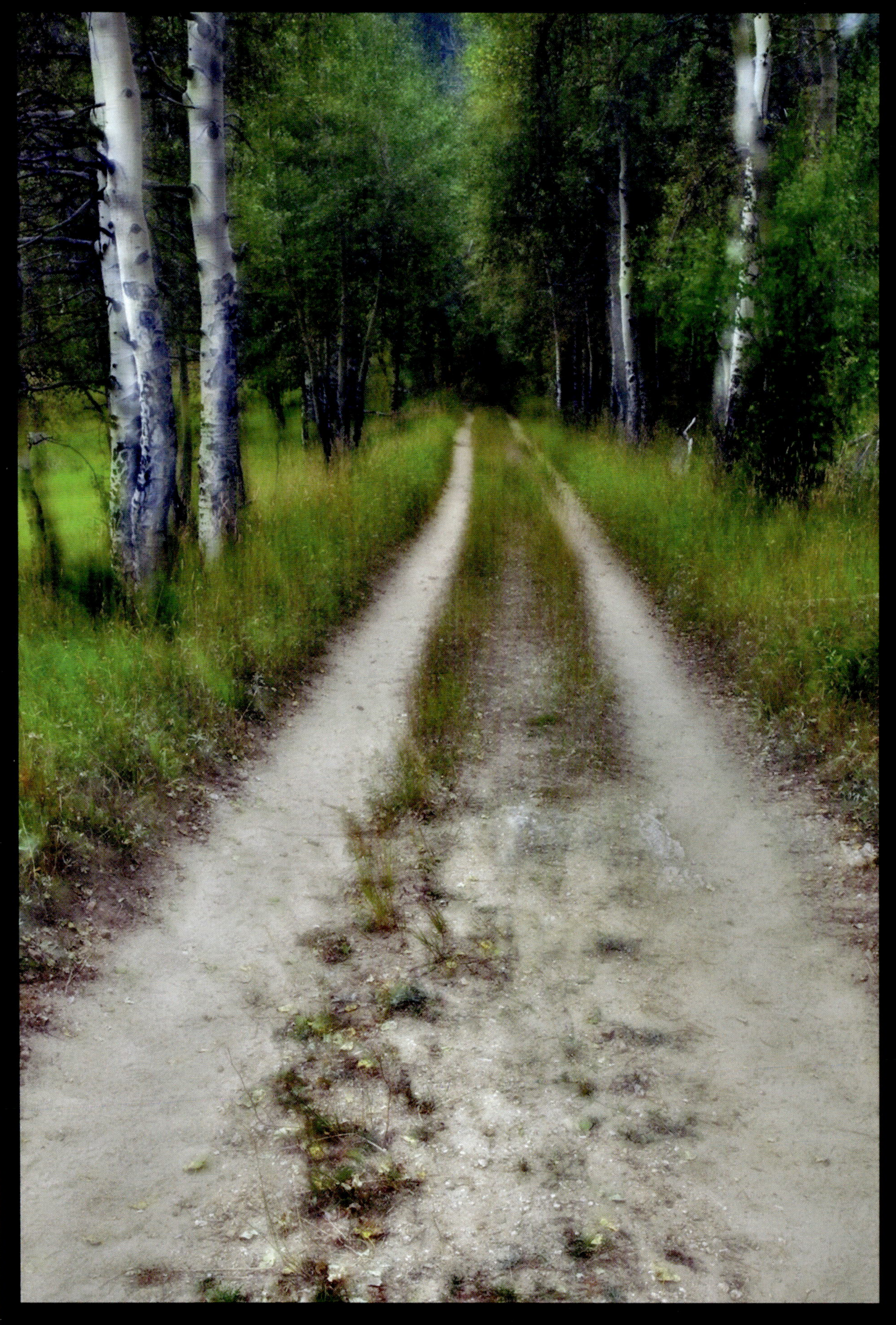

RIGHT BRAIN PHOTOGRAPHY

BE AN ARTIST FIRST

Eli Vega, Photo Artist

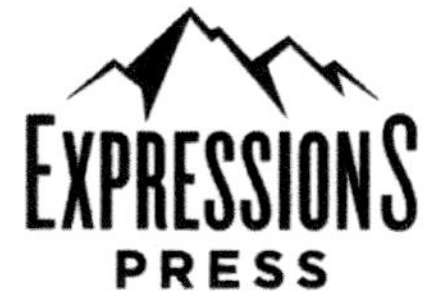

Front & back cover design by Rico Vega

ISBN 978-0-692-36543-4

Published by Expressions Press

Fourth Edition

Printed in the U.S.A.

Front cover: Garden of The Gods, Colorado Springs, CO. Five minute exposure. Technique used was "painting with light," using two off-road emergency flashlights.

ABOUT THE AUTHOR

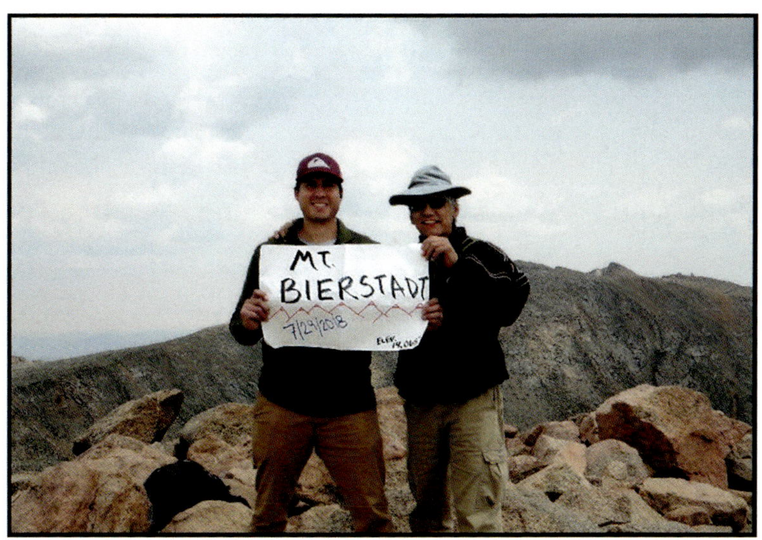

Eli and son Rico atop one of Colorado's 14ers (over 14,000')

Eli was born in a railroad boxcar, of poor migrant Spanish-speaking parents, in Kane, Wyoming. He knew little English during his formative years, except for a few basic phrases. Not surprisingly, he failed first grade because of that language barrier. It was that humble and daunting start in life that forced his creativity to surface and develop some unimaginable survival skills during his youth. His early life circumstances, out of necessity, required a high degree of creative coping skills.

By the time he was in second grade, his creative juices had found their way into his little mind and hands. He was already drawing colorful and detailed blue jays and cardinals. He was known throughout his school years as a good artist. His family's local Catholic priest was quietly taking notice. He later convinced Eli to attend college and major in art. The thought of going to college frightened Eli. The idea alone was like being asked to go to the moon. He didn't even know what a college major was, but the word "art" caught his attention.

Eli majored in art for three years at South Plains College, and Texas Tech University in Lubbock, Texas. Although he did not get a degree, those three years exposed him to several internationally renowned painters like Cezanne, Renoir, Rembrandt, Monet, Van Gogh, Marcel Duchamp, Albrecht Durer, Picasso, and Salvador Dalí. The two art movements that resonated with him most were Impressionism and Surrealism.

Eli made two friends in college who were novice photographers. One of them had a darkroom in his mother's basement, which triggered silent curiosity within Eli. His other friend, also an art major, was always toying with his camera. Those two life-changing friendships made an indelible impression on him. It was no surprise that he soon thereafter started fiddling around with simple Polaroid cameras, the kind that would produce pictures within seconds.

It was during that period that the combination of Eli's exposure to art and his interest in photography began taking shape. Even with a simple Polaroid camera he would experiment by holding an empty roll of toilet paper in front of the lens just to see what he could create. His future in photography, unbeknownst to him, was in its embryonic stages.

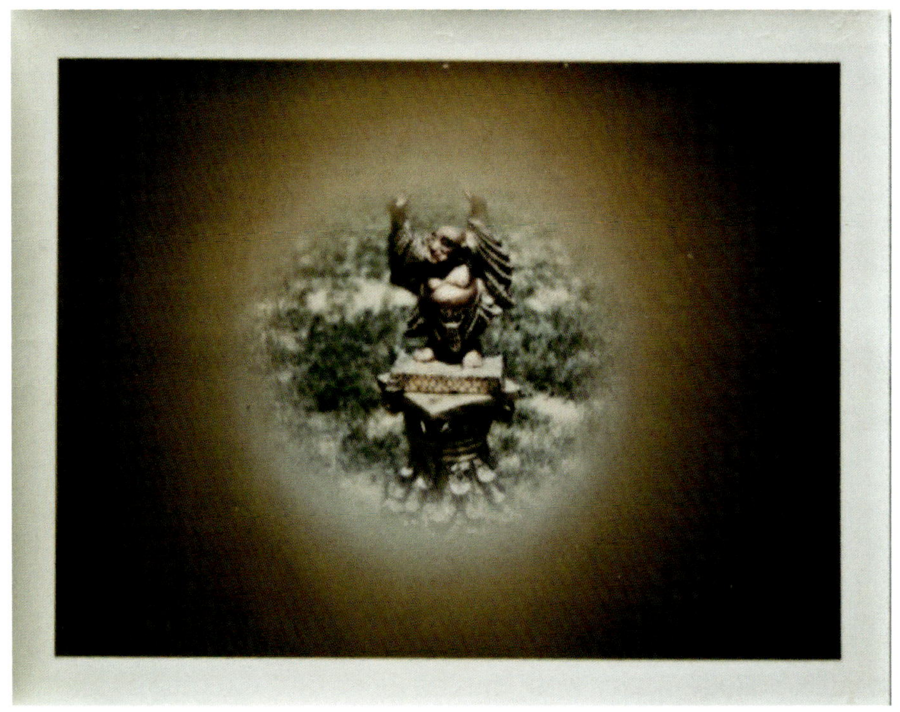

"Little Man," photographed by Eli through a toilet paper roll.
Taken with a Land Polaroid instant film camera

June 7, 1971

Fast forwarding the picture about fifteen years, Eli bought his first high-end 35mm camera, a Canon A-1 film camera. He still owns a body and two compatible lenses to this day. One of his current and best-liked images, of aspens in autumn in Colorado, was created with a Canon A-1 and Tamron lens, in 2008, years after the advent of digital photography.

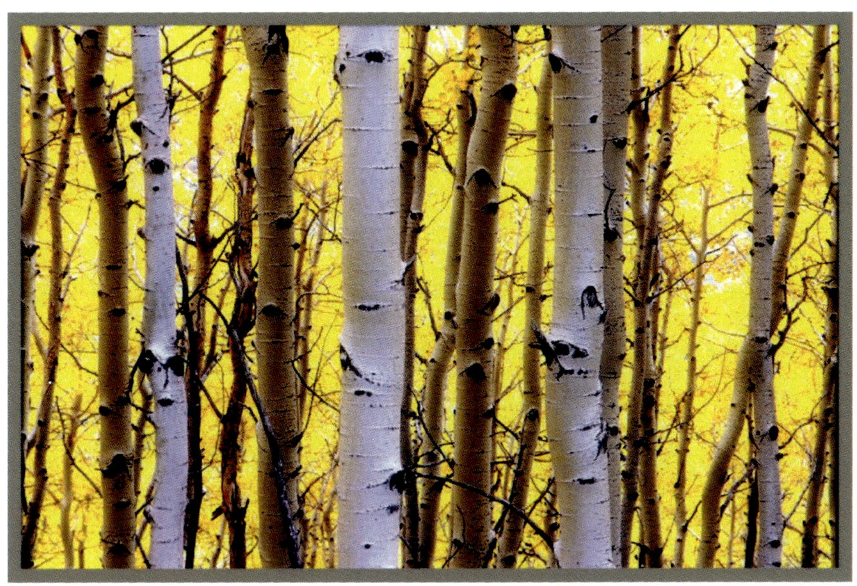

"*Owl Creek Pass Aspens*" 2008, with an old Canon A-1

Eli was in the middle of his former career in Human Resources and living in Fort Worth, Texas in 1986 when he joined the Fort Worth camera club, with his new Canon toy in hand. During that time, he read every photography book in the Fort Worth library, used up a lot of film while experimenting with his newly discovered passion, and took copious notes. It was just six months after joining the camera club that independent judges were awarding him first, second, or third place honors for his art. Only a year after joining the camera club, he started selling his first photos in his spare time.

By 1993, seven years after he started getting serious with photography, Eli started teaching his first photography classes in Dallas, Texas. Facilitating the learning process was easy for him. His specialty in Human Resources was Learning and Development. He had already designed and facilitated several HR workshops, including Time Management and Leadership Development. Four years before he taught his first photography course, he received his certification as a workshop facilitator, obtained through a one-week certification course.

The combination of three years as an art major in college, his HR training background, and his involvement with the Fort Worth Camera club began shaping Eli's photographic philosophy, approach to photography as an art form, as well as his photography teaching methods. He was well on his way to creating right brain photography and teaching others how to do it.

Eli lived in Colorado and for now is based out of picturesque Eureka Springs, Arkansas. He offers photography classes and field workshops in Arkansas, Colorado, and other locales. In addition to his classes and workshops, he facilitates small group and 1-on-1 field lessons and offers educational slide presentations to local camera clubs and other art groups. Camera clubs often ask him to serve as judge for their monthly competitions.

In addition to his photography instruction, Eli is an award-winning and highly published photographer. His work has been published in vacation magazines, travel guides, calendars, postcards, brochures, and other publications.

Eli gets a lot of fulfillment when he offers free slide shows to independent and assisted living communities. It's his way of giving back to those who no longer have the luxury of seeing the beauty our earth has to offer.

"You can't use up creativity. The more you use, the more you have." Maya Angelou

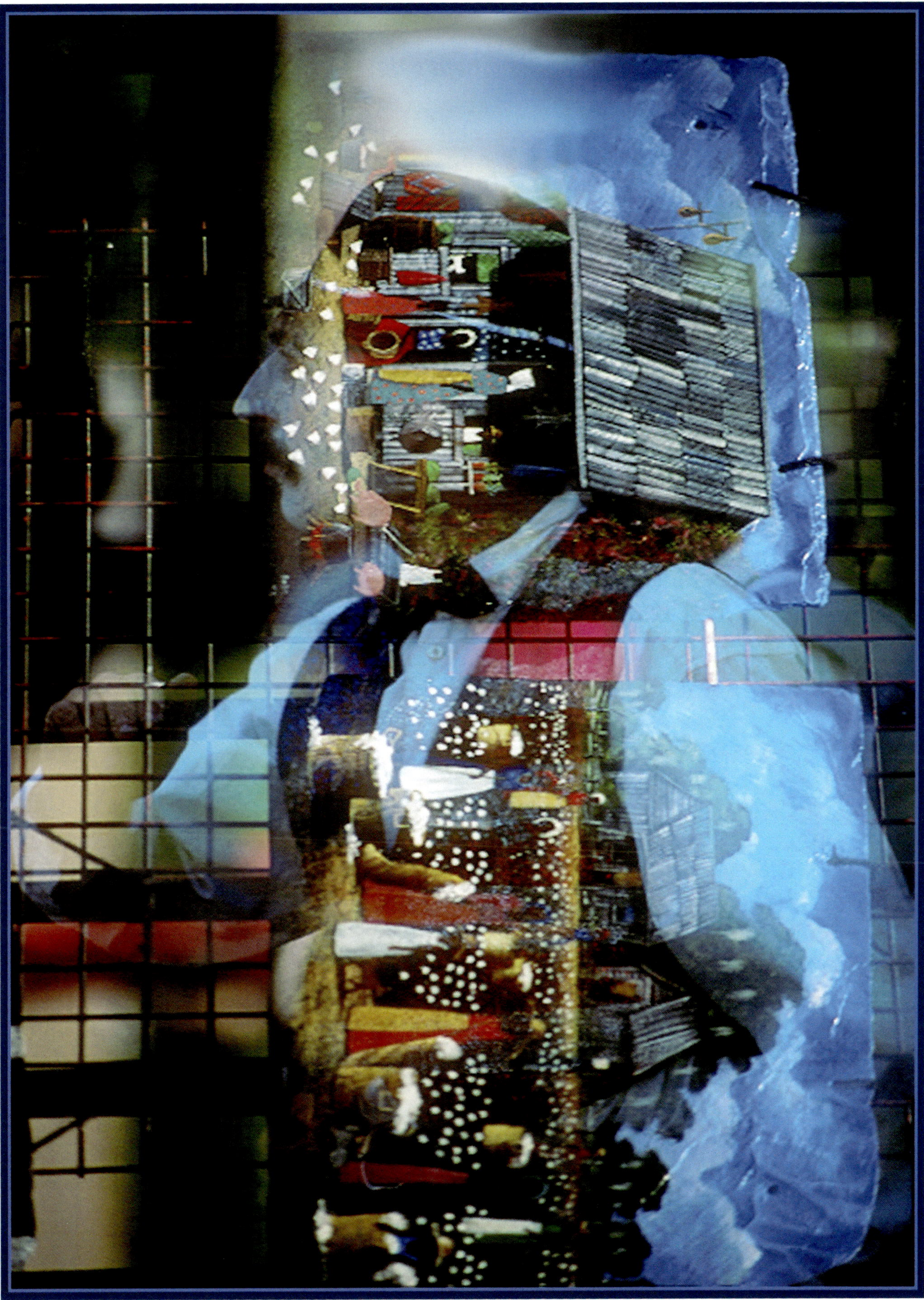

CONTENTS

DEDICATION

To my grand kiddos, Carson, Nicolas, & Joaquín. May you read this book and stare at my photo art someday. My hope is that my book will make you, your generation and those to follow, realize that photography is more than just taking pictures—it is an art form.

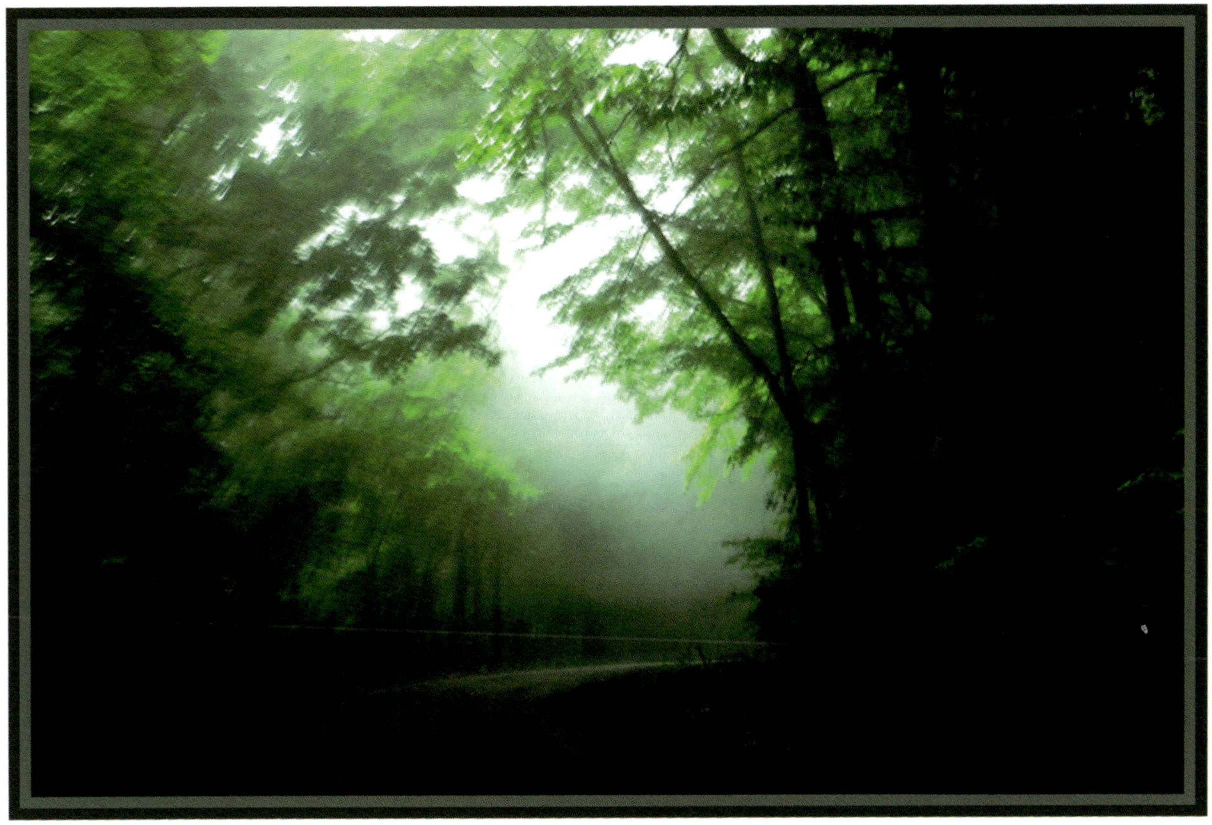

"County Road 306"

ACKNOWLEDGMENTS

I thank all my former students. Your kind and positive feedback inspired me to expand my efforts and continue to teach, touch and inspire others through my photo art.

Thanks to Tom and Gail Isikyan, Louis Brad, Chris Roth, and Jack Zivic in Colorado for your most valuable input. Your comments helped me with the design of *Right Brain Photography*.

Thanks to Peggy Williams, who attended my photography classes at Front Range Community College in Westminster, Colorado. Your positive testimonial resulted in my offering two 3-day photography workshops in Rocky Mountain National Park.

Jeff Hershberger, my part-time assistant, for being curious about my photography. You often ask me, "How did you do that?" It is that kind of questioning that keeps me thinking crazy and wildly. You, more than anyone else, heard me say over and over again, "I see something."

Thanks to my good friend Andrew Smith for saying, "Your photography is like visual poetry." Your comment helped me to keep rhyming.

Thanks to my sister Eva, who once asked me, "How do you make your photography talk?"
I didn't know I could do that.

Thank you Ron Buckner (B-6), bass player for Buckner Funken Jazz in Denver. My image of your bass will help me teach photo enthusiasts and professionals alike.

Thank you Cindy Kirby for your attention to detail. Your editing skills helped me enhance the way my words sound on paper.

I thank Kim Larson-Cooney at Arapahoe Community College in Littleton, Colorado for giving me the first opportunity to offer Right Brain Photography as a classroom course in 2011.
I later expanded that class into a 3-day workshop at Rocky Mountain National Park and Garden of The Gods. The third metamorphic stage was this book.

PREFACE—WHY I WROTE THIS BOOK

This book is a written companion to my current offerings of Right Brain Photography classes and workshops. I offer both 8-hour classroom courses and my popular 3-day field workshops in Rocky Mountain National Park near Estes Park and my 5-day workshop at the Eureka Springs School of the Arts. My purpose for writing this book is the same as my purpose for offering classes and workshops on right brain photography—to encourage photographers to use their imaginations and cameras to create photo art. Imaginative thinking and creativity, before we go “click,” seems to be a dying art today.

I am self-taught, having learned photography mostly through reading, practice, practice, and more practice. I distinguish between learning photography and learning photography post processing. Everything I learned about photography was during film days, with an emphasis on available light photography. I had no monitors to preview my results—I had to get it as right as possible, without a preview! Instead of menu items to set in a computer-like camera, I had the choice of filters and films for different situations and lighting scenarios. I also learned in-camera improvisations and short cuts that helped me improve my images.

We did not have the in-camera technical advancements that allowed us to adjust the film’s ISO or adjust for different light temperatures. Today, we can change our ISO from 100 to 800 or higher and still get great images. We can make in-camera adjustments based on the temperature of available light sources. We are not using a different language, just different vocabulary. Examples include “noise” (we called it “grain”) and “white balance”--we called it light temperatures, like the Kelvin temperatures of fluorescent and tungsten lighting. Without all these convenient advancements, we had to become good photographers.

As a result, it was critical for me to learn key photography principles and concepts. Among them were composition, f/stops and depth of field, selective focusing, different types of light metering, in-camera exposure compensation, and several creative in-camera special effects. I learned to actually “paint” with light or use light to “paint.” I discovered the creation of in-camera multiple exposures.

I sold my first in-camera double exposure image as a postcard in the late 1980s. I called it "Heroes of The Alamo."

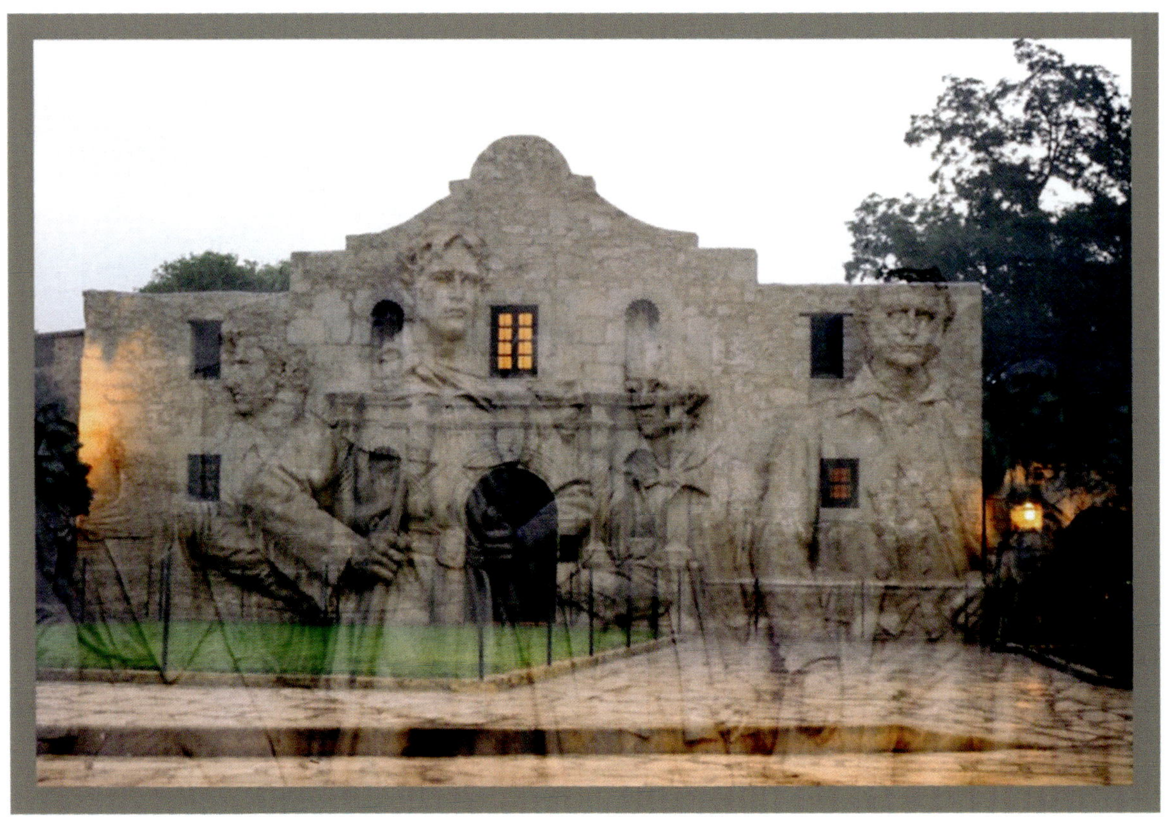

I learned how to get the most out of my camera. At times, I had to convince my camera that it could do things it didn't think it could do. For example, if I wanted to take an interior photo of a church, with ISO 100 film, sometimes it was so dark that my camera talked back to me. It told me, "I can't take this photo. I can only go to 30 seconds, and I need more light or more time, but I'm not sure how much time I need beyond 30 seconds." My solution was to simply change the ISO setting beyond 100 until I got a reading. If I finally got a light reading at, say, ISO 800 and it was for 20 seconds, I simply did the math--800 divided by 100 gave me 8. Therefore, 20 seconds times 8 equals 160. I would, therefore, need 160 seconds at ISO 100, or almost three minutes, to get that shot. I then bracketed around that "ballpark." I did just that for an abbey in Arkansas. When I showed the image to one of the priests who wanted to use the image, he asked me, "How many flashes did you use?"

Additionally, I learned all the tricks I could pull from my zoom lenses. I would zoom in, zoom out, or move the camera up or down while zooming. I learned how to convert backgrounds into backdrops by focusing manually and using selective focusing to add more blur to the backgrounds. I still use all those techniques today with digital photography. They are still as applicable today, and necessary to create what I want.

Let's not forget my art days, mostly at Texas Tech University. I learned about oil painting, charcoal, watercolor, pencil, pen and ink, and acrylic. What I learned from using those mediums was different ways with which I could interpret life, what I saw, and what I didn't see. The French impressionists taught me that not everything had to be perfectly detailed in order to create feelings and moods. The surrealists taught me to de-program my mind from the confines of what I thought to be true or even real.

It appears to me, from what I see and read today, that a lot of photographers with digital cameras have forgotten, or never learned, how to create their photography by using their cameras. It is as if photography, for them, is what they can do on their computers. Some have relegated control over camera to control over software.

So, to summarize, my creativity comes partly from my early days of trying to find ways to survive. My photography is rooted in my art days in college. In order to create my photo art, I had to learn what this gadget called a camera was capable of doing. I even devised ways to paint with it, which camera engineers did not originally have in mind. In college, I saw art students and instructors use the handle tip of their brushes to paint; to add a little accent to their paintings. It wasn't the paint brushes that created art; it was what the painters did with them that created art. This is also true of my photography. I need a good camera, just like a painter needs good brushes, but I, not the camera, create my images. If I have failed in doing that, not even the best photo editing software can create what I failed to see.

When I learned that the word "photography" comes from a Greek word that means "painting with light," I knew I was on the right path to creating what I now call my photo art. I guess you could say I am an artist with a camera. For me, photography is more art than science.

Right Brain Photography is not about the basics of how to photograph—I do that in my other classes. Learning about f/stops, shutter speeds, lenses, RAW, megabytes, histograms, and what software to use is primarily what the left brain needs to know. I wrote *Right Brain Photography* to encourage you to use your intuition and to see with your mind's eye. It is not even about *taking* great pictures. It is about learning how to use your magination to create images. Start with your right brain to imagine what your images might look like, to translate your feelings into those images, or to convey a message through your images. Then, have your right brain shake hands with your left brain and say, "Hey. I've got an idea, and this is what I need from you." I encourage you to get creative enough to make your camera do what you want it to do. Right Brain Photography will help you become a better photo artist in the field, not a better photo software user.

"When it comes right down to it, the secret of having it all is loving it all." Dr. Joyce Brothers

INTRODUCTION

One day, while in one of my many contemplative moods, I was thinking of all the comments I have received about my photography from students, peers, friends, and relatives. Several comments came to mind, which include the following.
"How do you make your photographs talk?"
"Your photography is like visual poetry."
"Your photographs look more like paintings."

I never thought of my photographs in quite those ways, but it made me wonder that if some people saw my photography that way, maybe others did too. I asked myself, "What *do* I do? How do I create my images?" Those questions, I have to admit, were not easy to answer. That thinking process took me back to my days in Human Resources when I asked job incumbents, "Tell me. What do you do?" I would get blank stares. When we do the same thing over and over for several years, we don't think about it too much. We just do it. For me, after over twenty years, everything I do with my photography has become second nature and subconsciously intuitive.

After forcing myself to answer my own questions, I started getting flashbacks to my college art days, the watercolors I created, Surrealism, and Impressionism. My forced self-analysis, which is not exactly a right brain process, also made me think about my readings in eastern philosophy, a topic that has intrigued me since 1998.

As I continued the introspective process over several weeks, I began thinking of a comment I make frequently when in the middle of my photo shoots, which is, "I see something," a statement my students and others often hear me say.

One day in late autumn, I invited my part-time assistant to go with me to Rocky Mountain National Park in Colorado. I had some ideas as to what I wanted. As we approached nearby Estes Park, I could tell that what I was hoping for was not coming together for me. I told him, "The sky is not right. The fall colors are gone. I'm not going to get the reflections I want. But, you know me, I'll find something." He quickly replied, "Yes, I know." I did.

I saw this that dreary gray day. Later in the book I will talk about the creation of this image and the importance of taking off the labels we assign to everything in life.

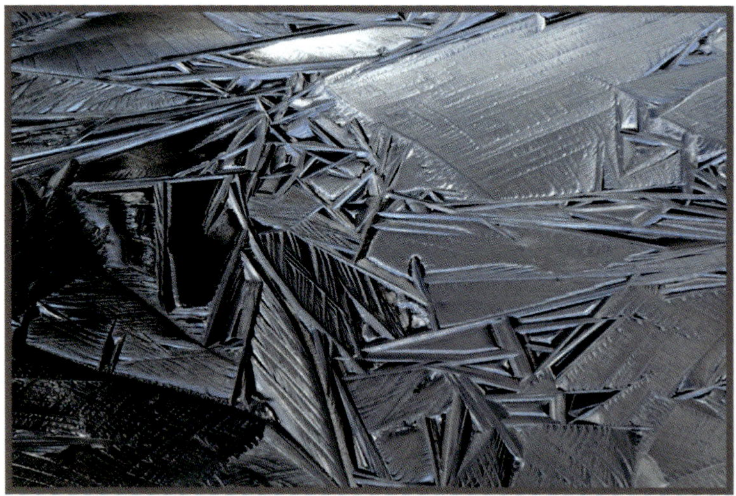

Now, back to what *Right Brain Photography* is all about. After I had put a lot of thought behind why and how I photograph the way I do, I started translating the building blocks that had always been a part of me. Clarity eventually evolved from my weeks of self-analysis, which led to the creation of my three photography models, or paradigms, which I introduce in my *Right Brain Photography* workshops. These three building blocks came together for me after working backward; after hovering above myself to see what I did with my photography.

The following are my three photography models.
I.S.E.E. SOMETHING™
ELI'S 5-POINT PHOTO ART MODEL™
THE PHOTO IMAGE CREATION PROCESS™

The world around us, especially when we look out at it with camera in hand, can seem very chaotic. It's too busy; too much stuff out there to see. Where do we start? The information I will share here will help you to artistically rearrange that world chaos. In this book, I will go into detail about each of my three models/paradigms. For each one, I will include thorough explanations and descriptions and share some of my images that relate to each model.

Additionally, I will challenge your right brain by giving you some assignments for you to try on your own. I encourage you to take the challenge presented by those assignments—it will help you exercise your right brain.

The three models I use are not independent of each other. There is some overlap and they all "feed" off each other. Although I treat them separately in this book, when I'm out in the field, they quickly merge. There is a thin line between them during actual application.

But wait. There's more! Several students have taken my Right Brain Photography workshops and classes. I have asked some of them to share with you what *they* have created by applying some of my Right Brain Photography concepts. You will get to see what they have created with their right brains. Some of the examples were well-planned by the artist; others were more intuitive or spontaneous.

Speaking of students, here are a few comments from students who have taken my Right Brain Photography workshops.

"I like the way you explain and show examples. I will talk warmly about this course."
"This was a wonderful learning adventure for me. My confidence & knowledge of photography as art have grown so much."
"This was amazing!
"You didn't make me feel stupid."
"Instructor enjoys teaching and sticks with the student <u>very patiently</u> until the student gets it."

My photography has evolved throughout the years. If you had asked me ten years ago what kind of photographer I am, I would have answered, "Landscape photographer." Today, although I still gravitate toward landscape and nature photography, I call myself a "life" photographer—I can find art in almost anything I see and experience.

Get ready to think outside the box that's *outside* the box. When you finish reading this book, you will understand why.....

> I am an artist first, photographer second

> I don't see with my eyes; I see with my imagination

> I see something before I see it

> I like to make the common uncommon, and the sane insane

Enjoy.

SECTION I

START WITH THE END IN MIND

Before I share the first of my three photography models with you, I want to massage your mind by showing you a few images. I won't say a word about them. Just look at them, think, wonder, and let your curiosity and imagination begin churning.

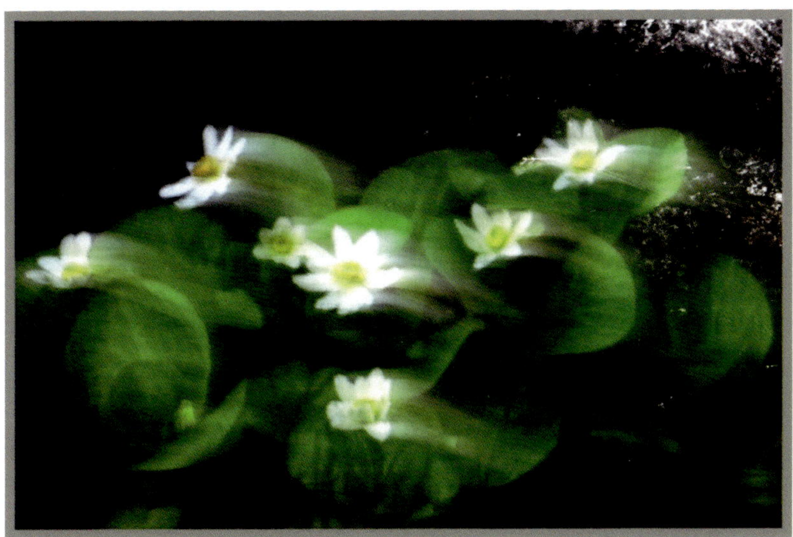

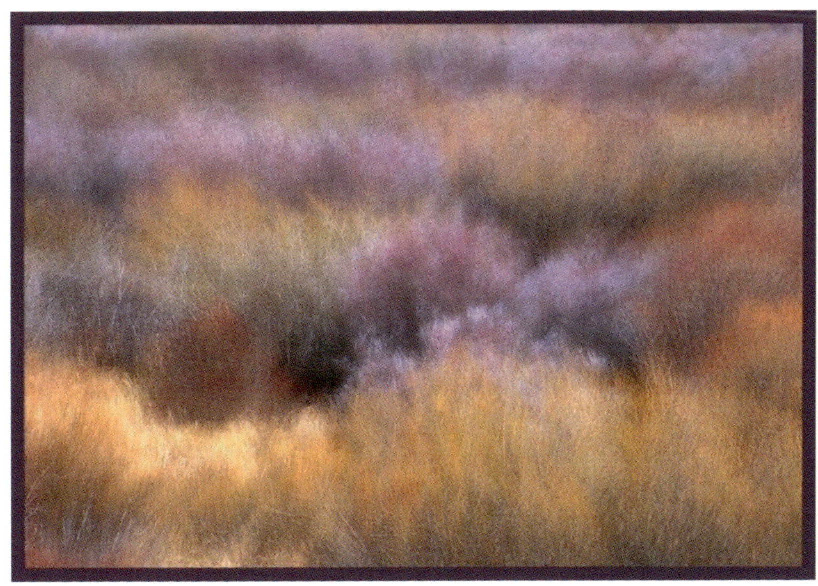

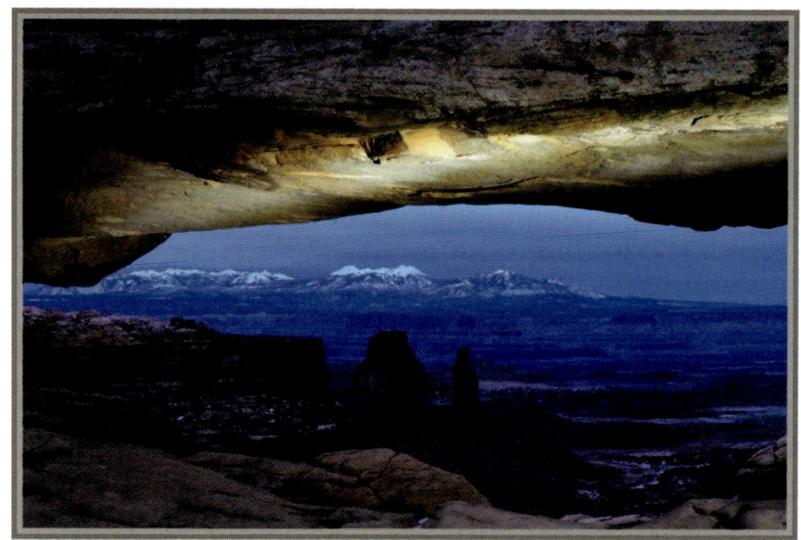

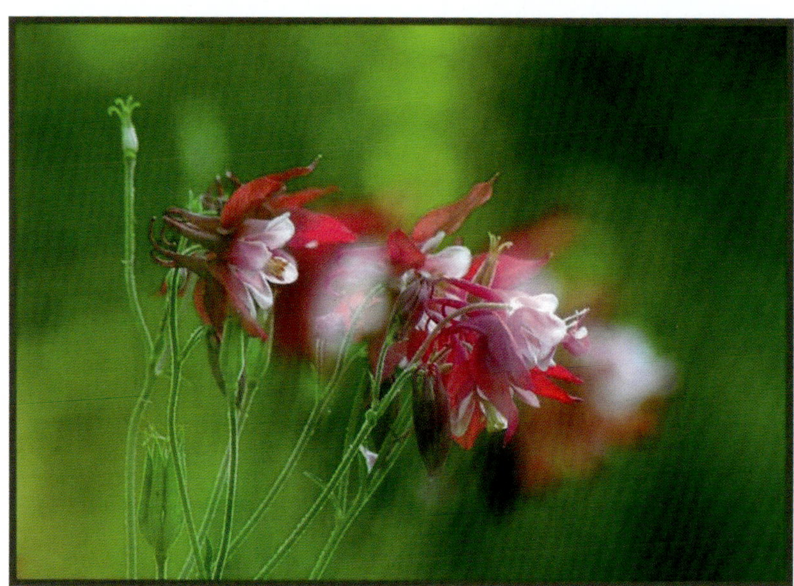

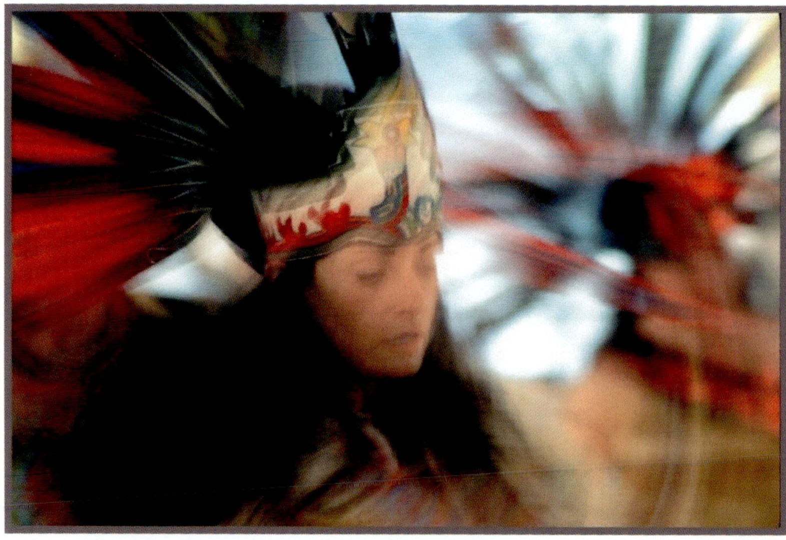

These are just a few examples of my right brain photography, without a hint as to what went into them--that comes later ☺

SECTION II

RIGHT BRAIN EXERCISES

There's nothing like a little brain stimulation to get those creative juices flowing. So, for starters, these exercises will flex your right brain muscles.

Exercise #1: Think of any nearby city, state, or national park you have visited before, especially those you have photographed. Now, think of yourself going back again. This time, however, you cannot photograph trees, rocks, formations, rivers, sidewalks, creeks, hills or mountains, waterfalls, grasses….well, you get the picture. What's left for you to photograph?

Take a few seconds to think about it. Write your answers below or on a piece of paper.

Now, look at the following page for just a few possible answers.

This is what I look for when I'm out scanning for something to photograph.

Shapes....colors...design...texture...form...patterns...mood...lines...feelings...etc.
These are the elements I see in art. The subjects my eyes see become secondary to these artistic elements. This approach to photography allows my mind to see life differently. My eyes limit me from seeing creatively.

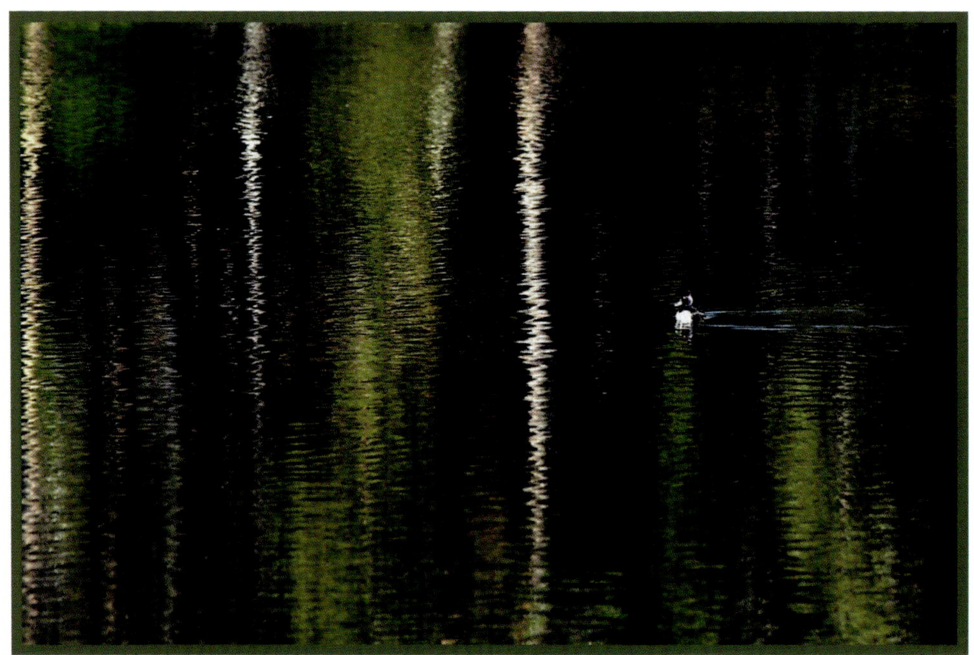

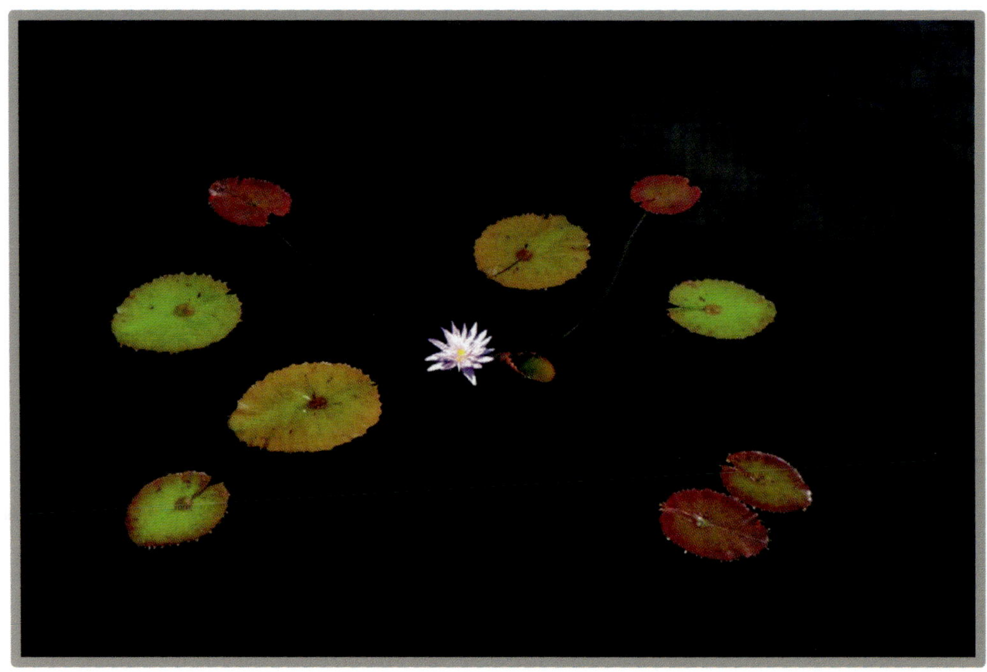

Although I could see subjects in both scenes, I saw shape, design, form, and texture first. To determine my best composition, I placed the physical, tangible elements in the most interesting, compelling or pleasing positions, just like an artist does on canvas. They are not pictures, but interpretations, or translations of what my mind's eye saw. I will expound on this later in the book.

It is important to remember that when it comes to photography, the eyes see too much. What they do see can complicate things by creating visual chaos for us as photographers.

Exercise #2: This one is called "Connect The Dots," but there's a catch.
For this exercise, connect all these nine dots following the criteria below.

1) You can only use four straight lines, but…
2) You cannot remove your pen/pencil from the paper at any time
3) All nine dots must be connected, with only 4 straight lines

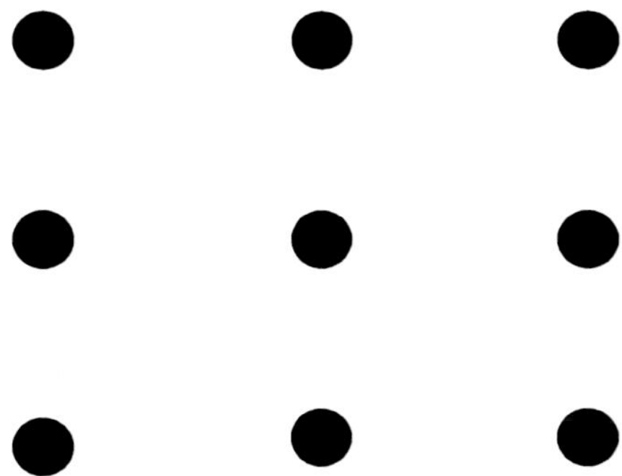

Don't feel bad. Don't kick yourself in the butt if it takes you more than one try.

If you think you got it, you don't have to look at the next page to see the answer. However, if you tried several times but could not figure it out, turn the page for the simple answer.

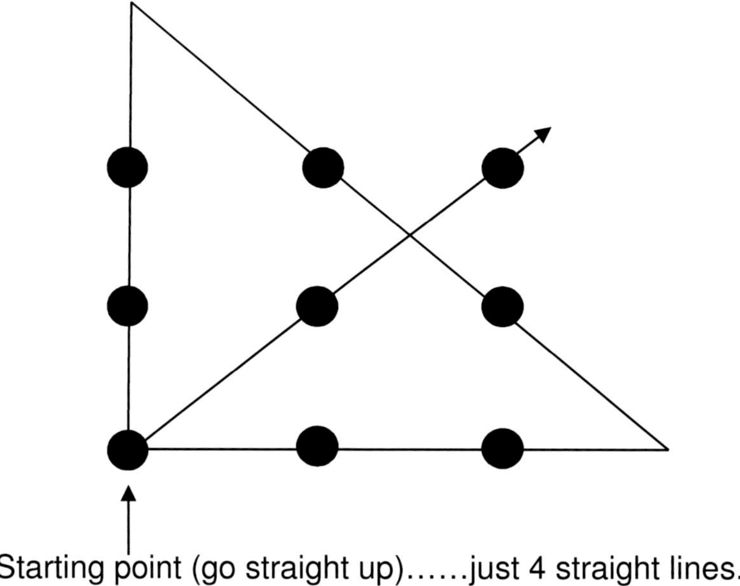

Starting point (go straight up)……just 4 straight lines.

This exercise may not seem like it's related to photography, but it is, in the sense that it forces you to "think outside the box." You will read more on this topic when I talk about my photography models later. For now, I can say this: the mind *is* the birthplace of limitations. The key is to photograph, not only what you see, but also what you don't see.

Confused? Don't be. I will fill in the blanks for you in the following sections.

SECTION III

I.S.E.E. SOMETHING

This is the first of my three photography models. I converted my commonly used phrase, "I see something," into a partial acronym. This model will show you how I see; how I look at the world around me. You will not see your world or world of photography the same after reading this section.

I said earlier that the eyes see too much when it comes to photography. Take this scene, for example. It is the type of scene we look at for an instant then keep walking, as we continue looking for something worth our effort—waiting for something to hit us between the eyes.

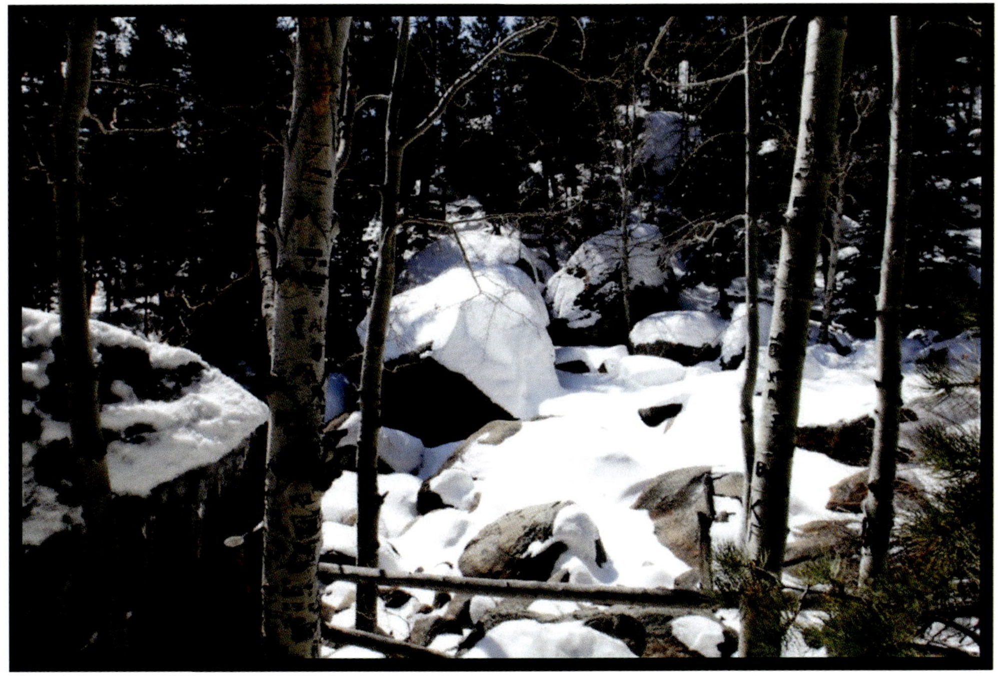

What the eyes see

This photograph is of the same scene, but explains how "I.S.E.E. SOMETHING" works.

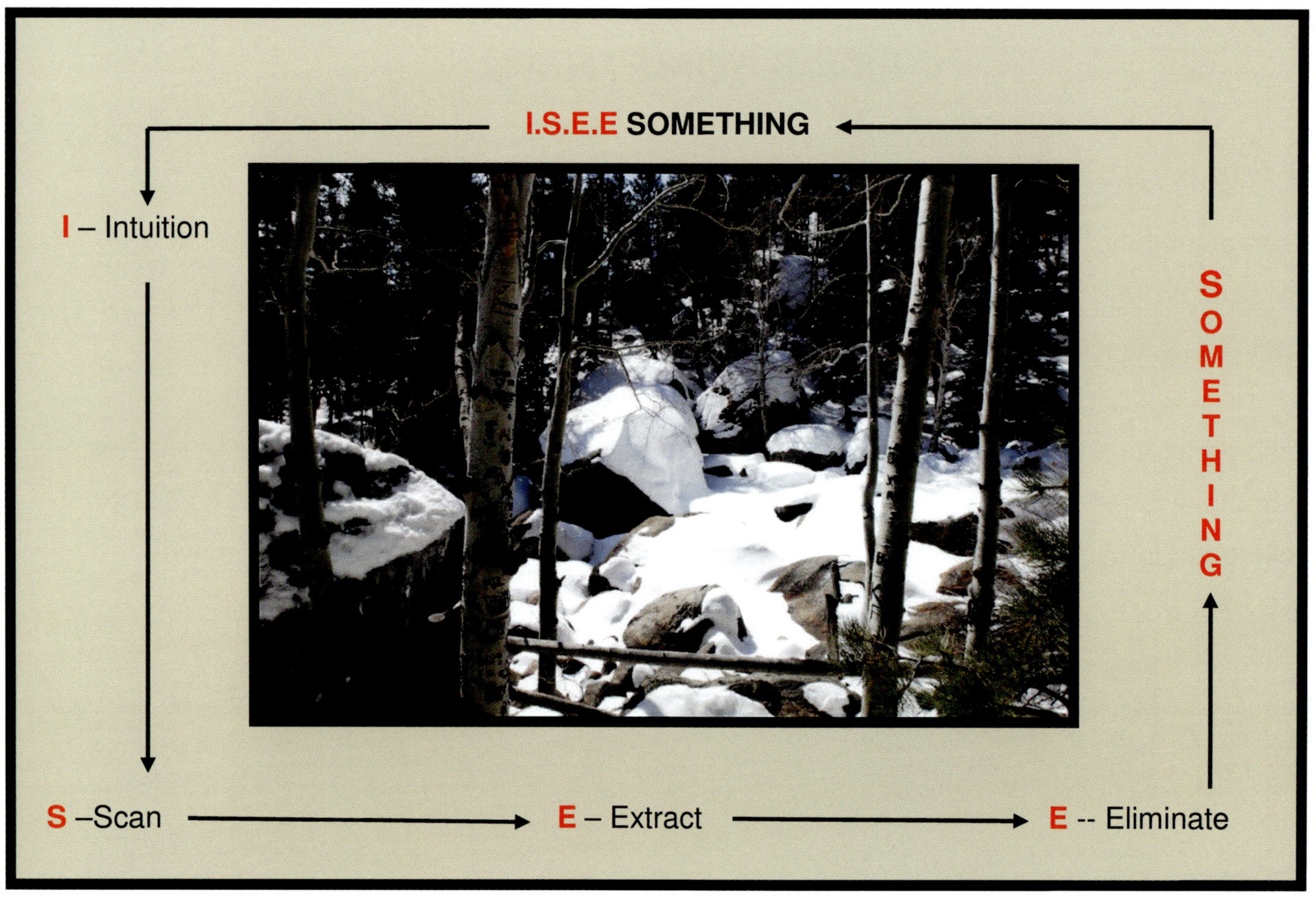

This process is what makes me stop and say, "Wait. I see something." It starts with *Intuition*, and then I *Scan* the scene. I then *Extract* from the scene. The last step is to *Eliminate* the rest of the scene, which allows me to focus on what I have extracted. I will explain each step one at a time and then show some examples that illustrate how I incorporate each of these steps to create my final images.

INTUITION. I have discovered, after offering several classes, workshops, and private lessons, that people have different degrees of intuition. Webster's defines intuition as "immediate apprehension or cognition…quick and ready insight." I like to describe it as having a sixth sense, or having a gut feeling. In one of my workshops, I asked, "How many of you, who don't feel you have good intuition, tend to walk fast when you're out shooting?"

We need to slow down, take our time to observe and absorb our environments. We are not hikers, vacationers, or simply travelers. We are that, and more. That does not make us special, or better than anybody else in any way. It just means that we see, or should see, the world from a different viewpoint.

I had an engineer in one of my classes who asked, "What if you don't have intuition?" I said, "Pretend you do." I said it jokingly, and then explained what I meant. If you really feel that you do not have intuition, assume that there might, just might, be something around you, maybe near you, that is silently waiting for you to aim your camera at it. Without intuition, we keep walking, hoping that something hits us between the eyes and says, "Hey, here I am." I like those moments too. Don't get me wrong. I have several of those "Here I am" type images. I am not suggesting that you steer away from them. However, you can expand your photographic collection by taking advantage of your intuition. Use it as your "water witch" to find something you might otherwise miss. It really comes in handy when you feel that nothing is coming together for you. I will add more to this later.

SCAN. When I listen to my intuition, I slow down, stop, take it in and start scanning the scene. I scan left to right, right to left, up and down, but slowly--that's the key. The eyes see too much, and if I scan too fast, I'm not really scanning for what might be there--I'm just letting my eyes see for me.

Scanning reminds me of those Sci-Fi movies when a robot scans a scene. The movie's director puts us, the movie goers, inside the robot's head as we see what he sees. As we see through his eyes, we see a grid on the movie screen as the robot moves his head left to right. Then, there it is! The robot sees something, stops the scanning, and zeroes in on his target.

When I scan, I let my mind, not my eyes, do the scanning. I look with my eyes; see with my imagination. As Mark Twain once said, "You can't depend on your eyes when your imagination is out of focus."

EXTRACT. When I slow down, I can begin my scanning. And, by slowly scanning, I often find those hidden treasures which I then *extract* from the big picture. Like the robot, I zero in on my potential target. Often, it isn't that in-your-face scene that becomes my catch of the day, but that hidden trophy I find by extracting from the much larger life canvas. Here is where my imagination really goes to work. I will expand on this in my other models, but my imagination always asks, "What would it look like, if…" Our eyes see too much.

ELIMINATE. Once I extract, I need to focus on whatever it is I extracted. In order to properly and slowly focus on what I find, I *eliminate* the rest of the scene from my conscious level. It might seem like an obvious step to take, but it takes deep, meditative focus to do this right. I can be in a crowded place, full of passersby, strollers, people talking and laughing, and children yelling or crying, and still stay focused. When I totally eliminate the rest of the scene, everything and everyone around me fades into the background. I am oblivious to my surroundings—except that one single focus of attention. It is this type of focus that allows me to create images that give the illusion that I was the only one there, or that it might have been created in a studio.

Please go back and look at the example photo again. Think of what I just said about Intuition, Scanning, Extracting, and Eliminating.

The image on the next page is what I was able to *extract* from the scene I showed before, after I followed my *intuition*, *scanned*, and *eliminated.*

We are in such a hurry to find the obvious that we often walk right by great opportunities that are just waiting to see the front of our lens.

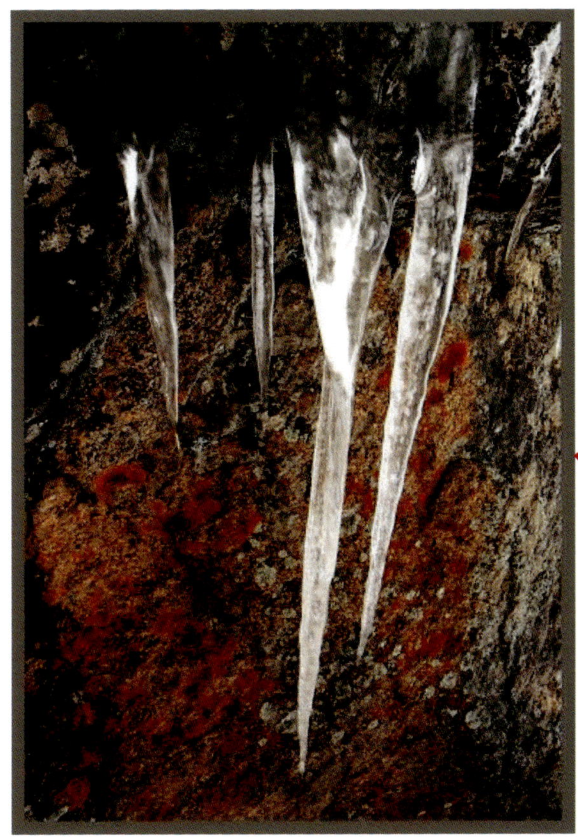

This image…

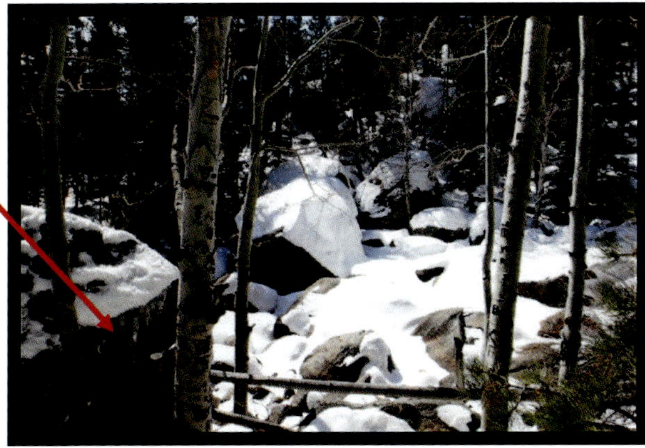

From this scene.

I liked the thin white lines that accentuated the edges of some of the icicles, and the way the middle one was actually two icicles that had merged and twisted to form a new one.

I will say more in a later chapter about how my right brain partners with my left brain to create what I want. It all starts with the right brain—what do I want this to look like?

So far, I have only given you one example of how "I.S.E.E. SOMETHING" works. Let me give you several more. I will show you "before" and "after" images, so you can see the big picture, and then show you my extraction. When you look at the examples, remember that it all started with intuition and scanning. After I extracted, I ignored, tuned out, everything and everyone around me.

The following images serve to show and explain how I move from concept to image creation when I'm in the field.

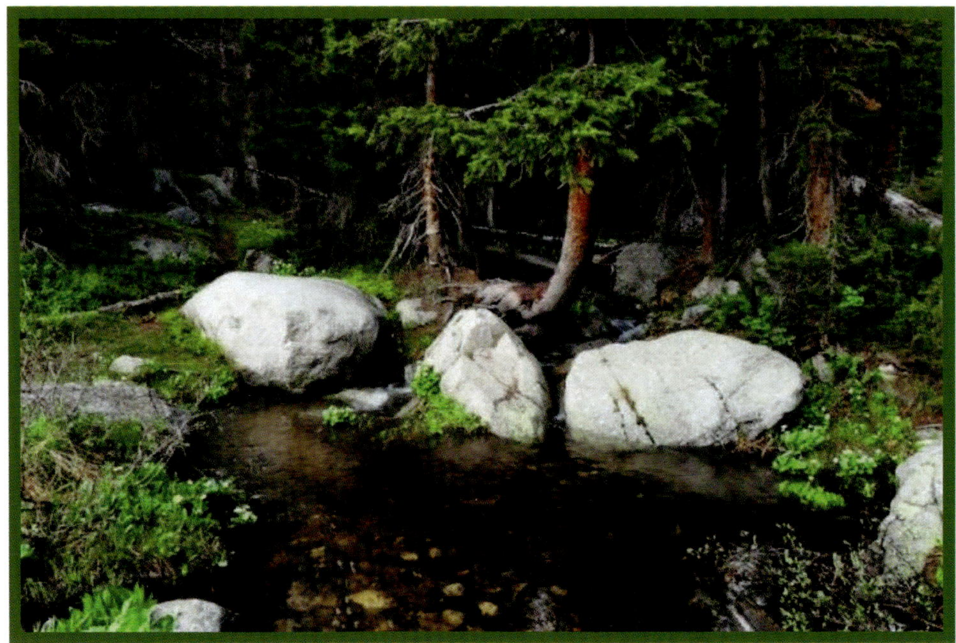

The scene above is near Long Lake in the Indian Peaks Wilderness area in Colorado, one of my favorite hiking areas. As you can see, there isn't much going on here. We see nice green trees, large rocks, and some standing water. The water originates from a small stream, as it makes its way from the nearby mountains. The scene makes for a nice snapshot, at best.

Even though this was a bland looking area, as you saw from the previous photo, my intuition made me stop. As I scanned the scene, I noticed some small white flowers. I kept staring at the flowers, and herein is the essence of extracting. After spending some time looking at them, they still remained just cute little white flowers. My imagination then kicked in. I started wondering what those cute little white flowers would look like if I could make them "move." What my eyes saw was unimpressive; what my imagination saw was art in the making.

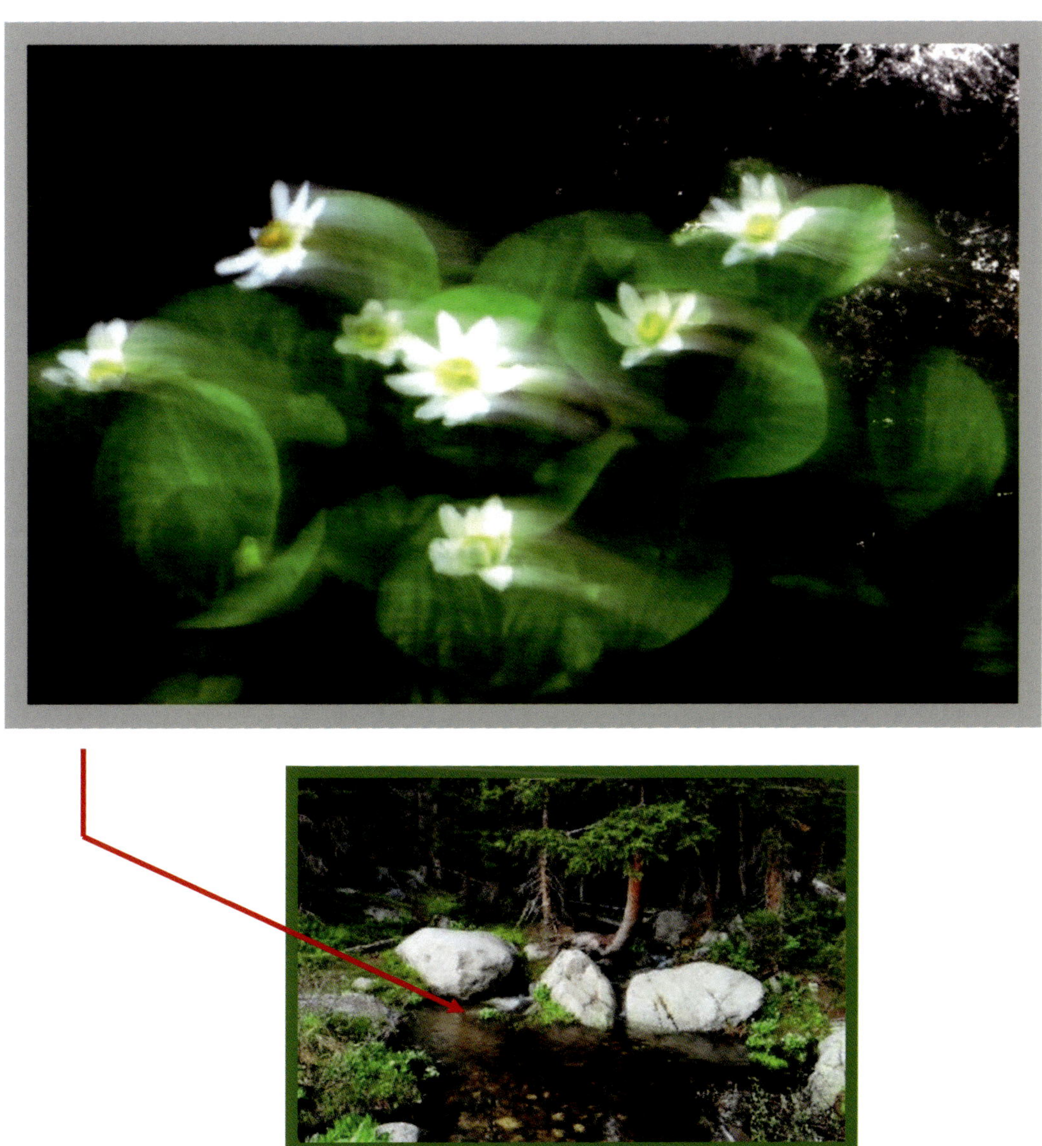

To create this image, I used my telephoto lens to get closer, and then simply moved my camera slightly and slowly to the left while the camera was on my tripod. A 1/5th second exposure allowed me time to make the flowers "move." A large f/stop number (f/36), small aperture, gave me that needed long exposure.

The message here is this: if I slow down, follow my intuition, scan, extract and eliminate, I will find these hidden gems. I will see something--that something that doesn't always jump out at me. I could have easily walked right by this spot on the trail if I was simply looking for something to hit me between the eyes. My eyes see things instantly; my imagination needs time to "see" what I could create, if....

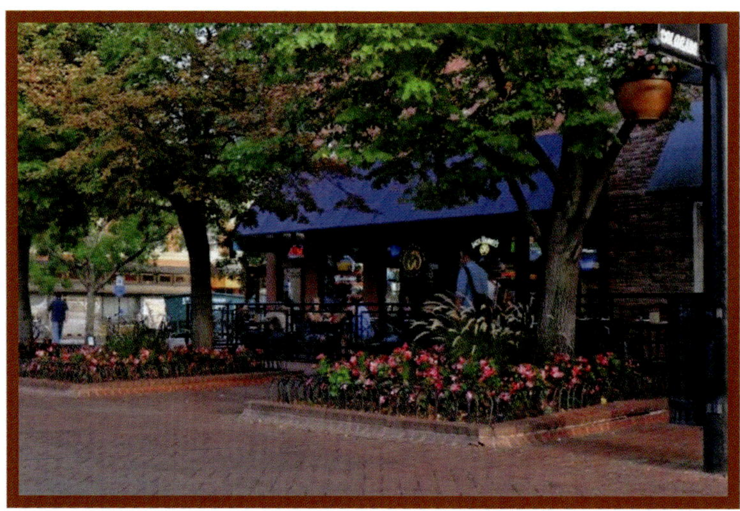

The eyes see too much. Here we see people walking around Pearl Street Mall in Boulder, Colorado. We see people, brick walkways, storefront windows, flower planters, and trash cans. I was attracted to the combination of tans and pinks. My intuition made me stop and ask, "Hmm? I wonder what I might find over there?"

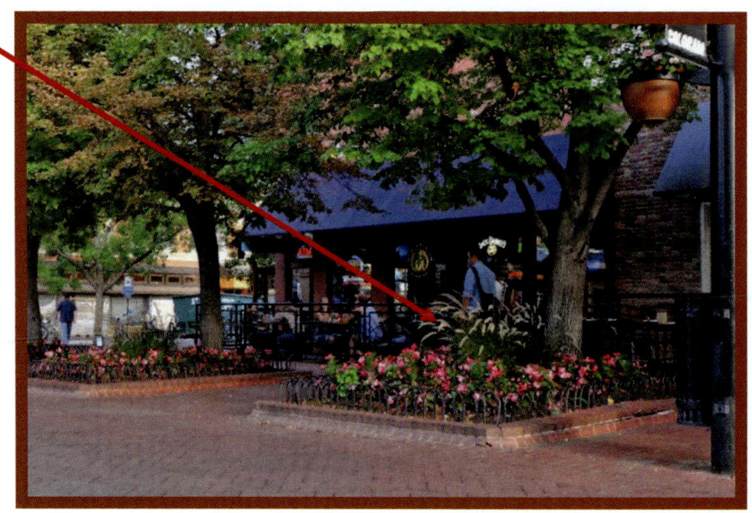

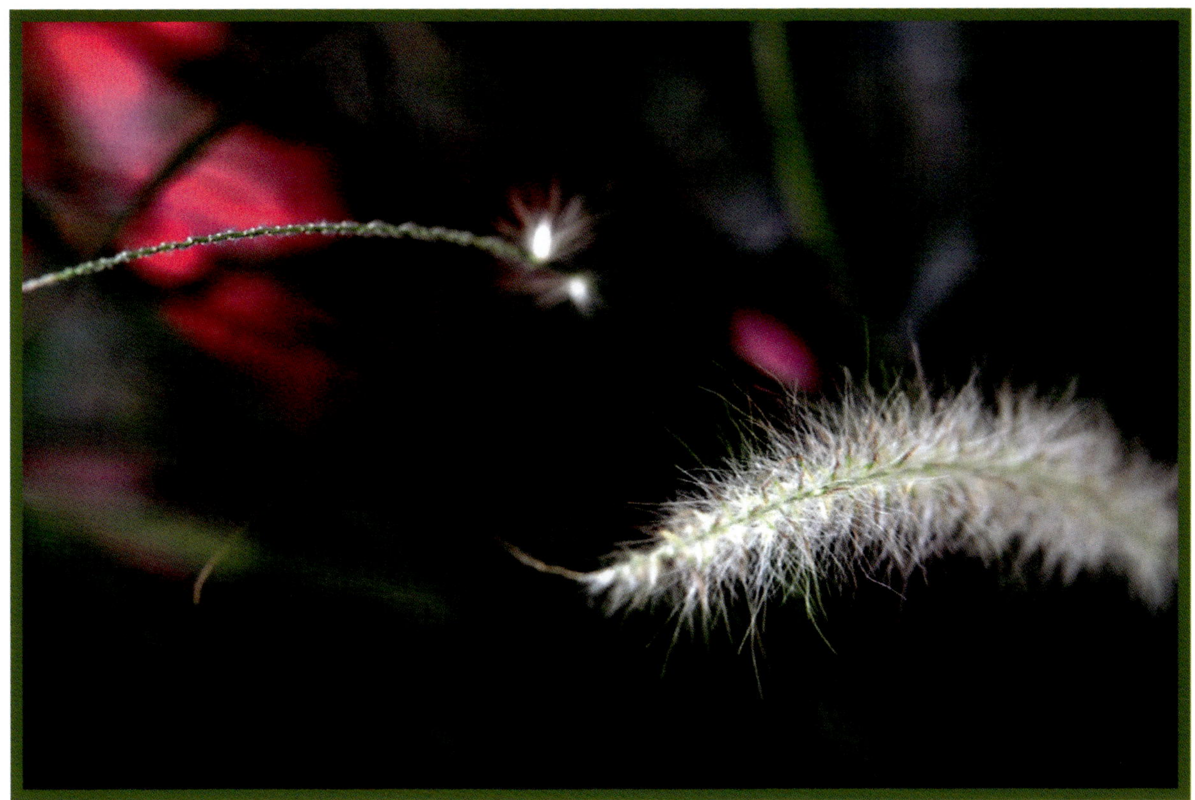

This is what I found “over there.” My intuition led me to the pink flowers and tan-colored plants by the tree on the right. My color theory from my art days kicked in. As I got closer to this area, I saw color, design, lines, and nice compatible color contrast. The rest just fell into place.

My right brain always initiates the process toward my final image. I ask, “What do I ‘see,’ and what do I want it to look like?” My goal is to interpret, to translate, not duplicate life. If I leave it up to my eyes to see for me, I will see as a photographer, depending on my eyes to help me see something. As a photo artist, I look with my eyes, but see with my imagination.

In this case, I saw the nice contrast between the light tan colors and the greens and pinks in the background, the shapes and lines those plants created and the direction of those lines—both leading the eye toward the center of the scene. The scene had more contrast than what my eyes could distinguish. Our eyes quickly adjust to high contrasts in lighting—we don’t see the contrast. I take advantage of the fact that the digital tools in our cameras cannot make that same degree of extreme light contrast adjustments. As a photo artist, I do not want to perfect what my eyes see—I want to interpret what my eyes see. If I only duplicate what I see, my images might end up technically right, but aesthetically weak.

Once my right brain creates an image in my mind, it shakes hands with my left brain and says, "I have an idea, and this is what I need from you." This is not the same as, "I have an idea. How do I do it?" I knew that if I intentionally underexposed the scene, I would make the light-colored plants "pop," because of the difference between the plants' light colors and the dark shade in the background. I also wanted to see what else I could add to the feel of the image with a wide open f/stop. After a few minutes of looking through my view finder and making some adjustments, including my focusing point, I determined what I wanted this scene to look like.

I settled on a minus 2 stops of underexposure for impact (that's severe in photography), and an aperture of f/6.3. The shutter speed, 1/40th of a second, was irrelevant, since I had the camera on my tripod and there was no breeze to disturb the scene. I locked my mirror up to minimize any possible camera vibration.

I will not go into this much left brain detail with most of my other images in this book. "Why?" you ask? Because, it is not a question of what f/stop, shutter speed, focusing point, exposure, or lens we should use. What we should ask are questions like, "What do I want it to look like?" "What message do I want to convey?" The answer to those questions will help us answer our left brain questions. We should not ask what we need to do. Wee should ask what results we want. That's what artists do. Start with the end in mind.

Do you remember the story of me and my friend driving to Rocky Mountain National Park? I told him that what I was hoping for was not coming together for me. I then added, "But, you know me. I'll find something." "Yeah. I know," he quickly responded. He knows me well.

We headed to one of my favorite lakes in Rocky Mountain National Park, Sprague Lake. We walked around, and still, nothing. To someone who is not used to seeing mountains, the scene on the next page might look spectacular. It looked "flat" to me—not much color, no drama in the sky, and no autumn yellows reflected in the lake.

Then, my intuition kicked in. I started scanning. I got closer to the lake and peaked behind the plants in the foreground. By that time, another photographer, with a huge wildlife-size lens, had crossed my path. We met very near this same spot. I asked him, “Any wildlife today?” “No, not today,” he replied as he left the lake.

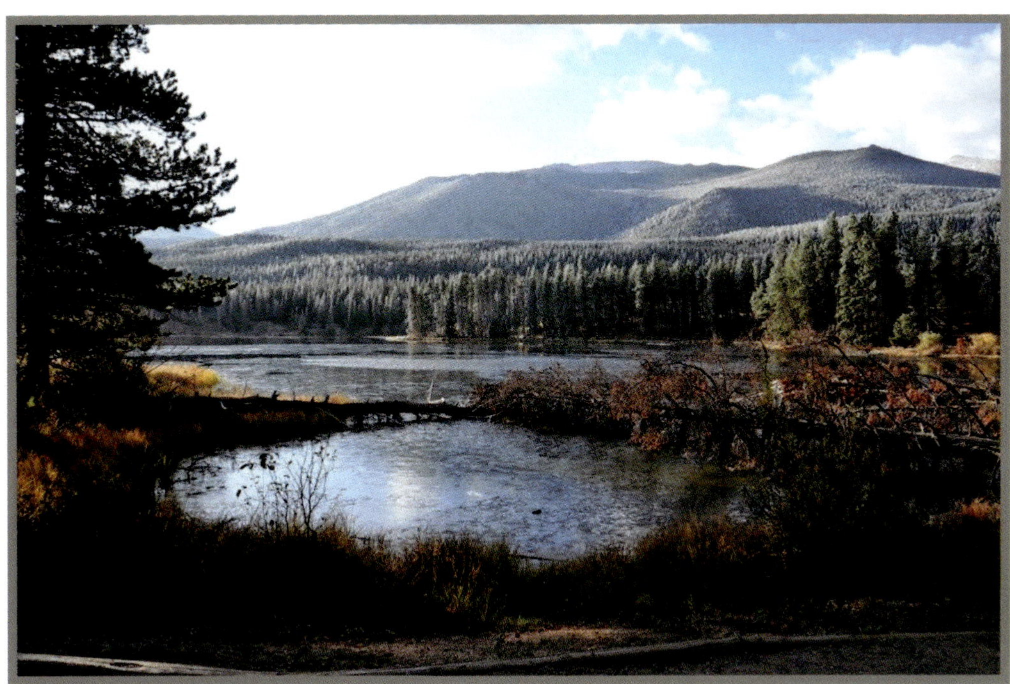

As I explored behind the plants and into a portion of the lake, I extracted from the rest of the broad uneventful scene. Everything around me became a blur as I zeroed in on my catch of the day.

The image on the next page is what I extracted from this generic scene. When I show it during my slide show presentations, I get a lot of stares that seem to say, “You’re kidding. You got this image from that scene?”

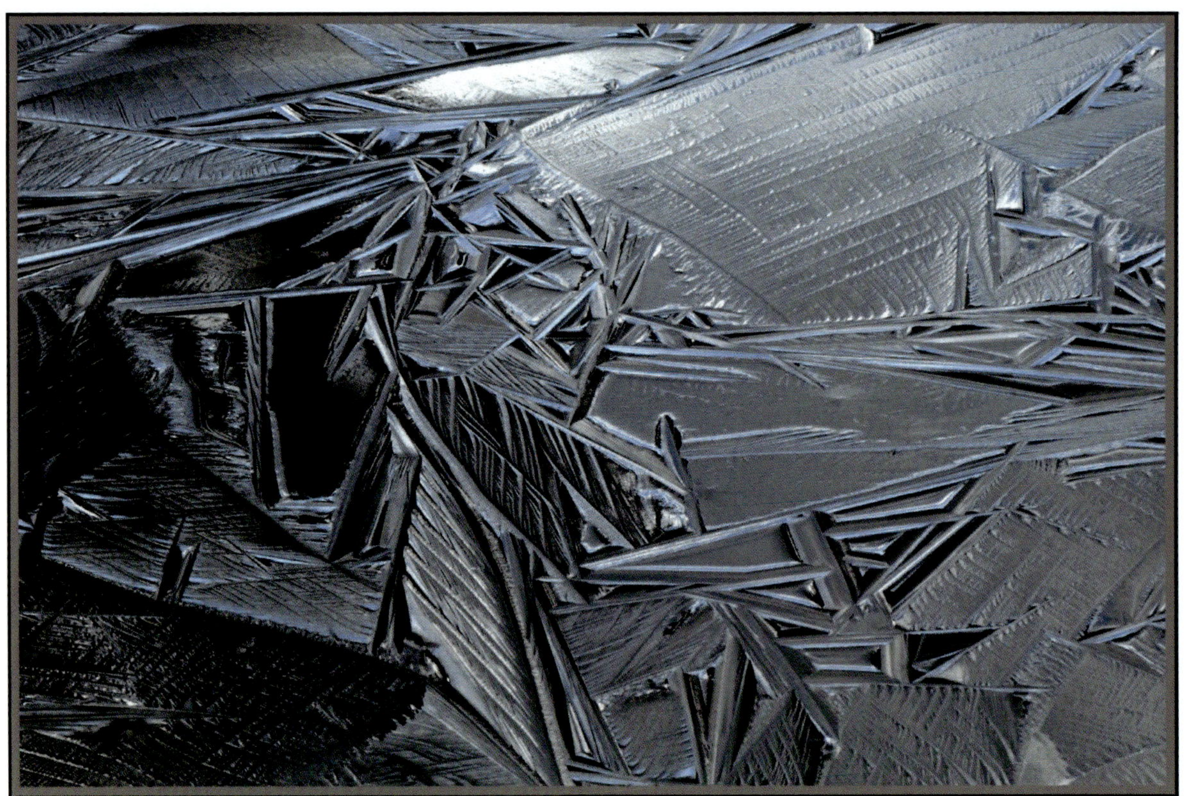

This extracted image is nothing other than part of the lake behind the foreground plants. Some of the ice on the lake had started to break up, creating interesting geometric and monochromatic shapes. I saw design, hues, lines, patterns, and shapes. I used my 300mm lens to get close to this particular spot on the lake that got my attention. It reminded me of Cubism, which I had studied during my art days in college. I call this piece “Wet Cubism.”

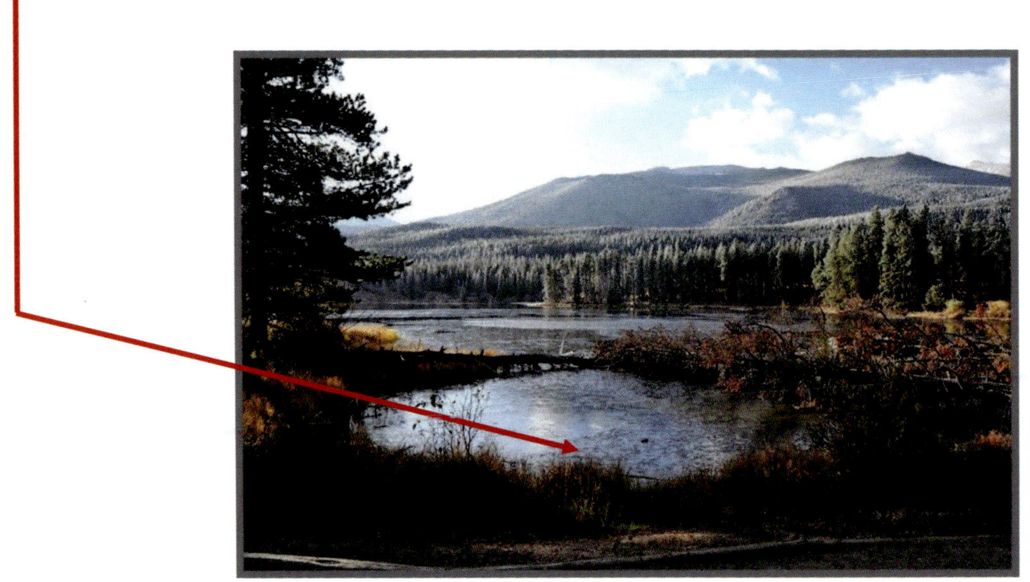

Now that I have explained how "I.S.E.E SOMETHING" works, I am now going to show you a few "after" images, without showing the big scene from which I extracted them. I will share only the end results I created after I followed my intuition, then scanned, extracted, and eliminated.

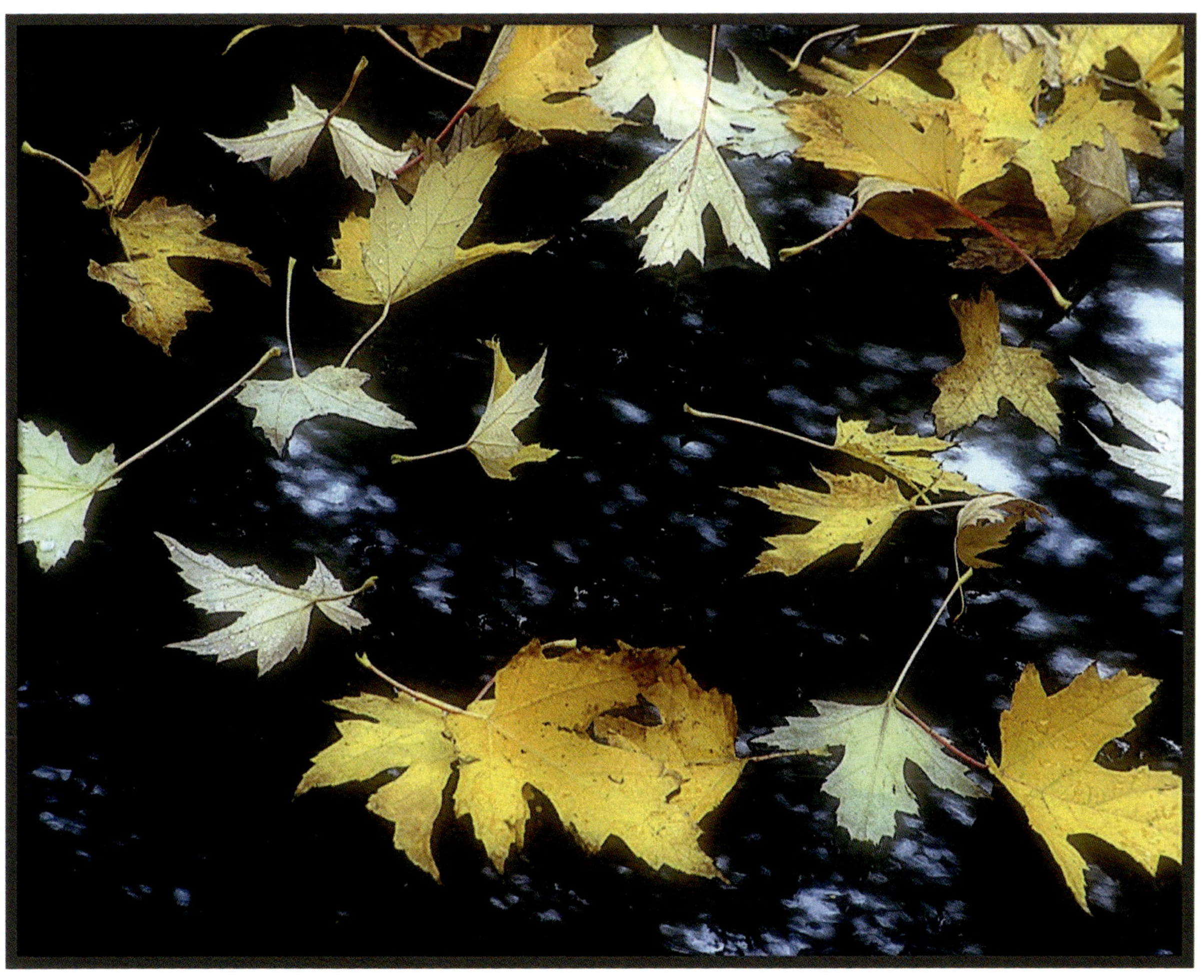

"Floating Leaves"

My timing for autumn colors was perfect. There is a great historic street in Boulder, Colorado called Mapleton Avenue, set on the foothills of the Rockies. The name is a hint of the colors you might find in autumn. It is a very wide street in one of the oldest neighborhoods in the city, decorated with a wide variety of beautifully sculpted trees. If you time it just right, you will see beautiful yellows, reds, and oranges along the historic neighorhood. Some of the colors cover the trees; some cover the ground like elegantly woven patterns in a carpet.

What you will not see on Mapleton Avenue are ponds. The autumn leaves seem to be floating on a stagnant pond, with the surrounding trees reflected in the water. Do you see a Porsche in that image, as in an expensive German car? I found these "floating" leaves on the hood of a black Porsche, on Mapleton Avenue. I kept my distance with my 300mm lens, making sure no one called 911 on me!

This scene was not on Mapleton Avenue. Let your eyes rest on this for a minute.

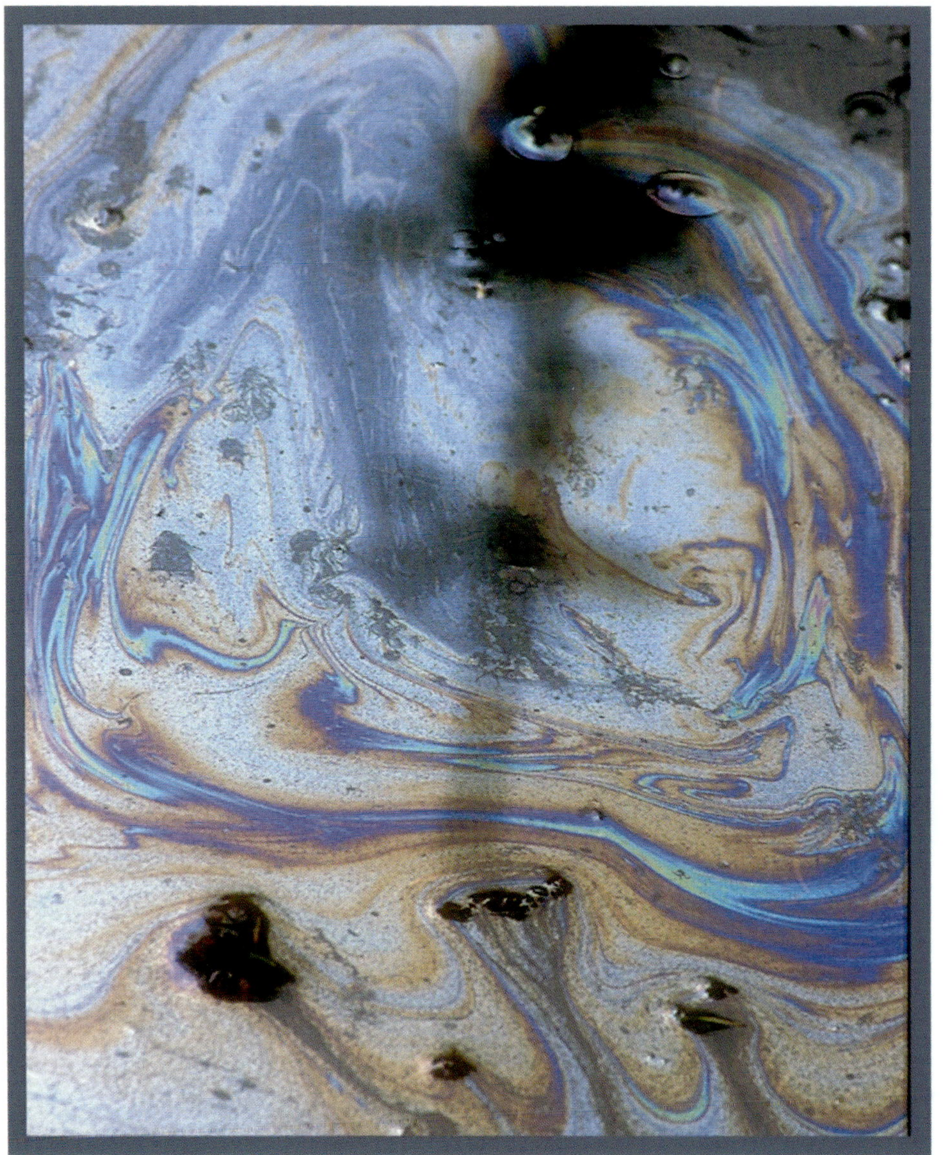

"On The Right Path"

An oil spill? Car oil stains in a parking lot? Hmm?

I'll give you a hint. This image was created at an elevation of approximately 10,000 feet—not a car in sight. I was on one of my many hikes in Colorado. It had rained the day before. On my way back to the trailhead, I started noticing all the puddles, which I and other hikers were trying to avoid stepping in. As I approached one puddle, I stopped, crouched down to knee level and saw art—nature's art. I set up my tripod. Several hikers noticed me and stopped to see what had grabbed my interest. As they stopped to stare and chat, I asked them, "What do you think this is?" There were several theories, but I think one guy got it right. His theory was that all the natural oils from the pine cones and trees had found their way down the trees and had collected in the puddles. As the breeze picked up, the colored patterns in the puddles shifted, creating interesting and colorful designs and shapes.

Sometimes when I come across a scene like this, I can't help but create an abstract. I see design, shapes, forms, texture, and colors—simple artistic blends, with no meaning per se. That same image, however, can elicit thoughts, feelings, or moods.

When I show this image, I get all kinds of reactions and interpretations. Some people have seen the face of a fox (dark area, in upper right), a blue eel, an angel's wing, a cross, and other interpretations. This is why I like abstracts—everybody sees and feels something different. What do you see?

"Anyone who says you can't see a thought simply doesn't know art." Wynetka Ann Reynolds

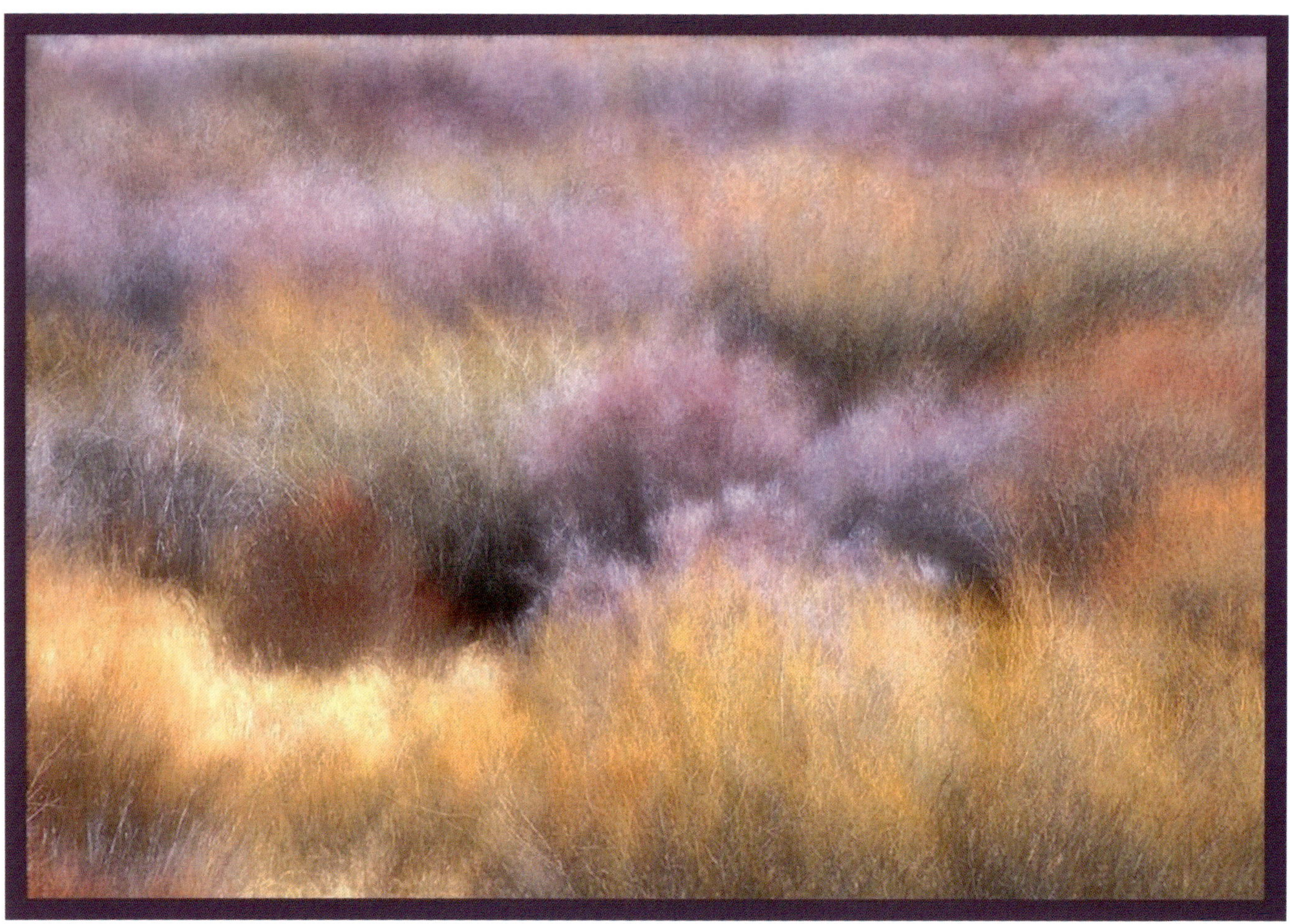

I usually don't invite others to go with me during my photo shoots. I made an exception one cold October day when I invited a friend. He was curious to see and learn about what I did as a photographer. He picked me up one early morning. Later that day we found ourselves in the high country in north central Colorado. We were heading toward Walden. Since I wasn't driving, I had the luxury of doing some scanning as my friend drove. All of a sudden, I looked to my right and saw something. "Stop. Pull over," I quickly instructed. "What?" he asked. "I'll tell you later," I responded as he respectfully pulled over.

I got out of his SUV, grabbed my camera gear, and carefully walked across the narrow two-lane high country road. I stared out at what seemed like miles and miles of colorful willows. The willows had lost their leaves, exposing their most hidden inner beauty. I saw yellows, oranges, reds, and purples! I thought silently to myself, "This reminds me of a watercolor." Immediately, instinctively, I knew I had to "paint" a watercolor from the scene.

My right brain talked to my left brain: "Okay. This is what I need from you." In order to create my watercolor image, I knew I had to do a double exposure. Luckily, I had the type of camera that allowed me to do that in-camera. Here is what I did. I had used this technique before with other subjects, so I had a strong sense that it would work well for this scene as well. After setting my multiple exposure feature on my camera, I first took the scene out of focus and created an out-of-focus image. Then, I created my second image. However, the second image was in crisp, sharp focus—all the way through. I usually create the sharp, in-focus image last so I can see more detail in the final image. It looks like a dream, like a water color, but if you look closely, you can see the willow branches throughout the image. I call this "Watercolor Willows." Surprised?

At the end of our day together, my friend made this interesting observation and comment. "Until today, I thought it was easy to be a photographer—you just look at something and take a picture. But after spending the day with you, I have gained a new appreciation and respect for photographers." Since he didn't know much about photography, I was okay with him calling me a photographer. Let that sink in for a minute.

"I just get an idea and follow it, and see where it goes." Ray Wyley Hubbard

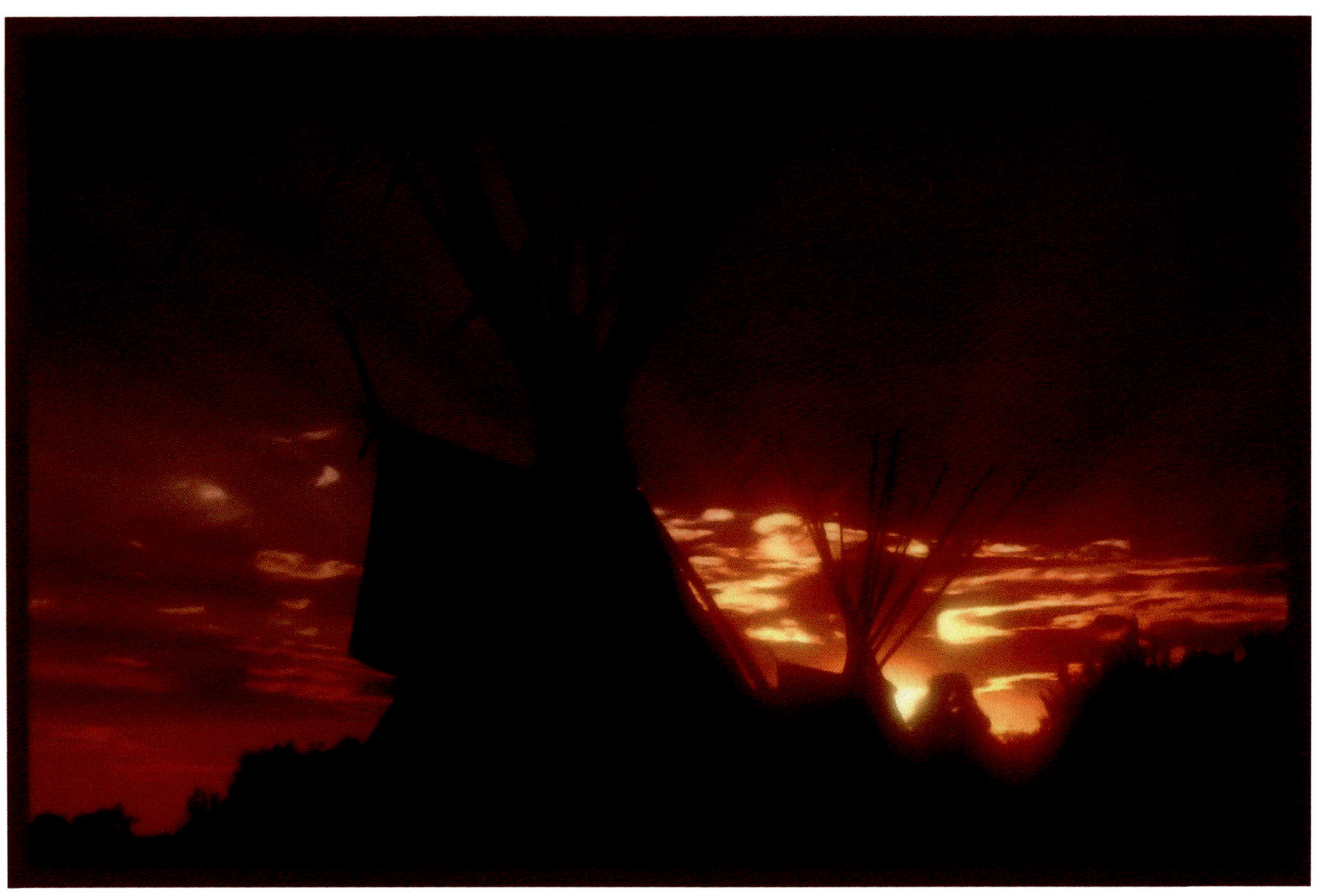

"Tepees at Sunset"

I was in Anadarko, Oklahoma during their annual American Indian Exposition. Part of the culturally colorful and exciting event included a great display of traditional American Indian tepees. The town had set aside a large park area for the awesome display. I got several shots during the weekend, but the scene was too "busy" for my taste---just too much going on. I felt that the artistic and colorful tepees lost their essence against the modern buildings, park trees, signs warning event goers of areas that were off-limits, and swarms of weekend visitors there for the special event. Although I got several good images, I just wasn't quite satisfied.

I decided to wait until late sunset to photograph the tepees against a colorful setting sun, imagining in advance that I was going to get some nice silhouettes agains high contrast dusk colors. I'm glad I went back later that evening. Those images ended up being some of my favorites from the visit.

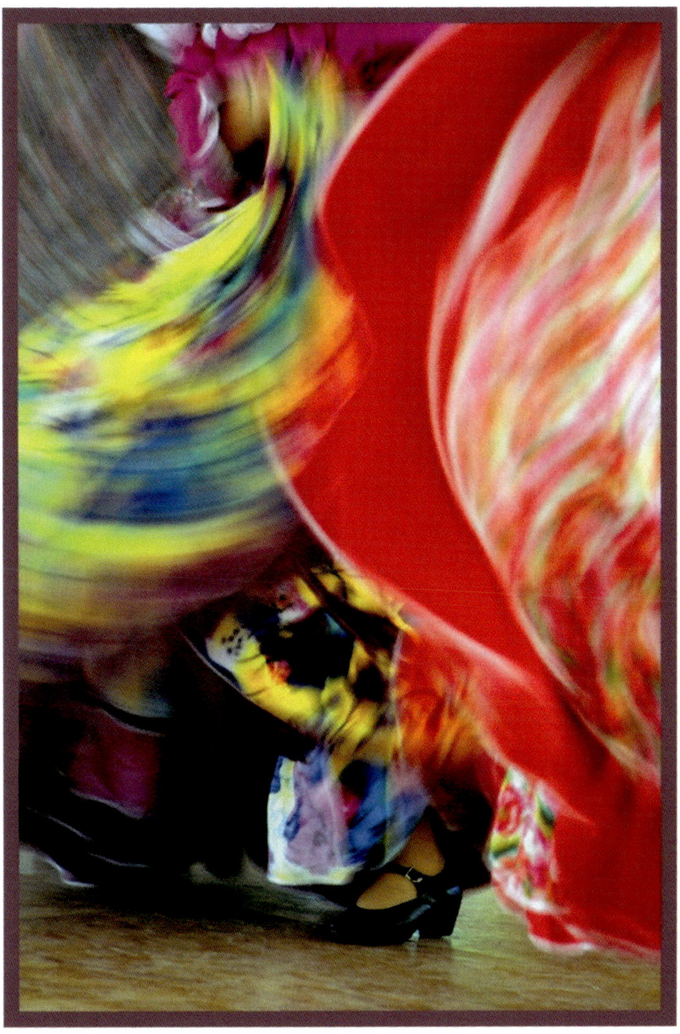

"Zapateale"

I attended a "Diez y Seis de Septiembre" celebration in Boulder, Colorado. One of the main attractions was the Ballet Folklorico program—an event with rainbow colors, brightly colored skirts, and lots of Mexican style fast stepping dances. There were tents everywhere, music, wall-to-wall weekenders, children, and vendors. In the middle of all that, I watched one of the dancing events for a few minutes. I quickly decided that what I wanted to interpret was not the dancers but the spirit of their dancing. I knew I had to get several shots off to make sure I created that spirit. My goal was to interpret the spirit by visually recording the color and motion of the women's colorful butterfly-like skirts. As I was shooting, there was a moment when a dancer planted her foot on the floor for just a split second, at the same exact time that I pressed the shutter button. Photography requires a lot of skill, some planning, and a little luck.

MY CHALLENGE TO YOU

Now that I have shared my I.S.E.E SOMETHING model in detail, here is my challenge to you. I have two exercises for you. So, go out and "see something" you are not used to seeing. Remember: the eyes see too much. Look with your eyes, but *see* with your imagination.

***CHALLENGE ASSIGNMENT* #1** Common Places. Different Perspective

1A. Go to your backyard, or a location you commonly walk or jog by every day or every week. Without your camera in tow, simply slow down and stop for a few minutes. Let your intuition take over for awhile. Let it flow. If you do not feel you have intuition, assume that if you slow down, even stop at certain intervals, there is something there just waiting for you.

Begin the scanning process, slowly. Extract something from the big picture. It might be a flower bed, a sculpture, figurine, wind chimes, a bench, or a fountain. When you find it, study it and ask yourself, "What could I make this look like? What's the message? Do I get a certain feeling from it?" That is your right brain at work. Once you get in touch with whatever "it" is, start thinking of what help you will need from your left brain to achieve what is in your right brain—f/stop, shutter speed, exposure, focusing point, lens, etc.

The camera can get in the way, especially when you are not used to this approach to photography. You are the artist. Your camera and lenses are simply your paint brushes. They don't create the art--that's your job. Start seeing with your imagination.

1B. Now. Go back to that spot, or spots, but this time with your camera and move from idea, or concept, to actual image creation.

Well? What did you find? What did you create? Fun, huh?

***CHALLENGE ASSIGNMENT* #2** Right Brain In Uncommon Places

Go to your state map and look for an area you have not visited before—maybe an area you have been wanting to visit, but just never got around to it. Circle it on the map and go there. Don't do any research on it, do not look for on-line photos. Just go. Be spontaneous. Get up at 4:00 some morning and just take off. It's refreshing do that.

When you get there, let your intuition guide you. You might see a park, an outdoor museum, or signs pointing to certain local destinations, like lakes and wilderness areas. Go. Don't think about it too much---just go! You might surprise yourself. Along the way, your intuition might lead you on a short detour. Follow your gut feeling; your instincts.

Whenever you're ready, begin scanning, extracting, and eliminating.

Well? What did you find? What did you create? Fun, huh?

"Vision is the art of seeing what is invisible to others." Jonathan Swift

SECTION IV

ELI'S 5-POINT PHOTO ART MODEL

As I mentioned earlier, there is some overlap between my first two models. I don't apply my models separately or treat them as independent models. They all link and syncrhonize when I'm in the field. I talk about them separately here for the sake of explanation.

That said, my five points are: **Intuition**, **Imagination**, **Impressionism**, **Surrealism**, **and Eastern Philosophy**—yes, eastern philosophy, as I apply it to my photography.

I will explain this model as I did I.S.E.E SOMETHING. I will discuss the concepts and show representative images. I will also give some details regarding the making of the images. At the end of the section, I will again give you some assignments for you to apply in the field.

INTUITION. This is the first of my five points. I covered this already in the previous model. However, so many of my students express difficulty with this concept that I am going to provide you with another illustration.

Here's the scenario. I was passing through the town of Hot Sulphur Springs in north central Colorado. I had this intuition that there might be something there to photograph—a quaint, out of the way little town, with a slow pace of life.

As I drove through the heart of town, on the main road that leads to and from the town, I kept looking left and right—following my intiution. After just a few minutes, I glanced quickly to my left and saw this next scene.

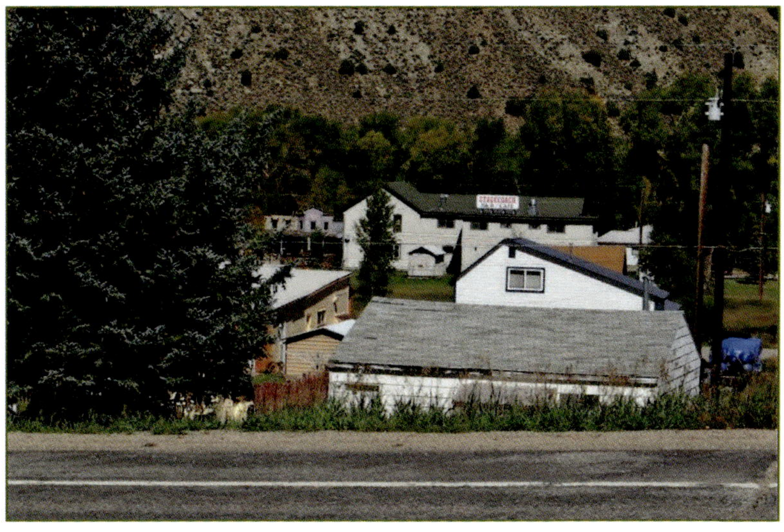

No, I didn't take this photo out of my window as I was driving! I can see you smiling.

Something caught my split-second attention as I passed by this part of town. I was driving by at about thirty miles per hour. I didn't get a chance to stare at it like you can as you look at this photo. But, can *you* see anything worth photographing by just looking at this?

I stopped and turned around soon after I passed this spot, parked the car, got out and started, yes, scanning. If you look closely at the photo above, there is a building, a structure in the far distance, with faint purple hues. Can you see it?

Well, I saw it and continued to follow my intuition. I drove up to the building and saw this scene.

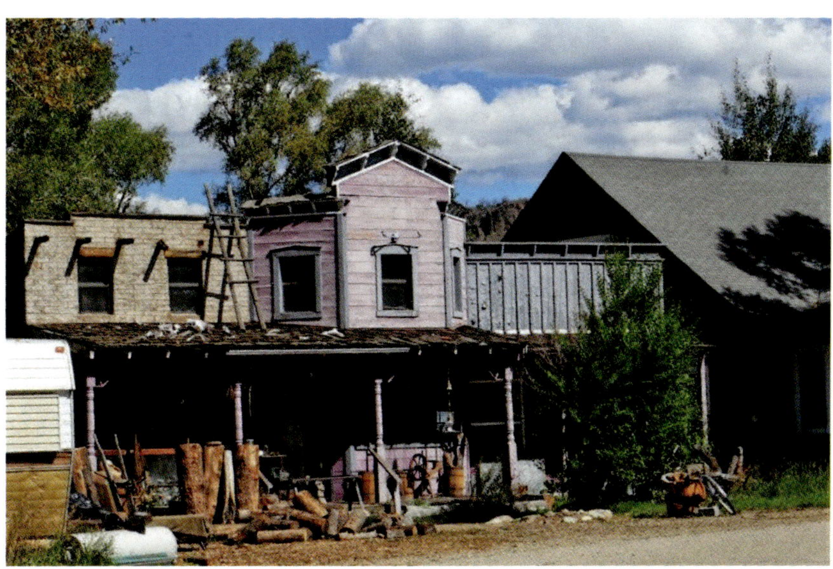

As soon as I saw the building close up, I started scanning and extracting. After I scanned all parts of the structure, I saw something. Then, after more scanning, I saw this.

Please remember that I saw the big picture on the previous page from quite a distance.

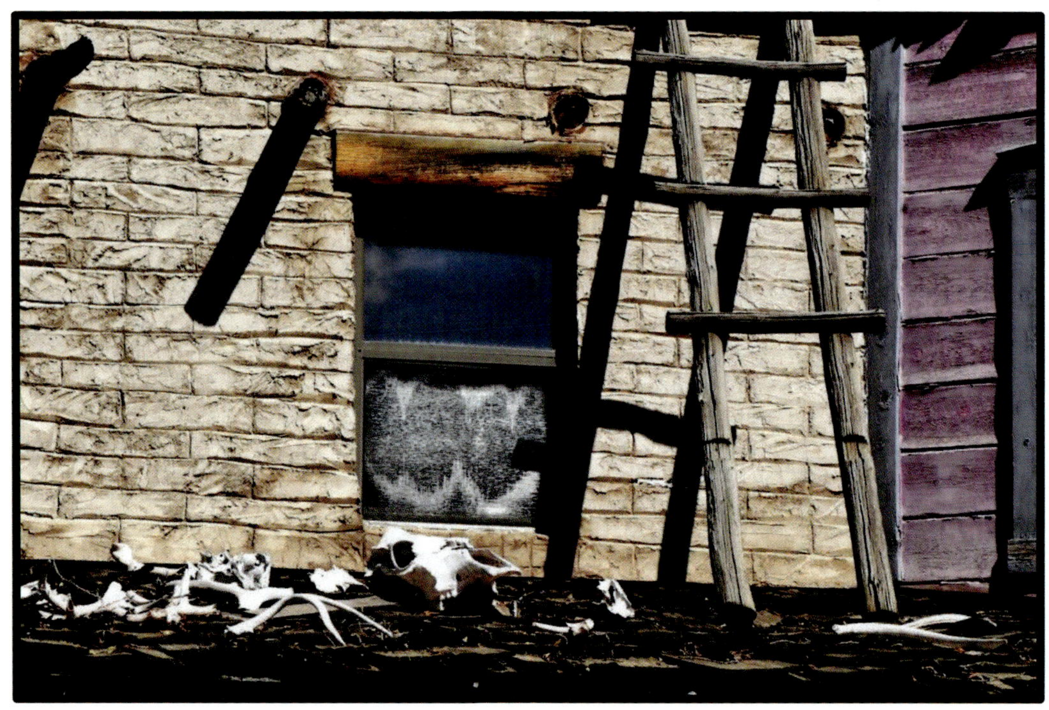

My point here is to re-emphasize the key role intuiton plays in photography. I cannot over emphasize this enough. Before we do anything with our photography, with our cameras and lenses, we need some sort of internal guide that will take us places our eyes don't readily see. We could say it's an internal GPS system, but that would not do it justice. A GPS system, which might be antiquated by the time you read this book, will tell us where it is that we want to go. Our intiution, however, does much more. It guides us somewhere too, but even before we know where it is we need to be.

IMAGINATION. Books have been written about this subject. Imagination and creativity go hand in hand. Which one comes before the other is for psychologists to figure out—I just know they are crucial and absolute necessities in my photo art tool kit.

A formal definition of imagination would read something like, "*The ability to form new images and sensations that are not perceived through sight, hearing, or other senses…*" In other words, it does not exist on the surface; at the conscious level. This leads to the thought that we need to dig for it in order to get in touch with it. Hmm? In which hemisphere of our brain does imagination reside?

My favorite author on the subject of creativity and imagination is not a photographer. "Chic" Thompson wrote a timeless book several years ago called *What A Great Idea!* I'd like to share just two quotes from his book.

"If everyone says you're wrong, you're one step ahead. If everyone laughs at you, you're two steps ahead."

"All behaviors consist of opposites….Learn to see things backward, inside out, and upside down."

I chose those two quotes because they remind me of what I do with my photography. When I tell people what I did to get some of my shots, they laugh at the absurdity, then quickly realize that is what we need to do to create unique images. I always try to see what my eyes do not. I look upside down, sideways, or obliquely.

Regardless of how we define "imagination," I want to address it in specific ways that relate to photography. It has to do with, yes, looking at things differently. What does that mean when we are trying to create photographic images? It means *looking* at something with our eyes, but *seeing* with our imaginations, asking ourselves what we could make it look like if we did this, or that, to the shapes, colors, or forms we see.

On the next page I list several possilbe answers to this question.

Below are several questions I ask myself; questions that originate from my imagination. They all start with, "What if I......"

......use a wide open f/stop?
......Use flourescent White Balance for a morning nature shot?
......use a slow, rather than fast, shutter speed?
......use spot metering on this subject?
......zoom in or out during a long exposure?
......paint it with light?
......move my camera during the exposure? Right or left; up or down.
......shoot into the sun?
......do a double exposure on this one?
......get on top of my car?
......swirl my camera during the exposure?
......use extreme under exposure? Maybe even -2 stops?
......shoot it horizontally, but show it vertically?
......show it upside down, or downside up?
......use myself as a ghost in the scene?
......put my camera on the floor?

The list goes on. It is limited only by our imaginations. As "Chic" also said, "Our minds are the birthplace of limitations." When I use my imaginaiton, I see things before I see them.

Let's continue on this "What if?" theme. Imagine, if you will, that you were a tiny little mouse living underneath an old abandoned house. Unlike other mice, you are a photographer mouse. As any good mouse photographer, you always take your camera gear with you everywhere you go---just in case a good opportunity presents itself. One day you make your way up to the abandoned house. Good—not a soul in sight! You find your way to the long-abandoned bathroom. You ask yourself, "Should I take this shot?" You've read Eli's book on right brain photography, so you decide, "Why not?"

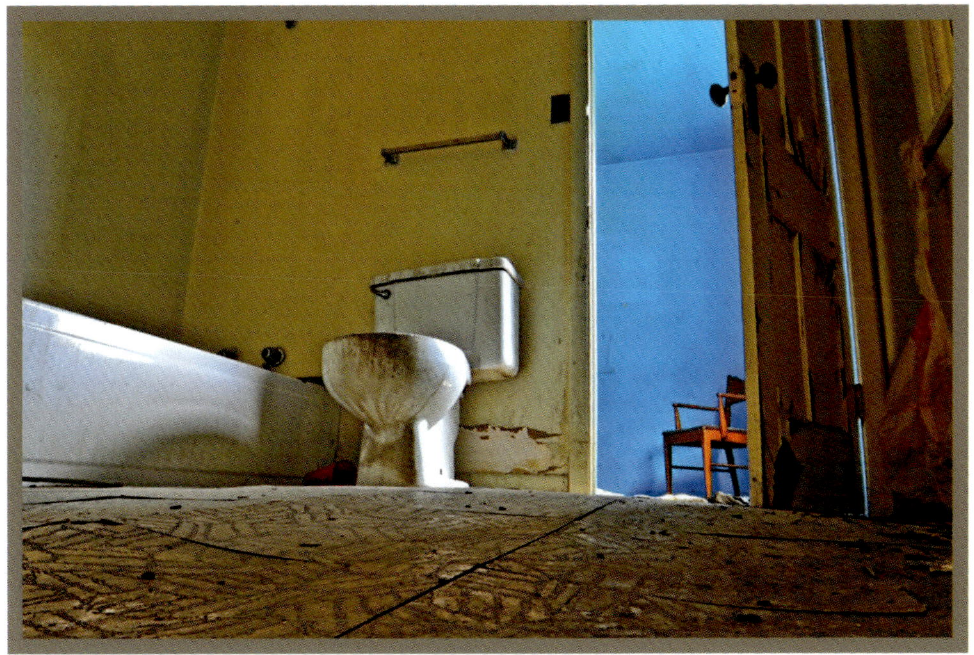

Well, okay then. On that note, I think we're ready to move on to Impressionism.

IMPRESSIONISM. Of all the art movements I studied in college, Impressionism was definitely one that grabbed my attention. I learned the styles and techniques of 19th century French painters like Renoir, Monet, Manet, Cezanne, and others.

The impressionists of that era were tired of just duplicating life on canvas. They entertained the notion of painting only an "impression" of what they saw, thus the term used to identify them. In fact, one of Monet's paintings has the word "Impression" in the title.

Some characteristics of, and ways of describing Impressionism include the following.

> Only a glance of the subject
> Use of visual effects, versus detail
> A sense of movement
> Blurring
> Bright colors
> Sketchy & unfinished
> Irregular surface texture
> An impression of what the artist saw

If you want to learn more about the impressionists, who they were, and examples of their work, you can scan the code below for more information.

Now that I have introduced Impressionism and the impressionists, let me share various approaches I take to create my impressionistic images. When I am out in the field, I don't analyze ways of converting something to an impressionistic image—it just happens. It's more intuitive; second nature. I just sense it and do it. It depends on the subject itself, the mood, and the feel I get from certain subjects or scenes. They "talk" to me. Depending on the moment, and the scene, it is as if I am an impressionist with a camera and simply follow my impressionistic instincts. That said, the subjects I find most conducive to impressionistic interpretations are florals and nature scenes.

I use specific photographic techniques or approaches to create images that have a sense of movement, have blur, seem sketchy and unfinished, and have less than perfect detail.

Sometimes it's **the scene itself**—a scene that convinces me that if Monet had seen it, he would have painted it. Such was the case when I saw this next scene near Steamboat Springs, Colorado. It was late September, late afternoon, and at the early stages of autumn. The whole scene looked impressionistic.

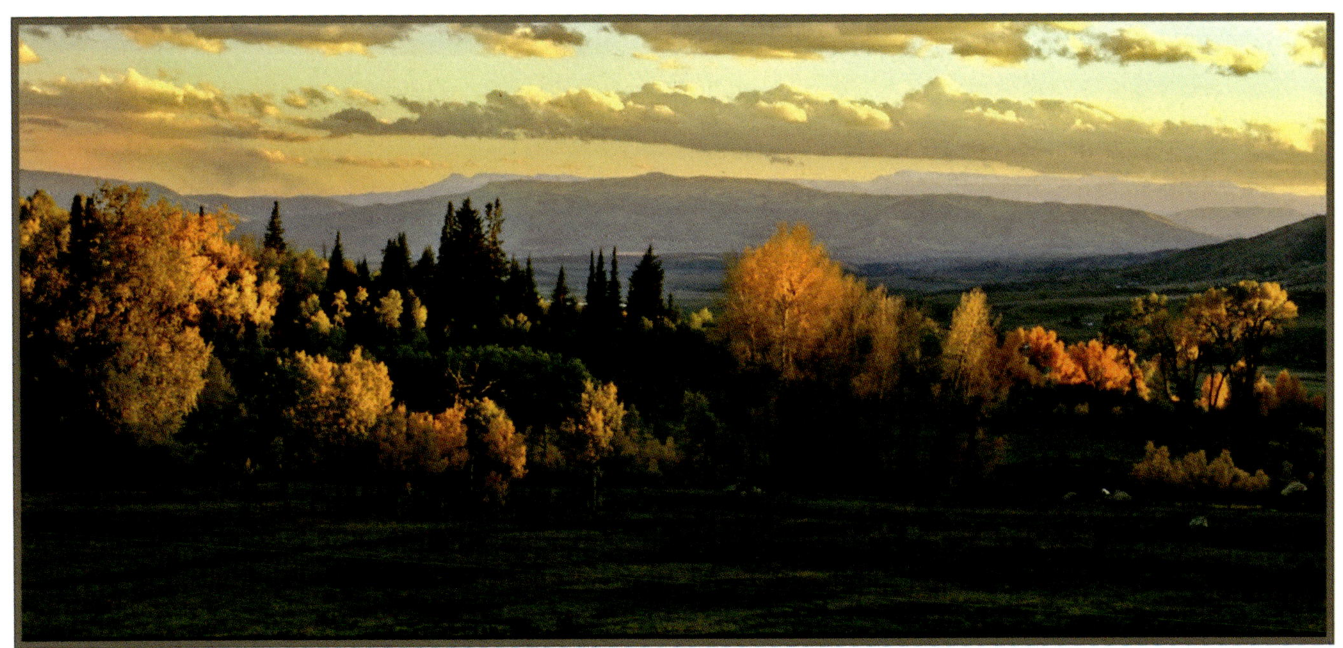

"Impressionistic Valley"

Double exposures. These are the steps I take when I create images like the one on the next page. 1) My camera is on a tripod and set for manual focus. I normally set my f/stop to f/5.6. I take the scene slightly out of focus. I take a test shot to make sure I like it. It should not be too much out of focus or too bright. If necessary, I make proper adjustments and re-shoot it. Now I'm ready for my double exposure. 2) I engage my double exposure feature for two shots. 3) I re-take the test shot, since I know what it's going to look like. Click. 3) I then set my f/stop to f/16 and refocus to get a sharp image. In addition to that I also underexpose the second shot usually by – 2/3. Click. I've got my impressionistic double exposure. This is more art than science.

"Watercolor Willows" is another example of this technique and effect, as is the image on page 66. Others are sprinkled throughout the book. You might call this the "Vega Effect," but to me it's about using the medium of photography to create what the impressionists created on canvas—an impression of what they saw.

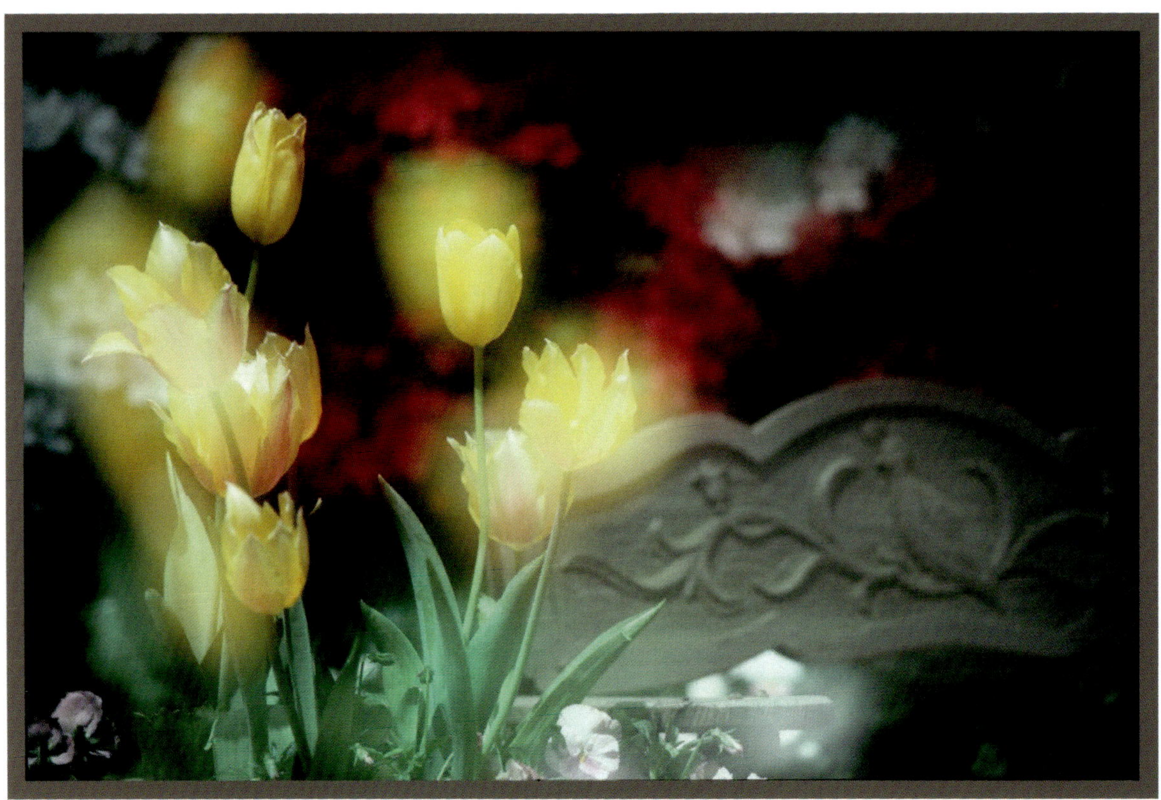

"Tulips Aglow"

Photographing **reflections** is another approach I take. Reflections of any kind grab my attention. I get a sense of peace from them. Some are mystical; some mysterious.

It was hard to decide which ones to share with you here. I chose "Trail of Gold" on the next page because, at quick glance, it's one of those brain teasers.

I was hiking one early morning next to a strong flowing creek near Rico, Colorado. It was late September and I was walking along a rugged 4-wheel road. I was looking for aspen autumn reflections that day. The image I had in my mind was a scene with clear aspen reflections in the creek or a nearby pond. All of a sudden, I noticed a trickle of water on the road. Several feet above me, to my left, was a mountainside sprinkled with nice golden aspens. I started scanning. Then I saw a portion of the road with a small stream-like flow. Following my intuition, I got lower, much lower. It was only then that I saw the mysterious aspen reflections, surrounded by contrasting sharp-edged rocks along the road. It was the aspen gold that really got my attention.

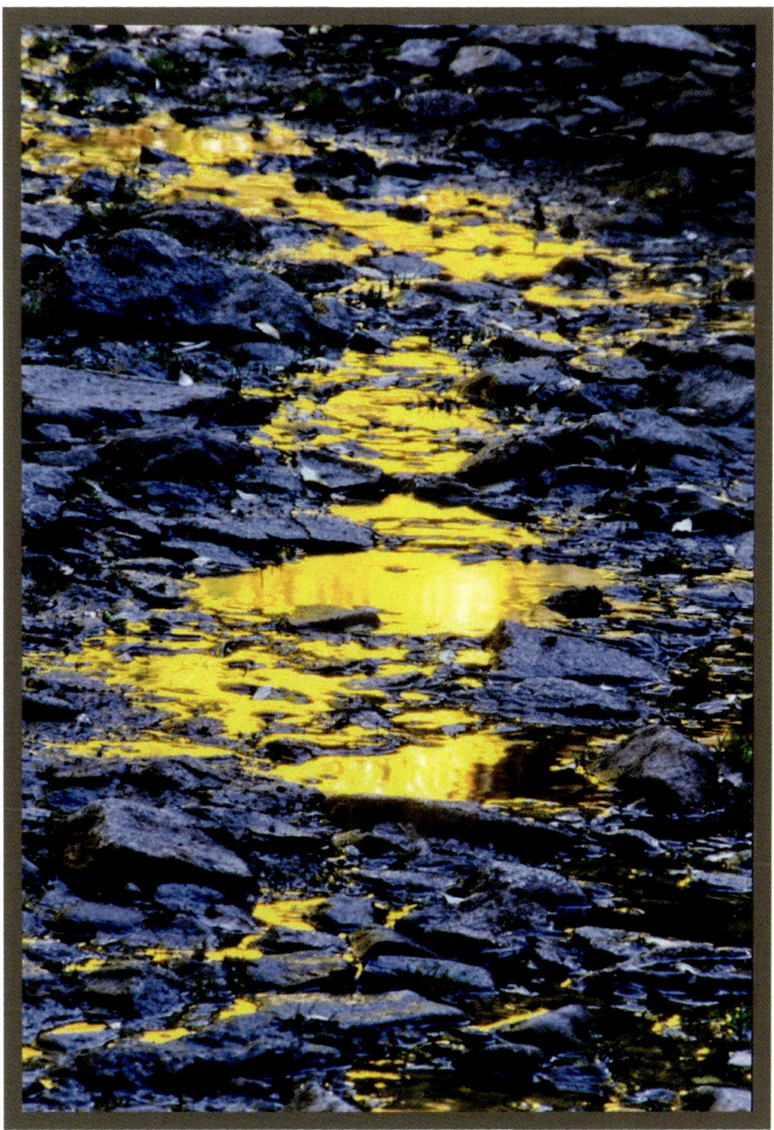

"Trail of Gold"

You will see other examples of impressionistic images later. I added them in a separate section to continuously challenge your thinking process.

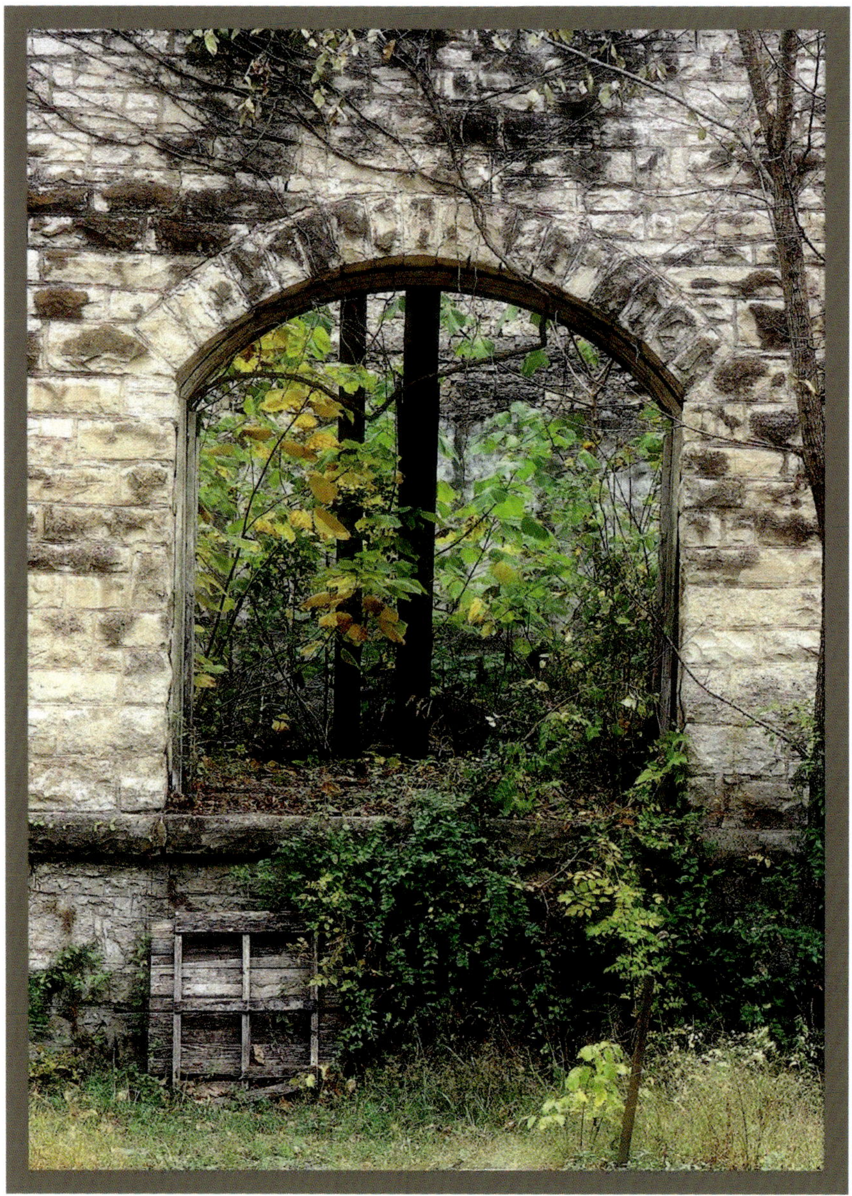

Are you inside looking out, or outside looking in? Or is there a stone wall with two exteriors? This is what makes surrealism so intriguing and mind boggling.

SURREALISM. I never forget the first time I saw *The Persistence of Memory* and *Christ of Saint John of the Cross* by the Spaniard Salvador Dalí. I saw the latter at the Art Institute of Chicago. Hanging high on one of its walls, the painting looked much bigger than 46"x81."

When I studied Dalí in college, I was instantly awed by his imagination and creation of out-of-body renderings of life. There were other surrealists, like Joan Miró, Marcel Duchamp, Max Ernst, and others, but it was Dalí that left an indelible impression on me.

I have been hooked on surrealism ever since. I use my intuition to guide me to the jarring, the unexpected, the surreal.

Some characteristics of, and ways that Surrealism has been described include the following.

> The juxtaposition of unexpected objects, themes, or ideas
> Things we usually do not associate with each other
> The element of surprise, or even shock
> Incongruency
> Perplexing
> Word association mix-ups

If you want to learn more about the surrealists, who they were, and examples of their work, you can scan the code below for more information.

I am instinctively driven to anything that meets the characteristics of surrealism. The subject or scene do not have to look as surrealistic as some of Dalí's paintings, as long as they surprise or perplex me. If it's surreal, it gets my attention. It is either already there for the taking, or I create it.

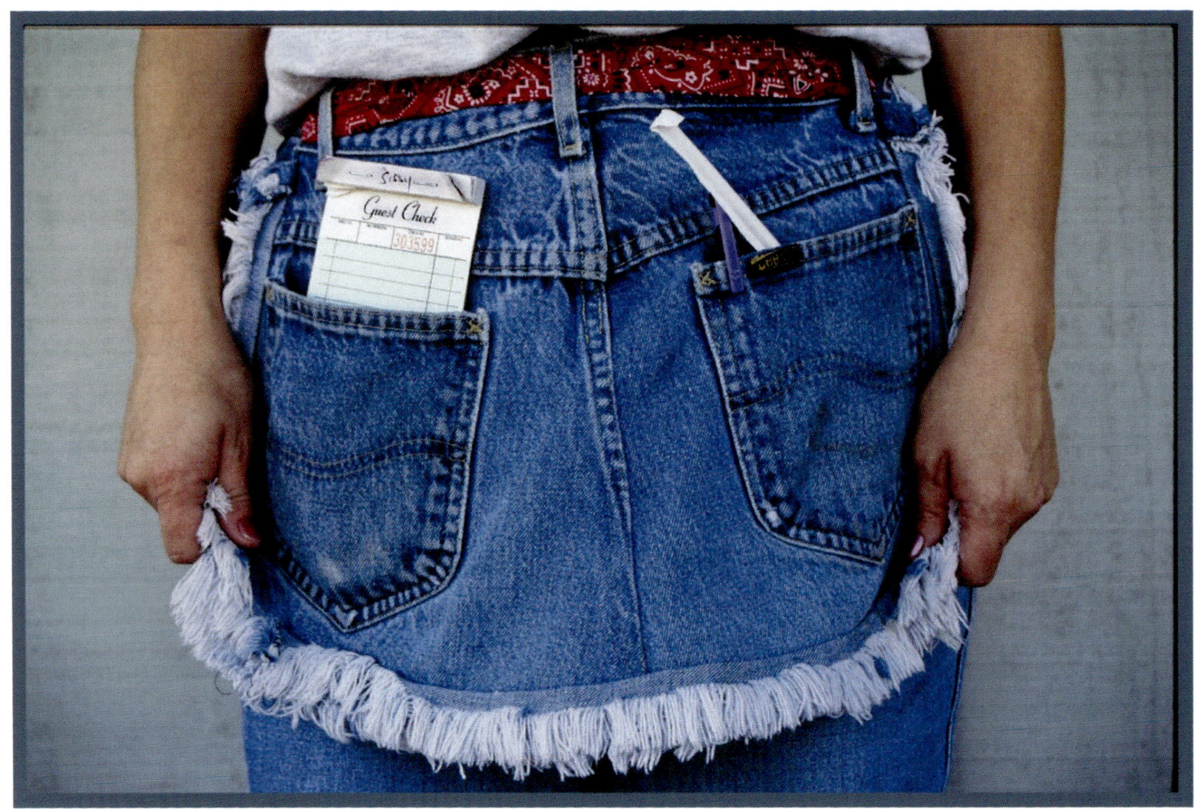

I got up really early one morning when I lived in Dallas, Texas. I took the small country roads east of the city. After two hours of driving and shooting, I stopped in a small country town and decided to have breakfast at a quaint cafe called The Roundup. As I relaxed and enjoyed my hot breakfast, I noticed the cute aprons the waitresses had on. After a few minutes of eating and observing, my surrealistic mind began kicking in. I had an idea.

When I finished my breakfast, I went to the front counter to pay. I asked for the manager. She said, “I'm the owner.” I introduced myself, explained that I liked the aprons, and told her I wanted to photograph one of the waitresses outside, if they weren't too busy. The owner, having no problem with my request, quickly yelled loudly across the room filled with early morning patrons, “Sissy! This man wonts you.” I heard her say, “wonts.”

I thanked Sissy for coming over, then walked her outside and told her what I “wonted.” The idea, as you can see, was to create a quick glance illusion of someone's backside, wearing jeans, with her hands turned backward on her hips. If you look closely, you can see the word Sissy scribbled on the top of her Guest Check book.

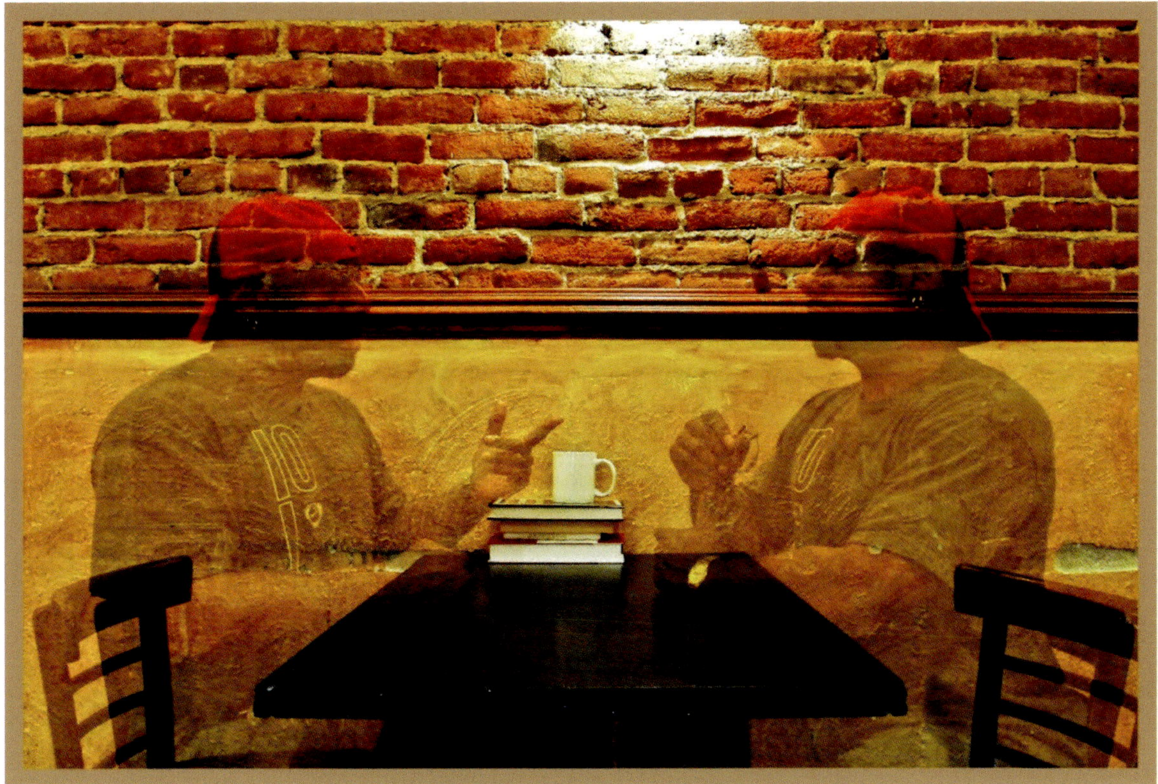

I call this image “Spirit Self-Talk.” I had done this before with a self-portrait, so I knew it would work. I asked James to first sit on the right side of the table, hold his glasses in his hand, and pretend that he was listening to someone. After I got that shot, I asked him to sit on the left side of the table and pretend he was talking to someone, like he was trying to make a point. He took it from there. The ghostly double exposure definitely looks surreal.

So, although I am not quite as bizarre as Salvador Dalí, I do like to incorporate many of the characteristics of surrealism into my photography. In the case of James, I created the surrealism in my imagination days before I asked him to model for me.

The scene I shared to introduce this section was from quaint Eureka Springs, in the Arkansas Ozarks. It is an abandoned power plant facility. One of the doors, weathered from decades of non-use, exposed its beautiful stone archway. Nature had taken over its huge interior through decades of decay. The inside looked the same as the outside.

The key to finding or creating surrealism is to remember its characteristics. I sprinkle a few more examples of surrealism later in the book. See if you can spot them.

My fifth point in my "Eli's 5-Point Photo Art Model" is **eastern philosophy**. You might need to meditate before I get started. No, I'm just kidding.

I have studied the concepts of eastern philosophy since 1998. It occurred to me one day that there is an interesting and creative application of some of its principles and concepts to photography. It goes beyond "Zen photography"—that term is too vague of a concept for me.

The following are specific eastern philosophy concepts and principles which I have applied to my photography. They are introduced from the viewpoint of my interpretations of those concepts. Applying them to my photography has become second nature to me now.

These concepts have great application to life in general, and I do apply them to my life. Books have been written about them. Seminars have been devoted to them. However, I will limit my descriptions and explanations to how I apply them to my photography.

Detachment. We need to detach ourselves from our life programming. Since kindergarten, we were taught in terms of right and wrong, black and white, this and that. "This, boys and girls, is called a……," we heard our teachers say. If we called a robin a blue jay, our teacher would immediately correct us. Since we were still in the early stages of our learning process in life, we were programmed to accept the teacher's corrections. We attach ourselves to symbols that represent ideas or beliefs we've been taught. As a result, we grow up to be adults and are now "attached" to recognize certain things in life for what they "are."

We need to detach ourselves from what we see, or think we see. In my study of eastern philosophy, I ran across this mind boggling concept: "No self, no problems." When you apply it to your photography, I encourage you to detach yourself from your "self." Sounds deep, huh? Here is one way to achieve this. When you're out in the field someday ask yourself, "If this wasn't me seeing this, what would the other "I" see? If that is too deep, ask yourself, "What would someone else see?"

I had a chance to visit with one of my Right Brain Photography students a few weeks after he had taken my workshop. Bob shared this interesting story with me. He told me he had gone to visit some relatives in Grand Junction, Colorado. He went to their backyard and started looking around. Disgruntled with the fact that he didn't see anything worth his time, he asked himself, "What would Eli see?" He made me laugh. He continued his story. After several minutes of looking around, he said that he started looking at the silver-like aluminum wind chimes hanging from the back porch. He kept looking at them as they swayed slowly in the breeze. Then, it occurred to him to get up really close and get some shots of them with a slow shutter speed, as they swayed in the breeze. He showed me the results of his "chimes." They were very abstract, with nice smooth swirled shapes and strong blurred colors picked up from the background. I really liked his image. They did not look like chimes. He had detached himself from seeing them as chimes. He confessed that when he was in his family's backyard, nothing impressed him; nothing got his attention, until he started thinking like me. He then added, "Who would think that wind chimes would make a good photo."

I show Bob's image, as well as the work of other students, at the end of the book.

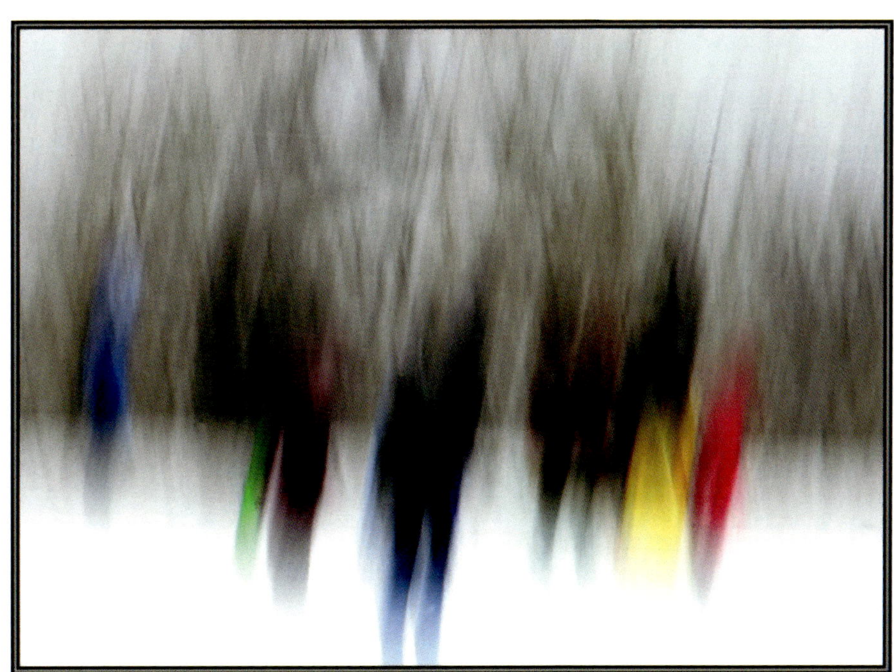

An example of detachment. People sledding on a hillside.

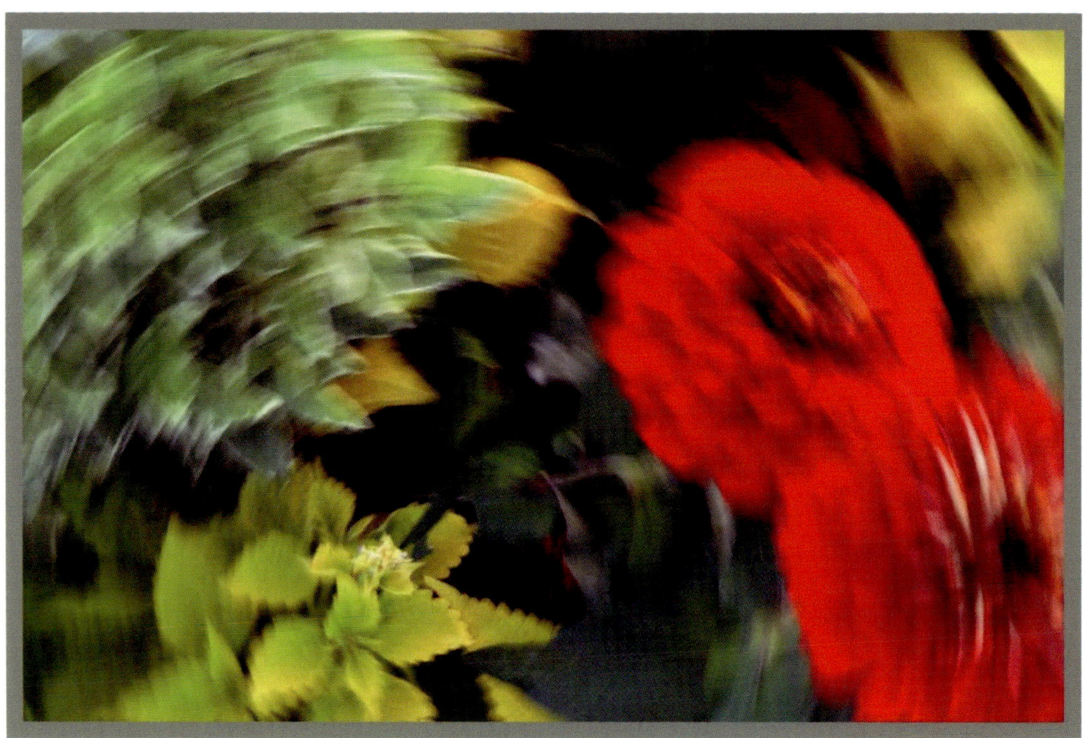

"Dimensions"

When I detach myself from my mental programming, I start seeing differently. I don't see with my eyes; I see with my imagination. When I do that, I realize I can make "flowers" look like this through my photography. By detaching myself from what I am programmed to see (flowers/plants), it frees me up to create whatever I want or feel like creating at the moment. If I do not detach myself from the construct and symbols related to "flowers," all I will end up doing is getting some great images of flowers. That, in and of itself, is not a bad thing, but I can add a totally different dimension when they are no longer flowers or plants. In this case, my imagination took over and asked, "What can I make these colors look like if I move my camera in a circular motion?" In this case, it worked better without a tripod. Since there was going to be motion, a high shutter speed was not of great concern. In fact, I wanted a *slow* shutter speed, to allow me time to swirl my camera during the slow exposure—in this case, 1/25th of a second.

"By letting go, it all gets done." Lao-Tzu

This takes me to the next eastern philosophy concept-- a close cousin to *detachment*.

Un-labeling. We need to detach ourselves from the labels we have learned. "This is called a tree." "This is called a caboose...." "This is a butterfly...." "These are tulips…."

Un-labeling can be difficult to do because we have been programmed to attach labels to whatever we see. For example, "bottle," "tulip," "tree," "light fixtures".....and the list goes on.

Labeling is directly related to how we describe things. If we see a lake, we see a lake because that's what we have been taught it is—a "lake." If we see a duck swimming in the lake, we describe it as such—a duck in the water. And, when all we see is a "duck in the water," the tendency is to keep walking until something really good hits us between the eyes and screams, "Here I am! Is this what you're looking for?" When it comes to photography, the eyes see too much. If we couple that with our programmed labeling, we can easily go home without some great images which we did not see.

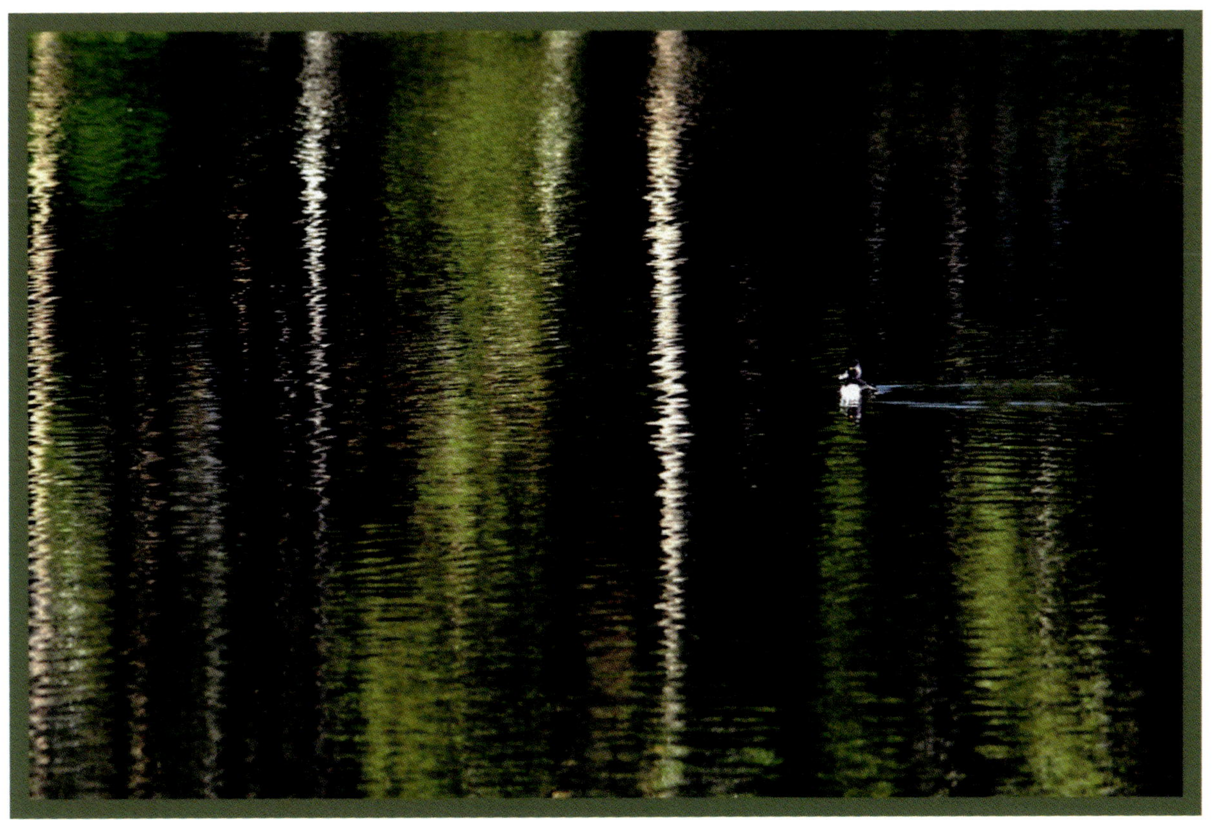

"Swimming in Abstracts"

The thought of a duck in the water does not sound too appealing, does it? It is important to understand that the previous scene did *not* look like this to my naked eye. It looked like, well, just a duck in the water.

There was a lot of right brain/left brain hand-shaking going on with that scene. At the top of the list was imagination—what would this look like if….? Anticipation and planning were the next steps. I saw the water on the lake and saw the reflections from the trees above. I could see the water moving, and knew what I had to do to darken the water and “freeze” the designs and shapes my eyes could *not* see. I used a fast shutter speed and under exposed the scene, which gave me the abstract shapes and rich colors not visible to the naked eye.

I saw the duck several yards to my right, moving toward the area on which I was focused. After I took a test shot to make sure I was going to like the results from my under exposure, it was just a matter of waiting for the duck to come into view. I was *creating* the image in my imagination, not taking pictures or “capturing” anything. I knew I wanted to introduce the duck when he reached a light area in the scene, so he would stand out and not get lost against a dark background. Planning, imagining, anticipating, and applying the elements of art paid off for me that day.

When I took away the labels, the scene no longer contained a lake—I saw shapes, lines, design, and color. The duck was but another shape to include in my design, as were the patterns he was creating behind him. Be an artist first, photographer second. This is right brain photography.

I rarely share or talk about my camera settings. It is not because I want to keep them a secret, but because photography is more art than science. To get the same or similar results depends on the scene—the time of day, lighting, motion in the water, the perspective, weather conditions, or the speed of the duck. I don’t use formulas in photography--only guidelines, principles, and concepts. That said, I under exposed the scene by a -2, or two stops under exposed, which is severe for photography. The aperture was f/9, and the shutter speed was 1/640th of a second. I used my 70mm-300mm lens to “reach out” to that particular area of the lake. That’s what it took to *create* the image.

Here is another example of detachment. All of my images incorporate more than one aspect of my paradigms, but, for now, let me focus on detachment and un-labeling.

I walked around Silver Lake, near Salt Lake City, Utah in Big Cottonwood Canyon. As I walked around the lake I saw these grass-like weeds or reeds that seemed to float on the lake surface. There were tons of them, sprinkled throughout the lake. They looked like this.

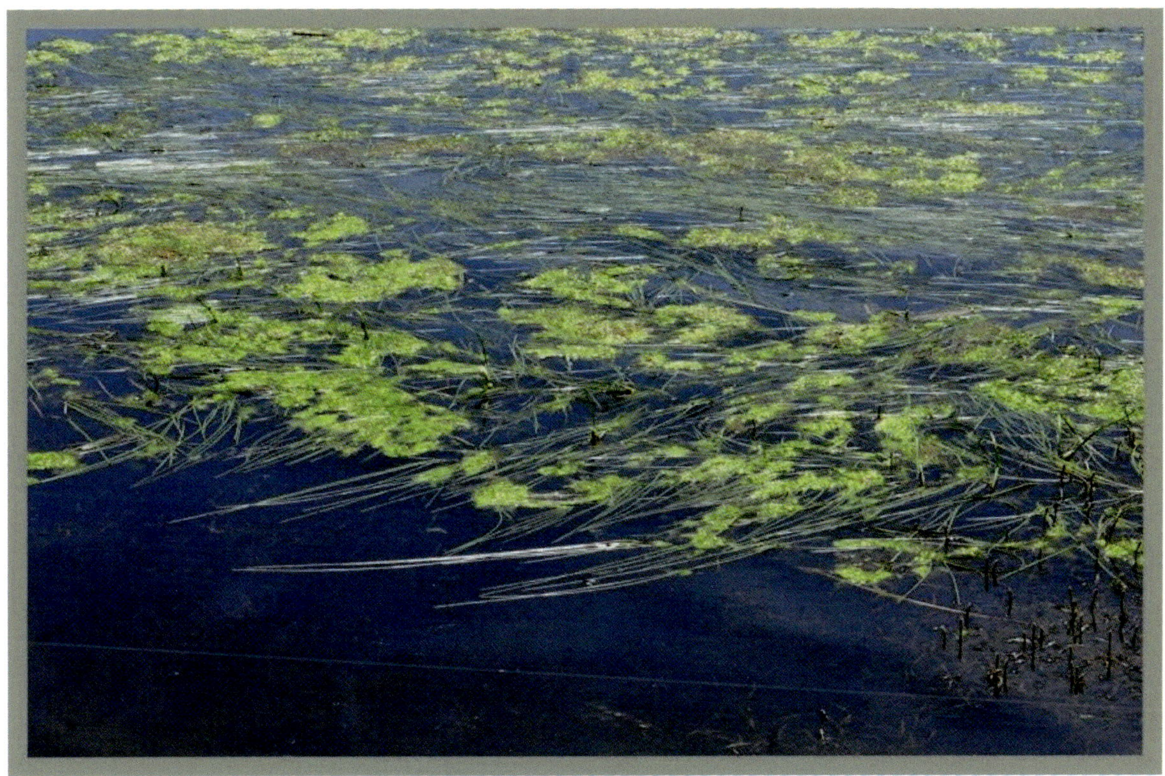

As I continued my walk, the labels began melting off. I no longer saw reeds, or even a lake. The more I walked around the lake, the more I started seeing shapes, designs, colors.

Then, bingo, I got enlightened. I could see it in my imagination. My right brain then shook hands with my left brain and said, "I've got an idea, and this is what I need from you."

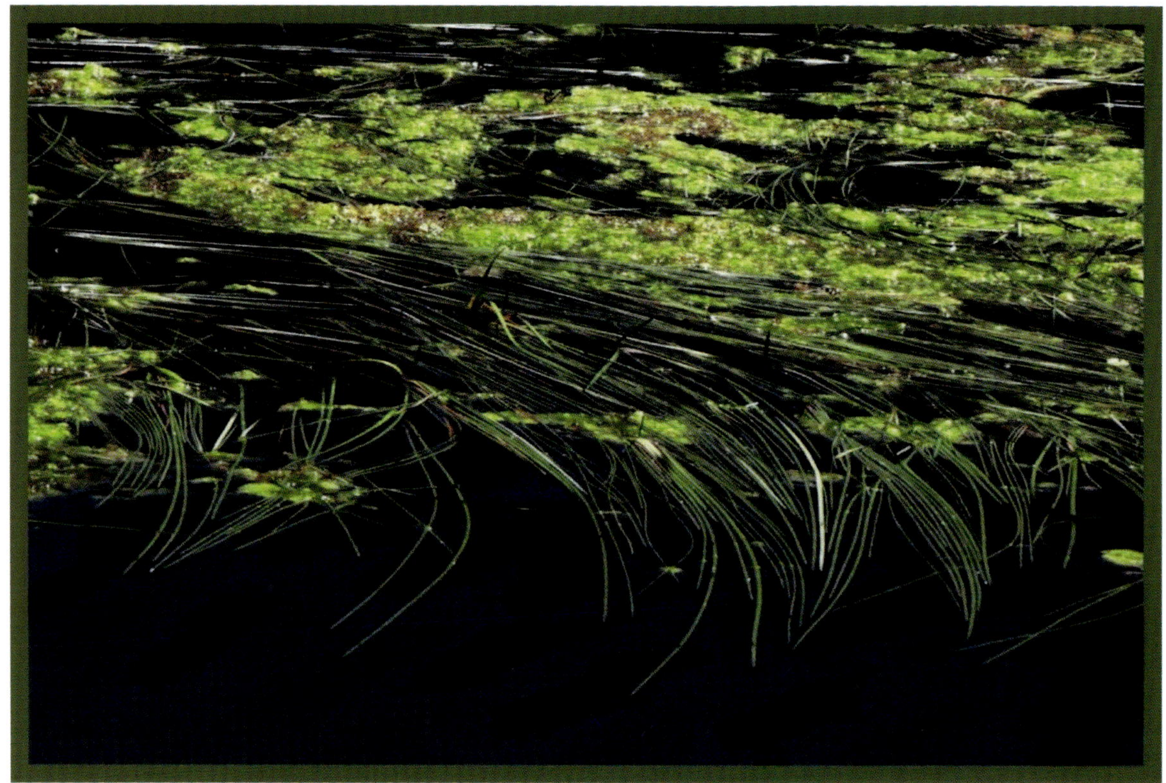

What my eyes see becomes secondary to what my imagination sees. In this image, the reeds are no longer reeds; water is no longer water. They are now shapes of color. I knew that an extreme under exposure (-2 2/3 stops) would give me what I imagined.

Impermanence. Life is in constant change. Nothing is permanent. I believe that a lot of people go through life, and then end it with, "What happened? Where did time go?" In order to get the most out of the short lives we have, we need to take advantage of every day, every hour, every moment. It is not enough to take advantage of every year or decade. If we do not deeply understand and accept our own impermanence, and act accordingly, we will miss out on living. Too many of us are just alive.

Similarly, in photography, everything around us is ever changing, now, as we speak. When we are out shooting, we need to take advantage of what we see, at the time we see it.

Place yourself in this scenario. You drive by a really neat barn built in the late 1890s. The red paint is barely hanging on, which adds to your interest. There are gaps between the wooden slats. The barn walls have less than 90-degree angles. Get the picture? You never bother to photograph it, thinking maybe next week, or next month. One late evening while you were sleeping, a strong thunderstorm rolled in. The old barn could not hold up to the winds that evening and just toppled over. Then you drove by a few days later, expecting to see the barn, and proclaimed with utter disappointment, “Oh, man, where is the barn?” Impermanence.

I cannot stress this particular concept of eastern philosophy enough, especially as it relates to photography. We cannot assume that either human-made or nature’s best subjects will be there the next hour, the next day, or the next year. Even if they are still there later, they might not look the same.

Some of my favorite images, including those on which I receive positive comments, were created with impermanence in mind. I will never be able to replicate them. Those precious moments, sometimes seconds, are gone—forever. I’m glad I have memories of them through my photo art.

I was in Russellville, Arkansas one early morning. I saw something I liked, but it was too early in the morning. I didn’t like where the shadows were falling. I decided to go back in a couple of hours, when the lighting and the shadows would be more or less where I imagined them to be. In that case, I took advantage of impermanence in a reverse sort of way. I knew the shadows would change with time. So, I went back two hours later and, voila! It was just as I had imagined. If I had waited any longer, the shadows would have changed again, but not to my satisfaction. In that scenario, I anticipated impermanence.

On the next page, you will see what I saw. You will see what my imagination saw, not what my eyes saw.

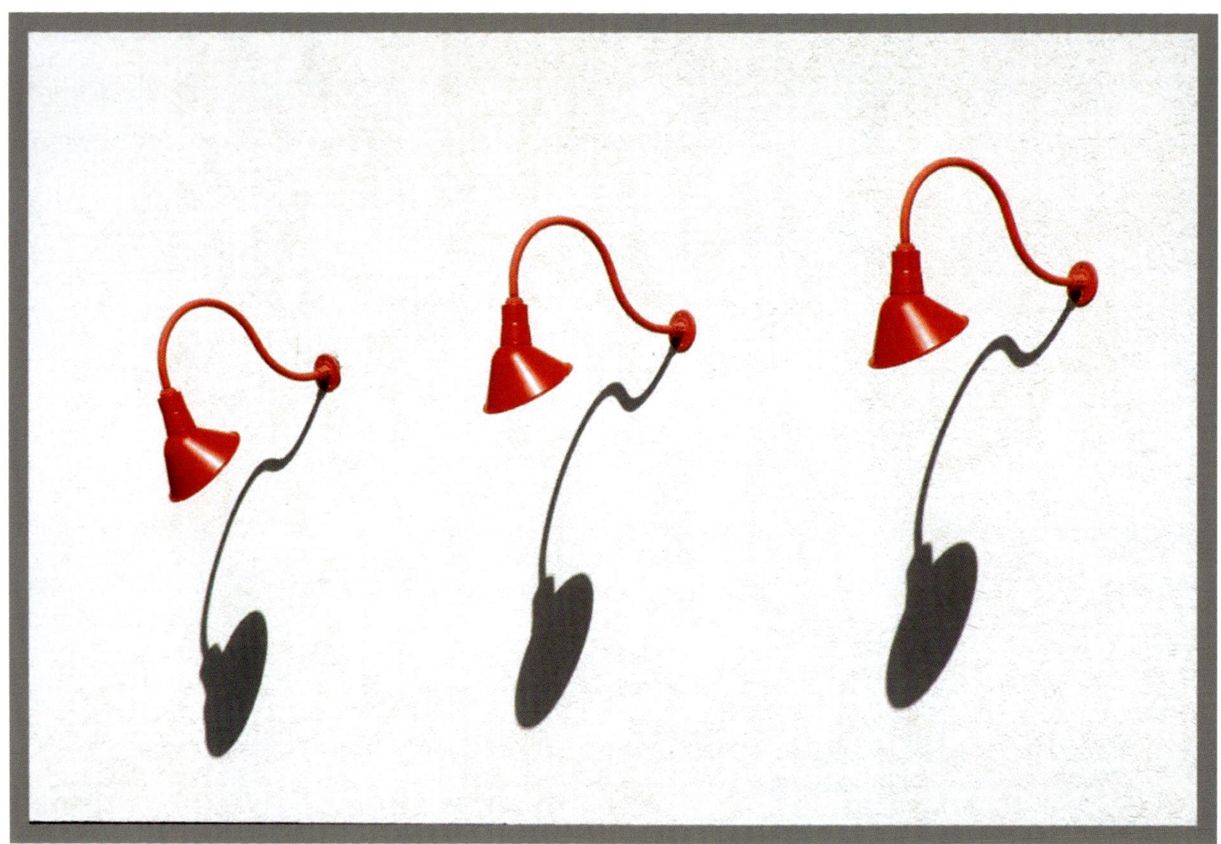

In addition to impermanence, detachment and un-labeling also came into play that day in Russellville. These shapes, colors, and designs were much more to me than simply light fixtures on the side of a Taco Bell.

Cindi, one of my most imaginative Rocky Mountain National Park workshop students, saw three identical dogs in this image. Can you see them?

Recently, also during one of my workshops in Rocky Mountain National Park, one of my students created an image of a spider web hanging from a dead tree stump. A few hours later she showed us the spot from where she had created it. She assured us that it looked much better earlier that morning. I said to the group, "Impermanence."

Interdependence. Everything and everyone are interconnected; interdependent. The colleges where I teach are dependent on me to offer my classes. I, in turn, am dependent on them to give me the opportunity to offer classes. We are interdependent. Employees are dependent on employers to provide them with a job and salary. Employers need their employees to get work done, to help them achieve their business mission. They too are interdependent. I could give more examples, but I think you get the idea of what I mean by the concept of interdependence.

I am usually attracted to interdependence when I see it occurring. In most instances, it is when the interdependence is happening in nature that really gets my attention.

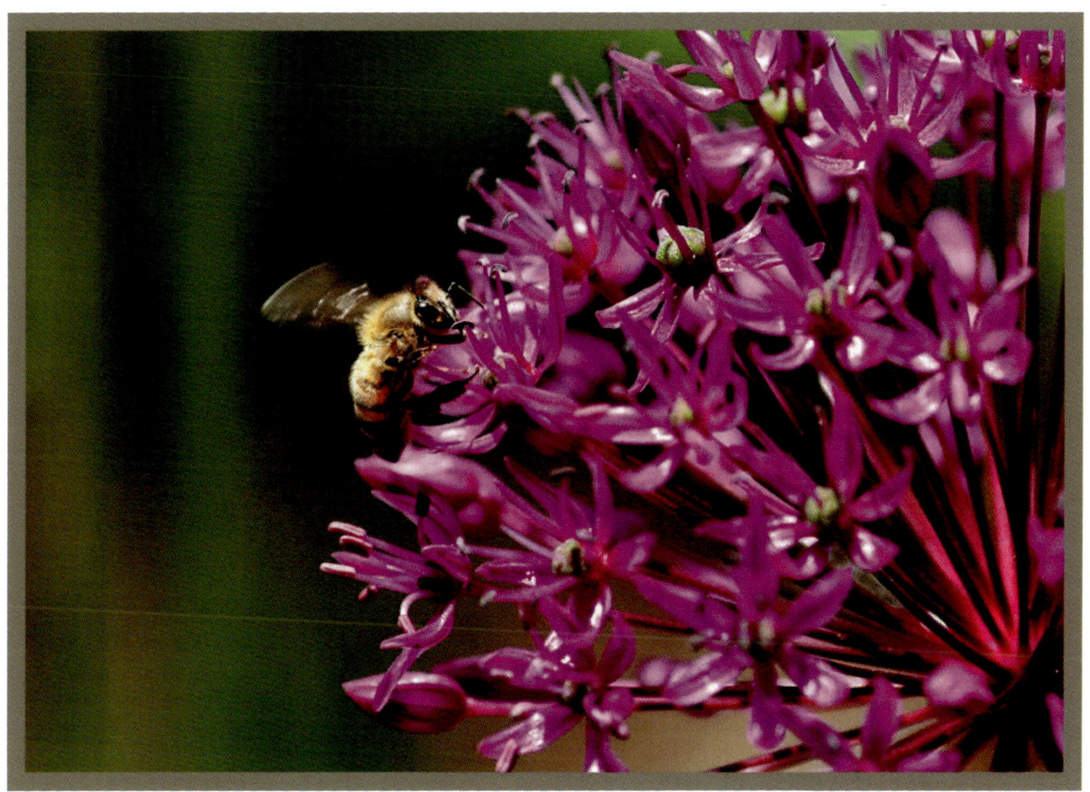

The bees need the flowers. The flowers need the bees. Interdependent needs.

Mindfulness. I introduce mindfulness in this section because mindfulness means being in the moment; in the here and now. I talked earlier about I.S.E.E. SOMETHING. I referred to scanning, extracting, and eliminating. After I extract from the big picture, I eliminate my surroundings, which allows me to stay "in the moment" with what I have extracted. When I apply deep and undisturbed mindfulness, I can focus better on the task at hand. As I mentioned earlier, everything around me becomes a blur.

This is why, with few exceptions, I do not create my best images when I offer workshops or 1-on-1 field lessons. I know this to be true because sometimes when I look at some of my images after the workshops, I look at the weaknesses and think, "I know better than that." My mindfulness during my workshops is directed more toward my students, making sure they are learning something, and assuring that all of them get my full attention.

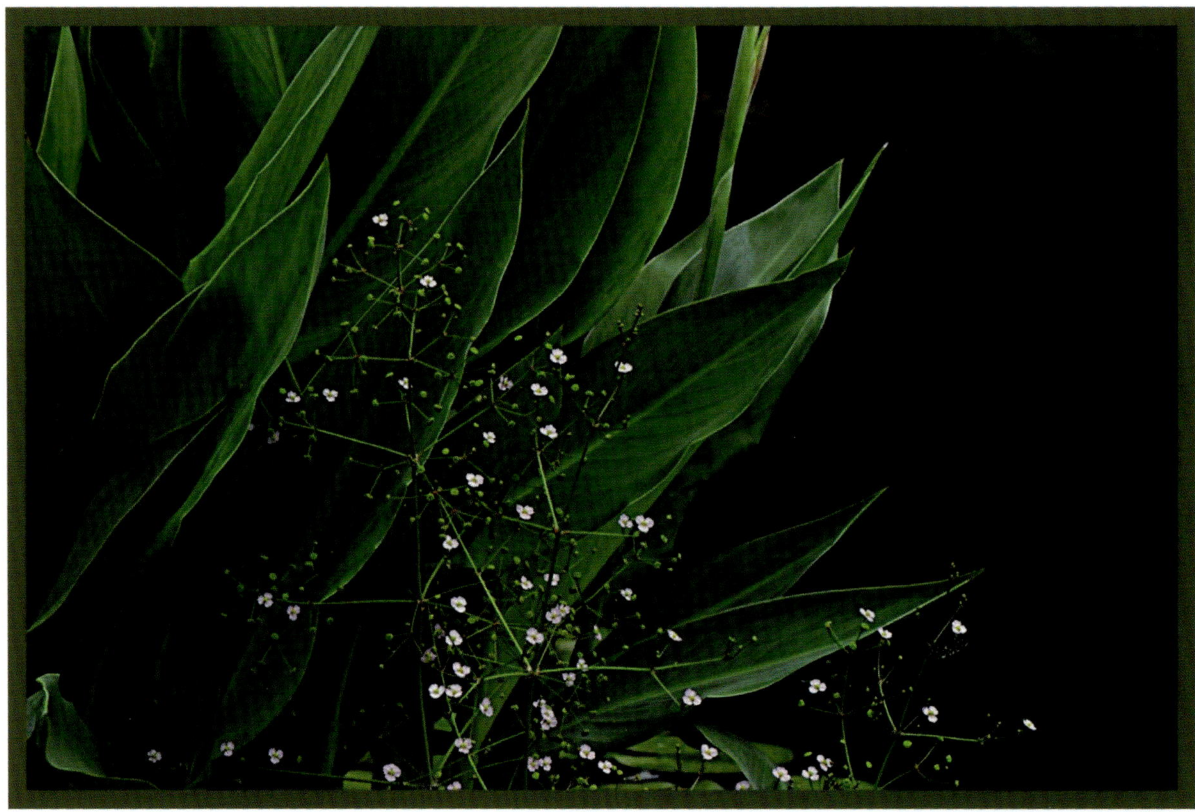

I call this "Standouts." It took concentrated mindfulness to get this. Even though my subject was far away from me, I imagined what it would look like if I was very close to it. I started examining its surroundings, the background, contrast in color, and lighting. Then I imagined what it might look like if ..... In this case, after my imagination took me closer to the scene.

I immediately detached myself from the labels "flowers" and "plants" in order to create what was left. I saw shape, color, design, and mood. I saw what my eyes did not see and told my left brain what I need in order to accomplish my artistic mission.

This next image is what the scene really looked like to my eyes. I have an under exposed rendition of this larger scene, but I favor the close-up, which I accomplished only by getting in tight with my telephoto zoom lens.

The image on the previous page is what I saw and extracted from this scene. My imagination can extract small details from large scenes—details that can easily be overlooked.

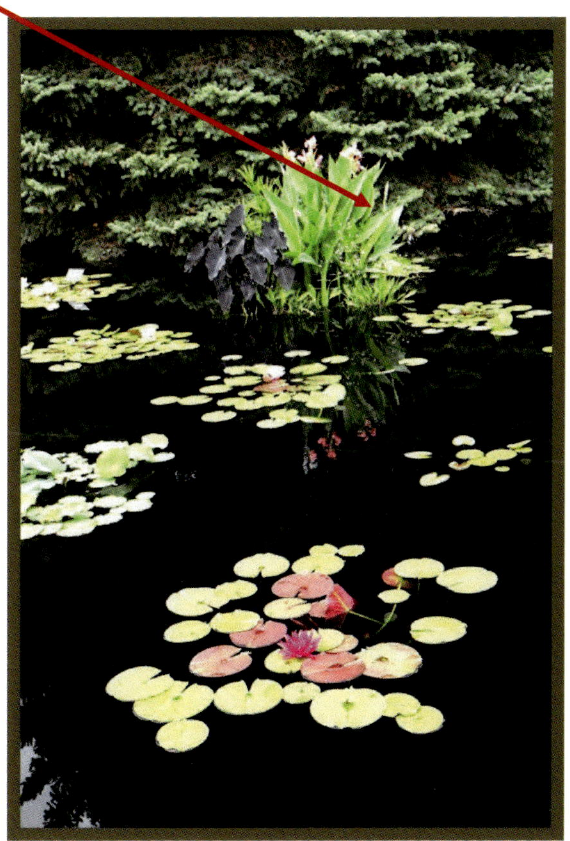

There are, by the way, other photographers who apply the same or similar eastern philosophy concepts as I do—they just articulate the approach they take to their photography differently. It's like applying eastern philosophy to one's life without realizing it. For example, people don't have to study eastern philosophy to apply compassion.

My last eastern philosophy concept is **meditation**. Meditation helps to clear the mind. Clearing the mind helps us to see more clearly, which helps us solve life problems more efficiently and effectively.

We need to keep our mind active, but we also need to give it time to recuperate from over activity. We need to sit still and not think of anything for a while. I have found that the clarity I get from meditation not only helps me with my life in general, but also eases the flow of my photography. If I am mentally relaxed, I can think and see more clearly. Additionally, my thought processes and reaction times become more efficient.

I talked about my five points separately in order to explain what they are and how I apply them. In reality, however, I apply more than one concept to my images. For example, the image with the light fixtures on a Taco Bell was created through the use of imagination, detachment, surrealism, and impermanence. The duck in the water included intuition, imagination, detachment, un-labeling, and even a touch of impressionism. "Watercolor Willows" had a combination of intuition, imagination, detachment, and un-labeling.

In the following few pages, I will show you examples of how I apply more than one of my five points to a single image. I will list the different concepts that apply to each image.

"Urban Sole"

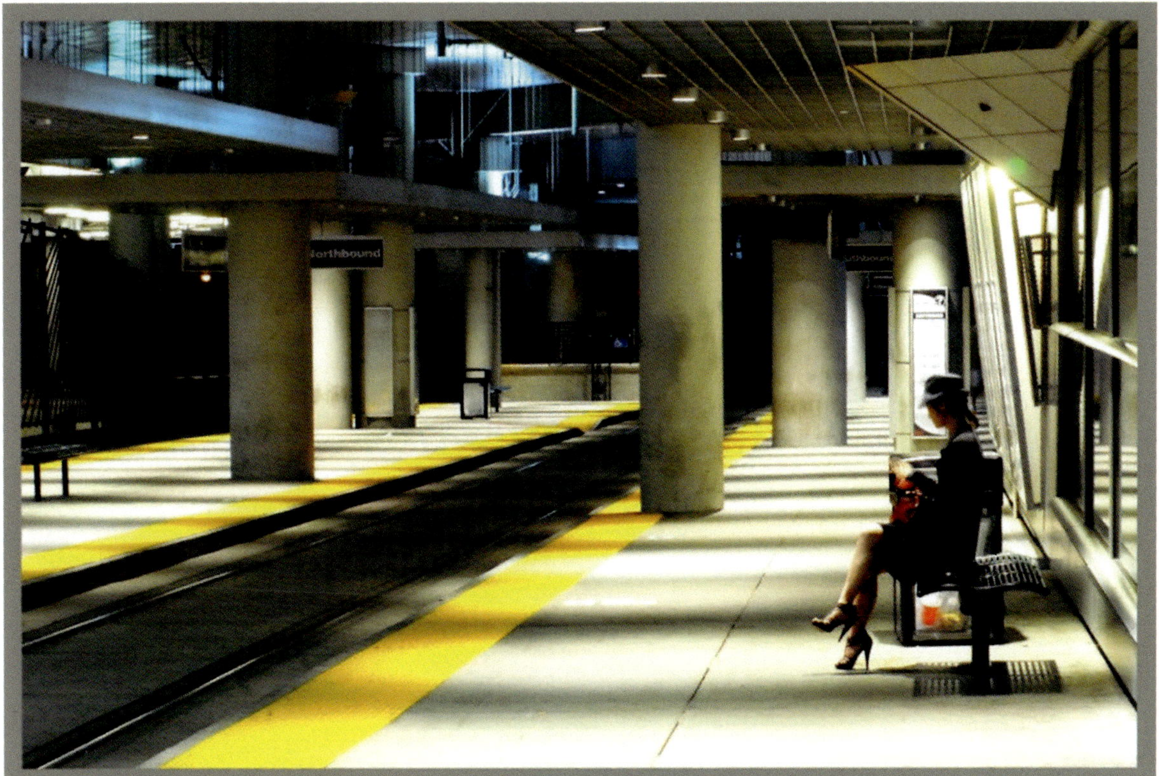

Detachment.....Impermanence.....Surrealism

I know it might sound strange, but I do not see subjects per se. In this scene, I did not see a train station. I saw color, lines, design, texture, geometry.

A couple of minutes before I created this surreal image, there was a lot of activity in and around this scene—bicyclists, trains, and commuters. All of a sudden, there was nothing left except this tiny, dainty figure against harsh and hard steel, concrete, pillars, and tracks. Just a few minutes later, the scene looked as busy as before. Then, everyone, including the lone figure, was gone.

This is the kind of image that begs questions. "Who is she? Where did she come from? Where is she going? Why is she dressed like that? What is she doing there by herself?"

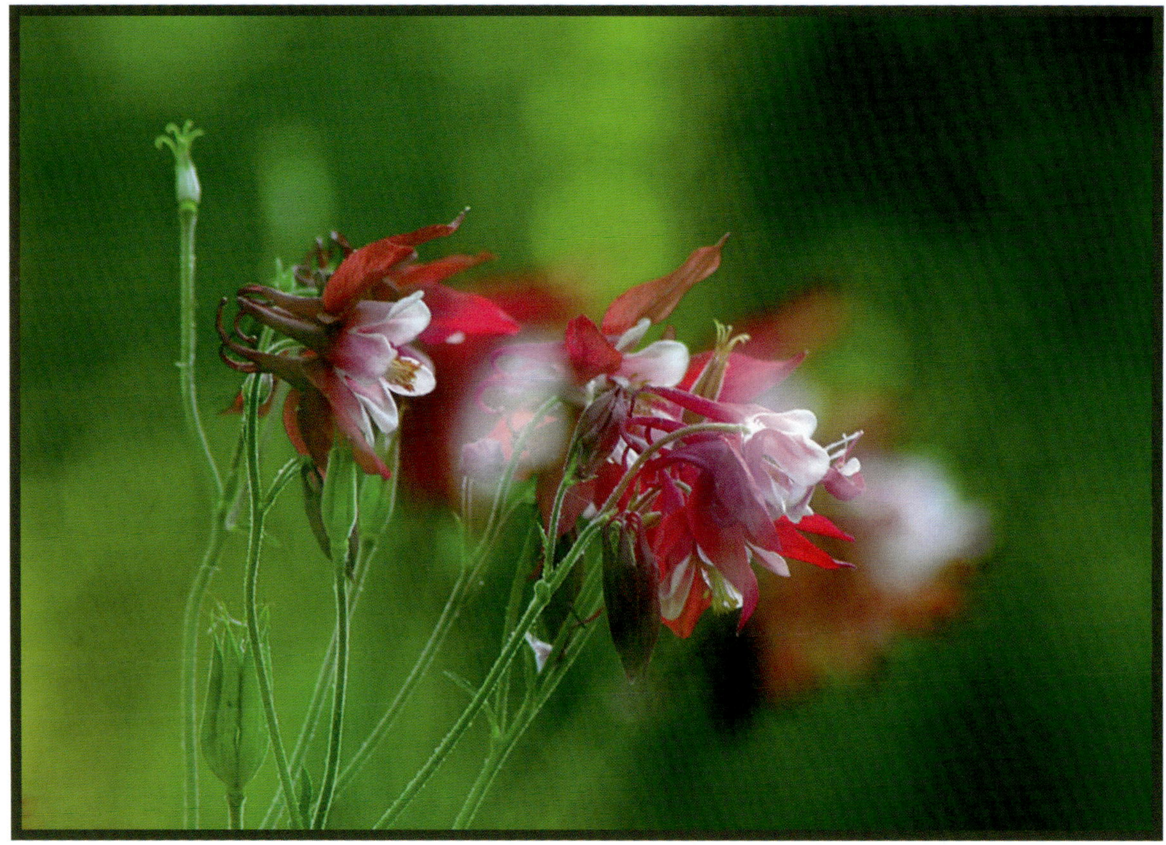

Imaginaton.....Detachment.....Impressionism.....Impermanence

Sometimes I create double exposures of subjects which most of us expect to see great sharpness through and through. Such was the case with these beautiful Columbines at Blue Spring Heritage Center near Eureka Springs, Arkansas. When I saw them, I just knew I had to do a double-exposure of them.

Imagination

Impressionism

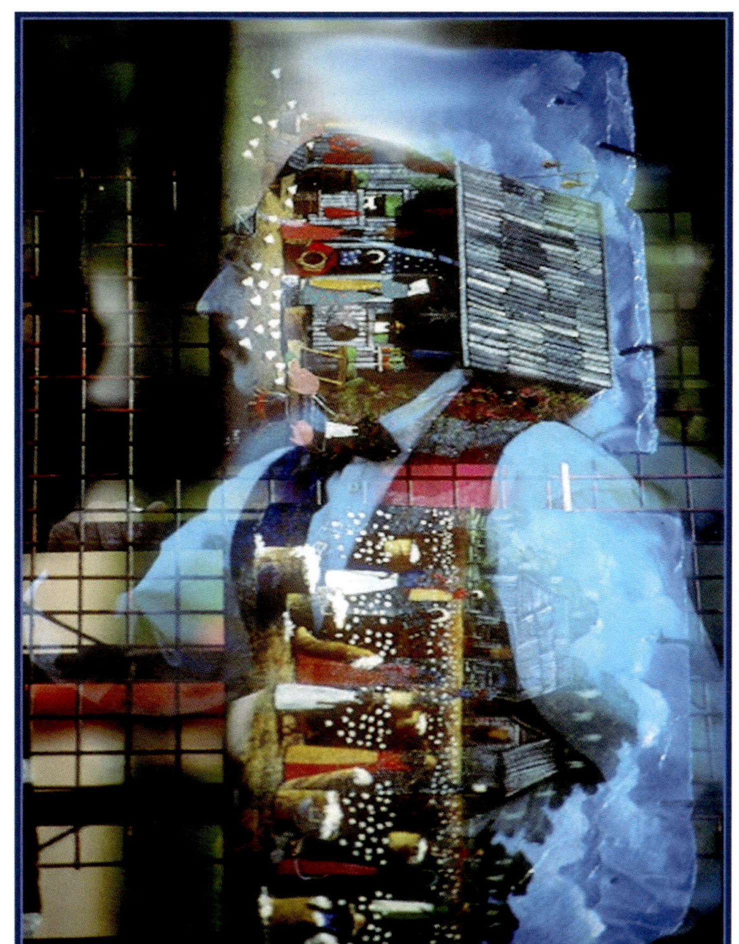

Detachment

Surrealism

Impermanence

What do you see? I call this piece "New Orleans Pantomime." Now that you have a hint as to where I created this image, let me share the story behind the lens.

I had been shooting around the French Quarter for several hours. It was filled with color, excitement, action, people, music, art and culture. After several hours, I felt like I had not captured the true essence of New Orleans. Then, while in Jackson Square, I saw a street performer on the corner across the street. He got my attention with his attire, white face, classy hat and bow tie, but it still wasn't enough—I needed to add more "New Orleans."

I turned around and not far from me was an artist whose specialty was the creation of small "deep south" themed paintings on small pieces of shale. I stared at several pieces she had painted. One of the most colorful pieces portrayed southern blacks picking cotton, with dilapidated shacks in the background, supposedly their living quarters.

My imagination woke up. Once I took the labels off the street performer and a painting on shale, I saw nothing but colors—colors that needed to be blended together. So I decided to create a double exposure of the street performer and that one art piece that caught my eye. I had to work fast because I didn't know how much longer he was going to be there. In order to mix in the colors and shapes, I first photographed the art on shale, horizontally. Then, I turned around and photographed the street performer vertically. The result was both impressionistic and surreal.

If you turn the book around 90 degrees counter clockwise, you will see the art on shale in the "New Orleans Pantomime" image.

"Let the beauty of what you love be what you do." Rumi

Intuition

Surrealism

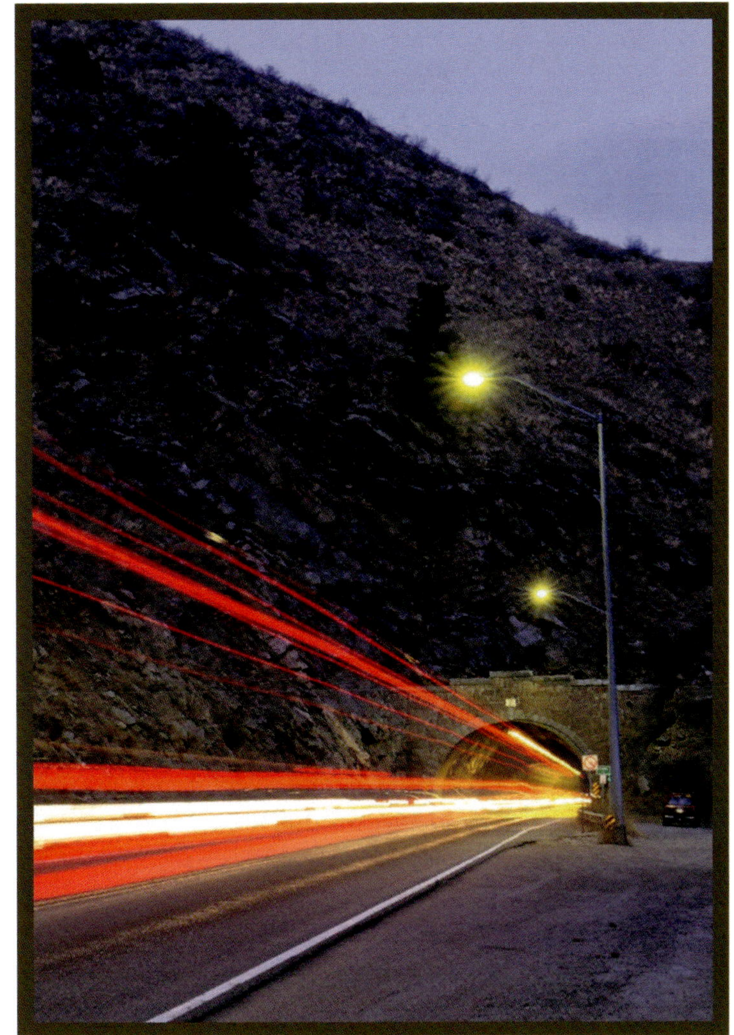

Imagination

Impermanence

Detachment

I was driving home from Aspen. I drove through the canyon on scenic Highway 6, along Clear Creek canyon between Idaho Springs and Golden, Colorado. There are a total of six tunnels in the canyon, the most of any canyon in the state. When I approached tunnel #3, my intuition and imagination began stirring. For years, I have deeply internalized the meaning behind the Greek word from which the word "photography" originates: "painting with light." That became my goal that evening—to "paint" with light, with a 20-second exposure.

I detached myself from the labels of "tunnel" and "cars." What I did see with my imagination were streaks of color that would seem to be coming out of the tunnel. The sight of a tunnel with cars going through it, really, is not that exciting. However, I made it interesting by setting the scene for a long exposure.

Timing was critical to create what I had in mind. The reason I wanted to wait for that specific moment was because I wanted white, yellow, and red streaks in the image I was creating. It took a lot of patience. For this particular image, I saw a big bus coming from my left. My hope was that the bus, with its lights high on top, would approach the tunnel at the same time that cars were coming out of the tunnel. I lucked out!

I am an artist first. I start creating images with my right brain. From a right brain perspective, I saw color, streaks of color bursting out of the tunnel. From a left brain perspective, it was late in the evening. The sun had just set, leaving the canyon in gray darkness. It was exactly what I needed to get some long exposures. The scene did not look this light to the naked eye. Because it was very dark, I knew that with a 20-30 second exposure, the fast-moving vehicles would disappear, but their continuous streaks of light would be recorded. The streaks of color were not from just one or two cars. There were several vehicles entering and exiting the tunnel during those several seconds. The higher streaks were from the bus entering the tunnel.

The end result is a very surreal feeling to the scene. A friend said it looks like a dragon's mouth spitting out fire.

Toward the end of the book, I will show you more examples of "painting with light." In those images I carefully "painted" my subjects, natural rock formations in the evening, using a flashlight as my paint brush. Keep your eyes open for those.

MY CHALLENGE TO YOU

You now know the components of ELI'S 5-POINT PHOTO ART MODEL. Now it's your turn. I challenge you to go out and practice; apply the components from this model.

It all starts with ***intuition***. I already gave you an exercise to practice applying your intuition, so I will skip that exercise. However, please keep in mind that it is intuition that often leads to the creation of some of the best images.

CHALLENGE ASSIGNMENT #1

IMAGINATION. First, please review the section on imagination, page 42, especially the list that follows the question, "What if I....?" Feel free to add more "what ifs" to that list—get creative.

This exercise may cost you a couple of dollars. Visit your local super market or grocery store. Buy three bell peppers--a yellow one, an orange one, and a red one. Hopefully you can find all three colors. Go home, study them, then come up with three different renditions of them.

I am not going to give you any hints, tips, or suggestions on this one. You are on your own. Well, okay, I'll give you one hint. Read, not only what I said, but what I did not say in my assignment.

Well? How did you do? Did you surprise yourself?

CHALLENGE ASSIGNMENT #2

IMPRESSIONISM. As a refresher, the characteristics of Impressionism include the use of visual effects, sense of movement, blurring, bright colors, sketchy, unfinished, irregular surface texture--an *impression* of what the artist saw. You might want to visit that section again on page 43 for a second look at my impressionistic creations.

I am sure you have your favorite subjects, or categories, in your collection of images. You might have landscapes, florals, portraits, cityscapes, or maybe doors and windows? Pick one of those subjects and go out and take a different approach than you usually take to photograph them. Using the characteristics above, create your own impressionistic images. Have fun with it. Get out of your photography comfort zone.

Well? How did you do? Did you surprise yourself?

CHALLENGE ASSIGNMENT #3

SURREALISM. Do you recall the characteristics of Surrealism? The juxtaposition of unexpected objects, themes, or ideas; things we usually do not associate with each other; the element of surprise, or even shock; incongruency; perplexing; word association mix-ups. You might want to visit that section on page 49 again as a refresher.

This next assignment will involve some creative in-camera techniques, maybe some you haven't tried before. Your right brain will need to shake hands with your left brain to pull it all together. Okay, here is your assignment.

Think of a common subject or subjects—subjects we see all the time but take for granted. Examples include spoons, toothbrushes, a flower vase, shoes, and other items. Applying the characteristics of surrealism, how can you make the common uncommon? How can you make the mundane insane?

Well? How did you do? Did you surrealize yourself?

CHALLENGE ASSIGNMENT #4 & $5

EASTERN PHILOSOPHY. Some of the key concepts I shared are *detachment*, *un-labeling*, *impermanence*, and *interdependence*. For your two assignments, I am going to pick the combination of *detachment* and *un-labeling* because they are interrelated—we have to detach ourselves from our labels. Those concepts are also the most difficult to wrap our minds around.

FIRST ASSIGNMENT. Go out anywhere you want and find a tree—yes, a tree. Ask yourself, "If it wasn't a tree, what would it be?" What's left to photograph? You've got all the time in the world, but you probably don't want to take that much time. Now go.

Well? How did you do? Did you surprise yourself?

SECOND ASSIGNMENT. Go out and find a 1959 Cadillac. This might be a little more difficult to find, but it will surely be fun to do. You will probably need to ask permission from the owner. 1959 Cadillac owners are very protective of their labor of love, and I don't blame them. After you detach yourselves from the labels "1959 Cadillac" and "car," what's left?

Well? How did you do? Did you surprise yourself with some classic images?

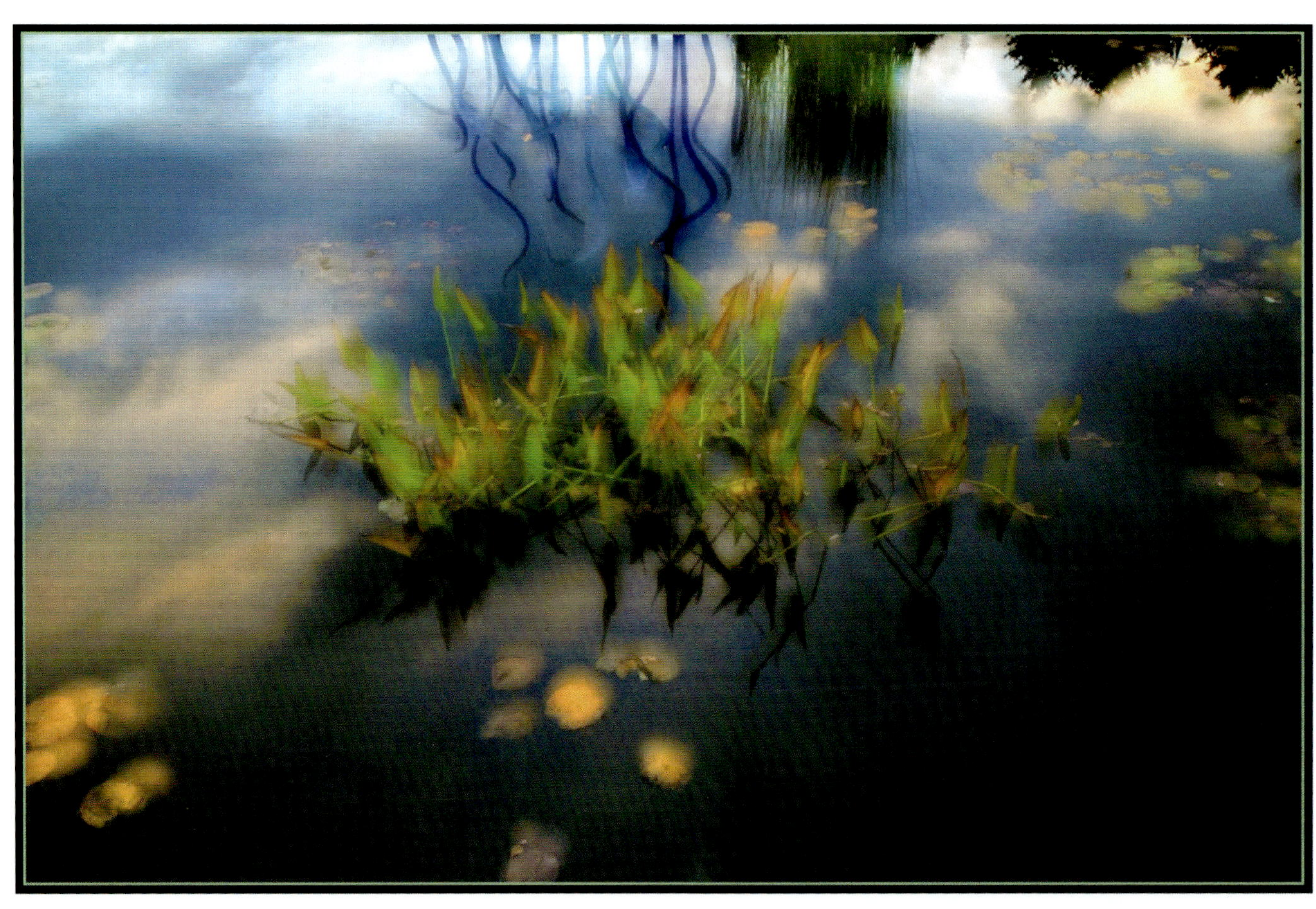

"Monet Pond"

SECTION V

THE PHOTO IMAGE CREATION PROCESS

For the most part, this is where the left brain resides. I introduce this model as the last of my three. My reasoning is this: I always begin the creation of my images with my right brain, as you have read already. Then, my right brain tells my left brain what I need. It is at that moment that I apply this last model.

I will first present the entire model, then go back and walk you through each of its components. This model will answer mostly left brain questions about the creation of my images.

The Photo Image Creation Process has two phases. Phase I, which has two parts, is all about what I do in camera to get what my right brain wants. Phase II is what I do back home with my photo editing software. On the average, 80%-90% of my end results are done in Phase I. 10%-20% are done in Phase II—that's the fine tuning phase.

Again, please let me emphasize that the reason I left this for last is because this is *not* my starting point when I create my images. My left brain simply responds to my right brain instructions, "This is what I need from you."

I encourage you to look at the one page overview of this model on page 114 as you read the following explanations. You can also make a copy of it and hold it in your hand or display it in front of you as you read the following.

PHASE I

THINKING. This includes a list of the various decisions I make after I ask myself, "What do I want this to look like?" As you notice, the first four decisions I make are highlighted in red. This is to emphasize that preceding everything else is the application of right brain elements, such as imagination, interpretation, detachment, and un-labeling. Actually, composition is always first on my check list, but I will cover that later in Section VI.

One of my students asked me, "Do you have a check list before you take a photograph?" You could say that my check list is everything under PHASE I. Although I will spend several sentences and paragraphs on them, when I am in the field, I go through them within a few seconds or a few minutes, depending on the scene and what I am trying to create.

Timing. There are so many aspects to consider regarding timing. I'll talk about them separately, but they are all extremely critical to getting it right.

Time of year. There are certain times of the year for which I plan some of my shooting. I even make notes on my calendar for future dates. I have my favorite places for those awesome autumn colors, but there are several other places I visit here in Colorado. I like to visit the Crested Butte area in late September. Telluride is my other favorite annual trek, also in late September. That trip usually includes stops in and around Owl Creek Pass, Ouray, Silver Dollar Road, and, of course, Telluride.

I found this next autumn scene along Owl Creek Pass, an awesome dirt road to take in the fall. It is southwest of Gunnison, off Highway 50. I understand some scenes in the John Wayne movie *True Grit* were filmed in that area.

The following is one of many scenes I have found along Owl Creek Pass.

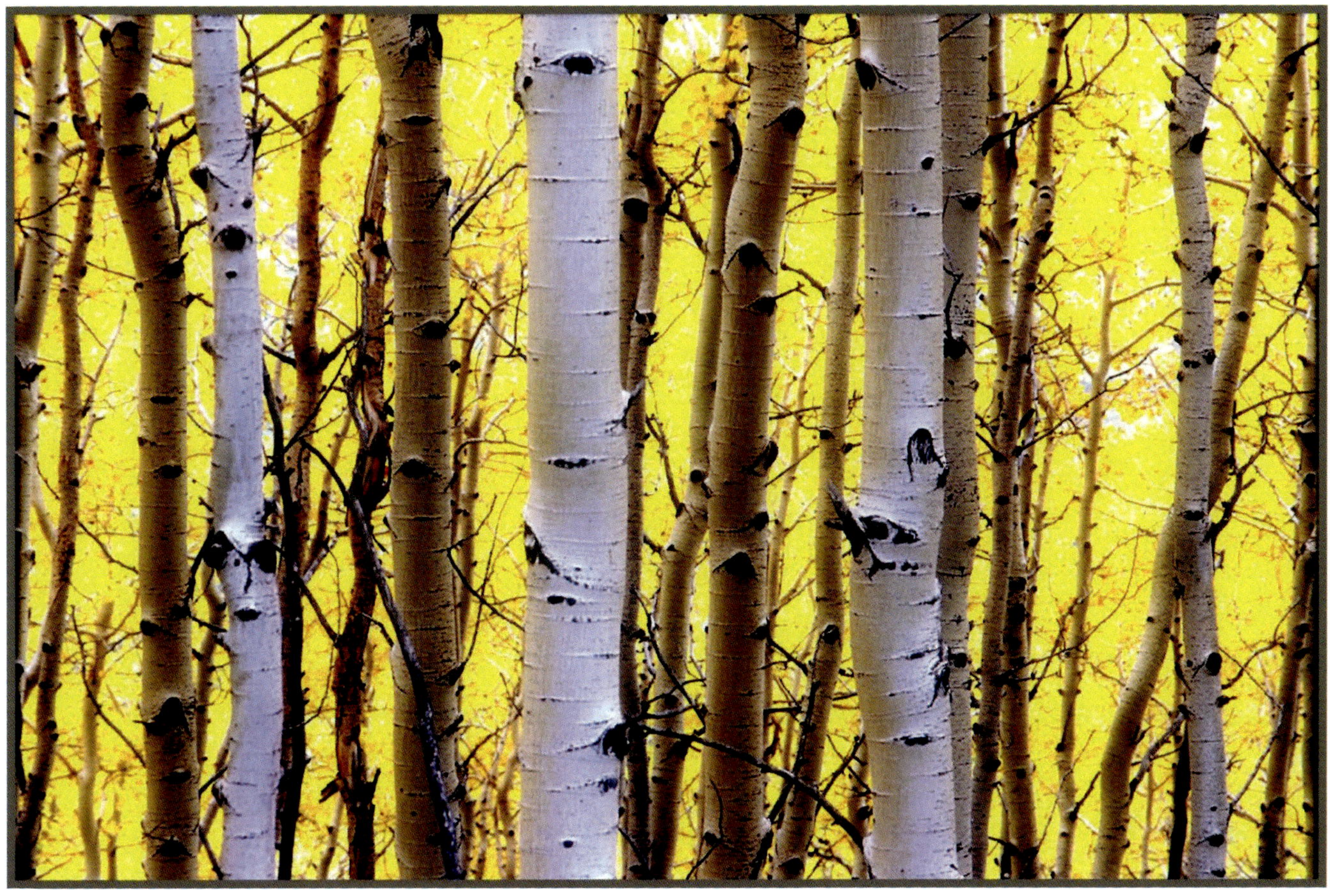

I will expand on *exposure* later, but I need to give you a heads up here. As I walked up to this scene, I was already making some left brain adjustments. I knew I wanted two specifics from this scene: blurred yellows and white aspens. I had to adjust my exposure compensation dial to a +1.3 in order to keep the front aspens as white as possible, which also kept the yellows in the background from going too dark. In order to blur the background yellows and not see detail in the yellow aspen leaves, I used a shallow f/8 aperture. I showed this image earlier, but now you know the behind-the-camera thought process needed to create it.

My other favorite place for autumn colors is Mapleton Avenue in Boulder. Colorado is known for its brilliant golden aspens, but I go to Mapleton Avenue to get my autumn reds. In this next image, late summer, autumn, and an early winter came together at the same time.

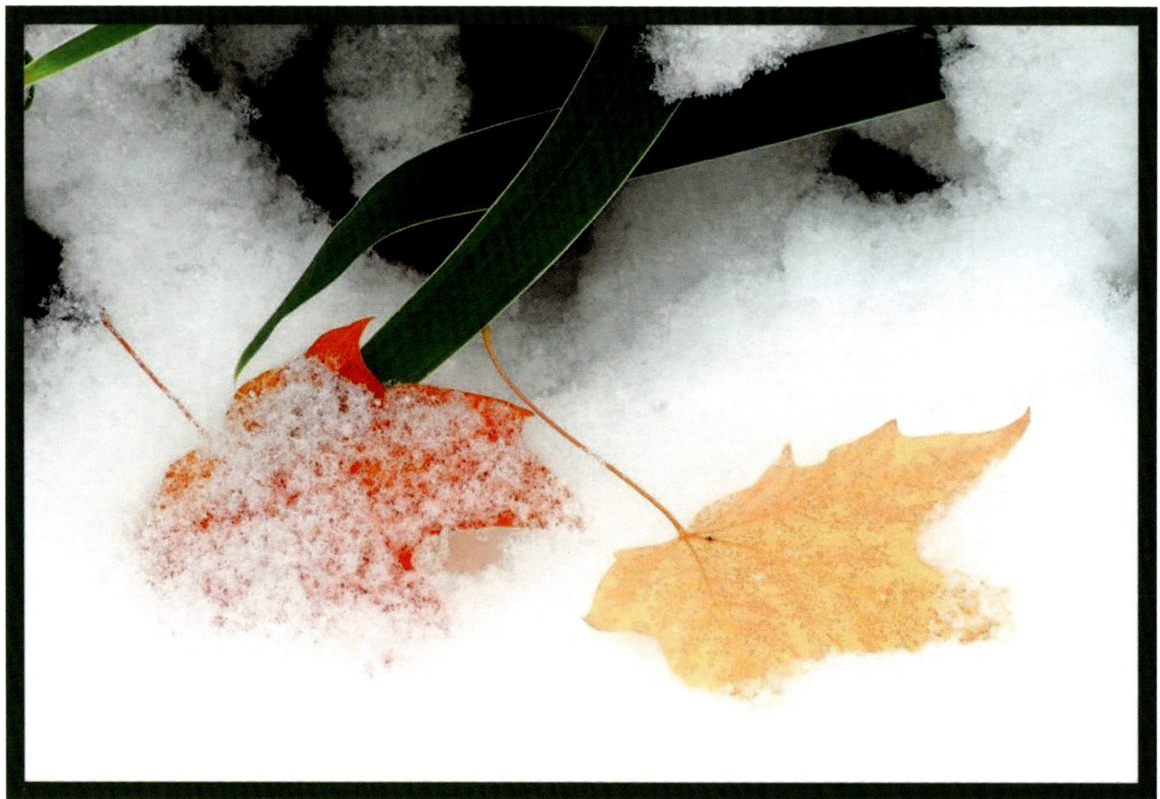

As with the aspens, I had to over expose this image, to make sure the white snow stayed white. When I expose correctly for the snow, the other colors will fall into place.

Time of day. For me, not only is it important to know when to shoot, but when *not to* shoot. I was in Zurich, Switzerland. It was around 3:00 pm when I saw a scene in the middle of the city. I liked the elements, as far as composition goes, but the timing was off. I liked the river, the historic architecture, the bridge, and the grand cathedral, but the lighting was only good enough for a basic “snapshot.” I decided to walk around town, do some more shooting, have a snack, and then go back at twilight. I love shooting at twilight, that 5-10 minute window we have between sunset and nighttime. My intuition paid off!

When I returned about three hours later, the twilight colors were perfect—just as I had imagined. As luck would have it, some awesome clouds had rolled in, which added to the feel of the scene and final image.

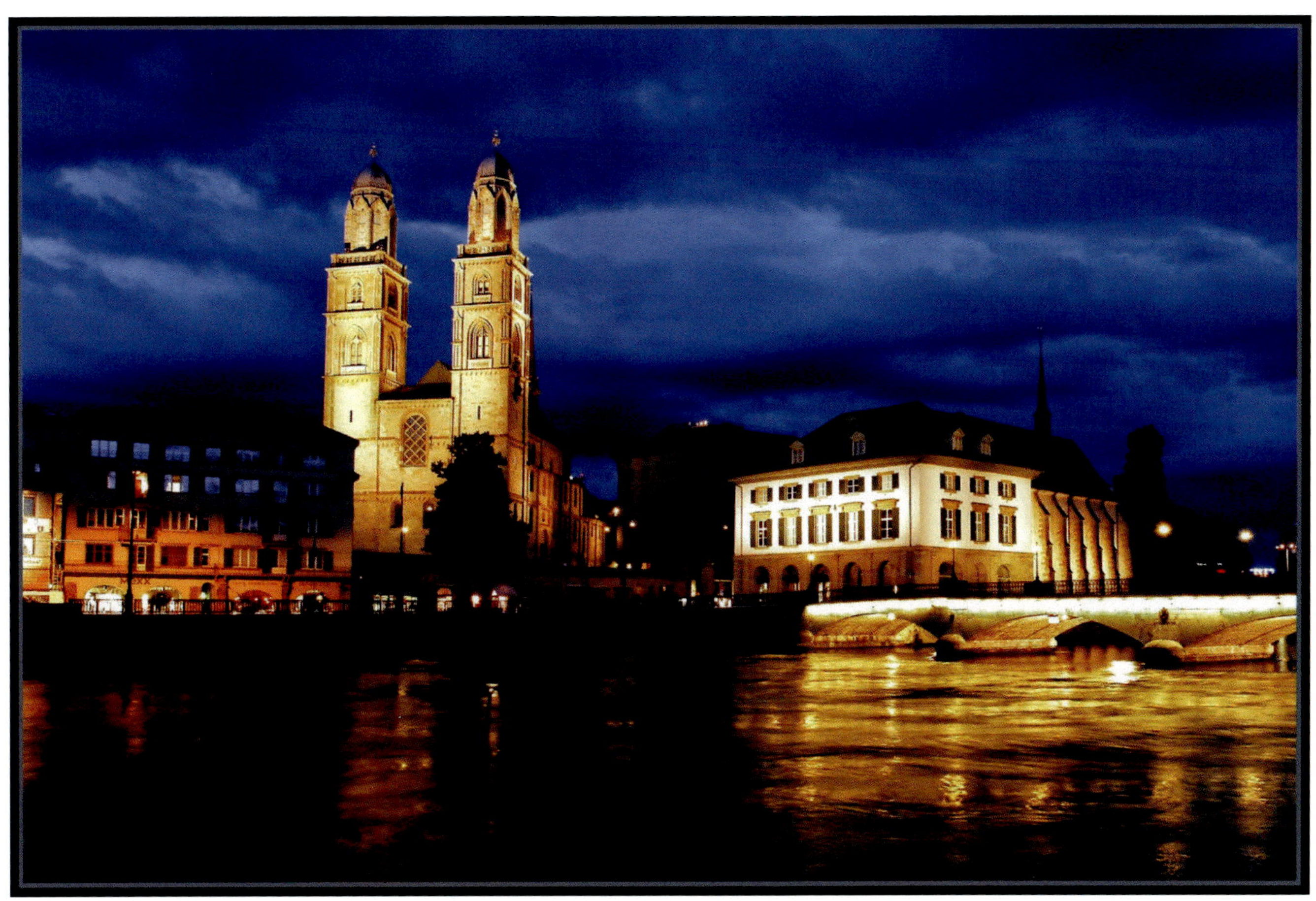

"Grossmunster & Reflections"

Timing. Sometimes it is not the time of year or the time of day, but the exact timing of that millisecond moment that will make the difference between a mediocre image and a good one, or between a good image and a great one. It was exact timing that was needed when I created the next image in Fort Worth, Texas in l988.

It is important to stress at this point that my models work in tandem, not separately. I treat them and discuss them separately in order for you to spend meaningful time digesting the specifics of each. All three models, as well as all the other concepts I mention, are part of the big picture. The whole is the sum of its parts, and then some.

The creation of this next image required strategic timing. The image is about something very common and unimpressive—construction. There was a major new freeway expansion on the southeast side of Fort Worth, a project in which the city took a lot of pride. I drove by it one day when all of a sudden I started seeing what was not visible to my naked eye. My intuition and imagination kicked in. I detached myself from the ugliness of the construction site and peeled the labels off "freeway," "overpasses," "workers," "equipment," and all other nouns associated with construction. What I saw were lines, design, forms, and geometry. I then imagined color. So far, all of that was only in my imagination. One day, I decided it was time to stop and take a closer look at the construction site. This is what my eyes saw.

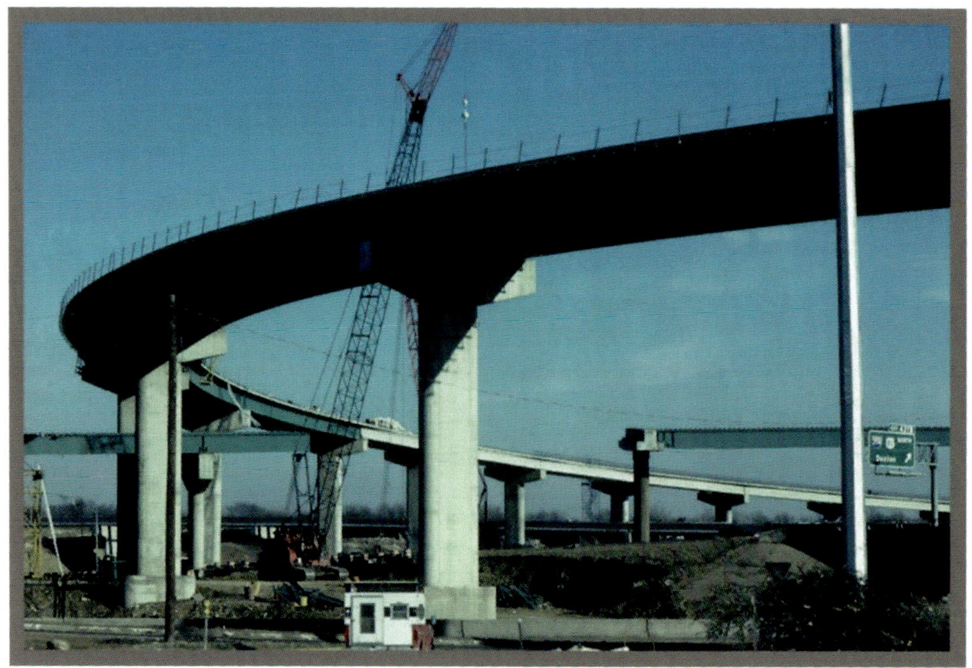

Not very pretty, huh? After looking at this harsh, colorless, and unattractive sight, my imagination came alive. I imagined geometric shapes silhouetted against an orange sky.

I knew what I had to do to create what I saw in my imagination. The only way to see what I "saw" was to go back someday, but it had to be early in the morning. And so I did.

About a week later, I went back to that same spot around six o'clock in the morning. I got there before the workers arrived. After I spent a few seconds looking at the great sunrise colors, I asked myself, "What if..." I then took out my FLD filter to enhance the brilliant colors already in the sky. It worked. I'll add a foot note here. During film days, there was no White Balance setting. We had to use different filters for different colors and Kelvin light temperatures. An FLD filter was used when shooting under **FL**uorescent lighting with **D**aylight film. They are also called FDL filters. I started experimenting with FLD filters many years ago and discovered that I can get some awesome colors at sunrise and sunset.

Now, back to my construction site scenario. I spent a few minutes getting some great shots, both horizontals and verticals. I was very pleased with the results, but felt that there was still something missing. It then occurred to me to wait until the workers arrived, hoping to see them walking on the top of this future freeway. A few minutes later I saw lights—head lights from the workers' vehicles as they began to show up for work. I patiently waited, knowing that if nothing materialized I already had some good images.

The workers took their time. I faintly heard them talking. I saw the scaffolding, which I had included in my earlier images, and mentally crossed my fingers, hoping to see the workers climb high, high above the construction. All of a sudden, yes! A few men started climbing the scaffolding. I knew they had to reach the top and start working up there. I instantly imagined more silhouettes—human figures against the great warm colors of an awesome sunrise. Impermanence was also a factor—the sunrise wouldn't last forever.

Then, it happened! It was almost as if I had written the script, "I want you guys to get up there and start walking from left to right." That is exactly what they did. I started shooting.

Then, like magic, they stopped, and one of the men dropped to his knees to inspect something. My instincts yelled, "Now!"

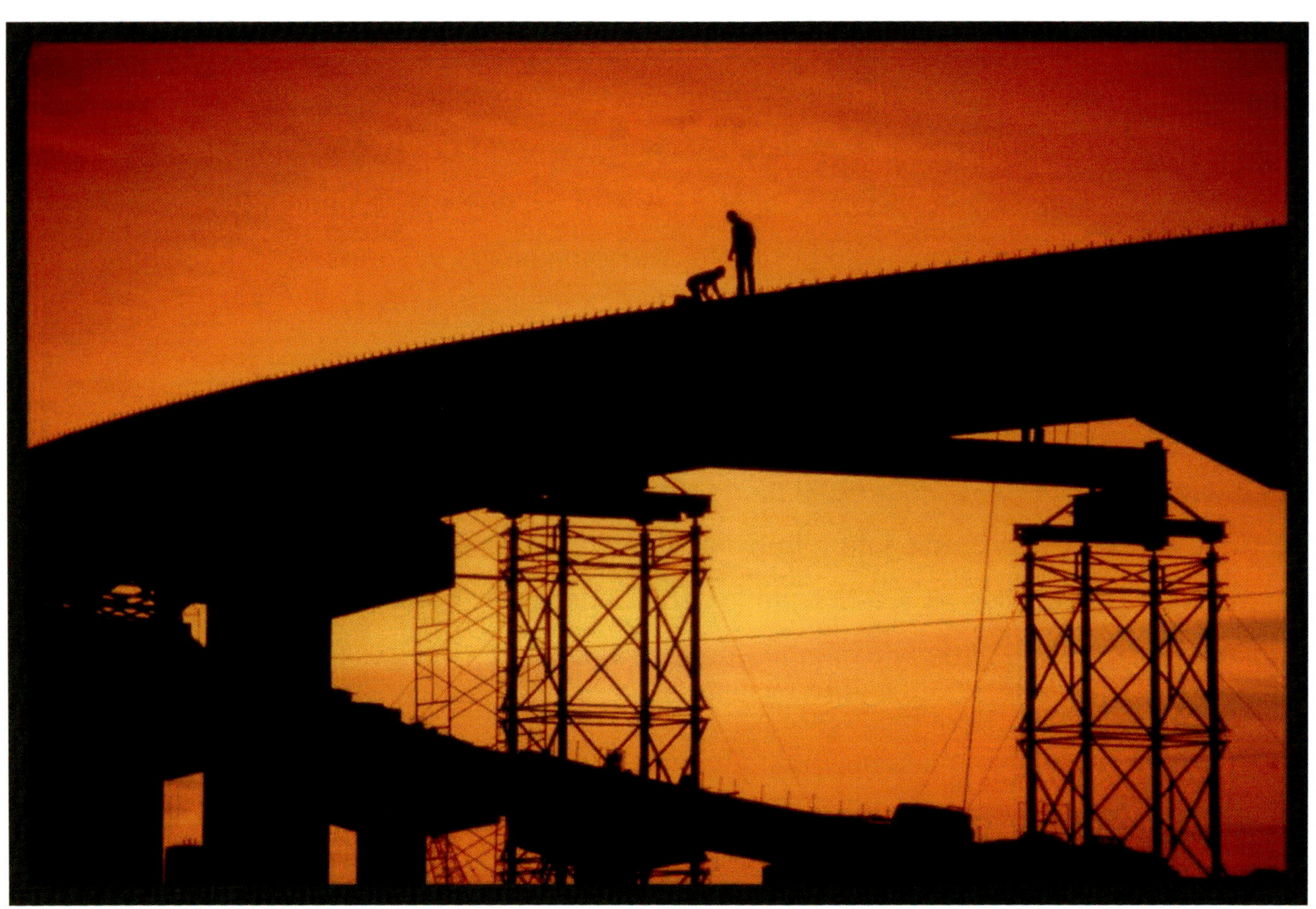

"Hard Hats & Concrete"

I don't see with my eyes; I see with my imagination. I see something before I see it. This concept is not just about reacting to the "decisive moment," but about previsualizing the right moment. This is right brain photography.

Although I show you examples of *my* work in this book, I provide them to teach *you* about what I do with my photography, and how I do it. I encourage you to practice the art of seeing with your imagination first, which will help you "see" something before you see it. I highly recommend that you take a basic art course. Doing so will help you see color, shapes, designs, lines, form, and other art elements, before you see the actual subjects—in this case, workers, pillars, bridges, scaffolding. And, if you sprinkle my three paradigms included in this book, no telling where your photography will go.

Wow, I've spent a lot of time on ***timing***, but I think it was necessary to demonstrate the important role it plays in photography. Are you ready to move on to lighting?

Lighting. As you saw from the previous image, lighting is everything in photography. No light, no image. In fact, from photography's own etymology, all we're doing is "painting with light." Timing and lighting often go hand in hand. Sometimes we have to wait or plan for the right time to get the right lighting.

I take three approaches with lighting. I plan for it, imagining how my subjects might look like at a given time of day. I also take advantage of what I am given on any particular day, and look for subjects that are conducive to that lighting. Sometimes I follow the lighting. As the sun keeps moving, I keep an eye on what it's doing to the landscape. There are several characteristics of light that are important to me. I look for the color of light, the angle of light, the amount of light, and the direction of light. Since I am primarily an outdoor available light photographer, I can be ridiculously patient in waiting for the right lighting. Sometimes it's not a matter of waiting, but planning for the right lighting, as in the following scenario.

There are some beautiful mountains in Colorado called the Red Mountains. They are south of Ouray, along the Million Dollar Highway. I had photographed them a couple of times before, but had never been quite satisfied with the results. I made plans to take my annual Telluride autumn trip, which often includes the Red Mountains. This time, I planned on being at the Red Mountains around 5:00, late afternoon, hoping to get that late afternoon warm glow on the mountains. I invited my part-time assistant to join me that day. I asked him to drive, which allowed me to scan the landscape around us.

We drove up the winding Million Dollar Highway out of Ouray that afternoon, as I kept my eyes on the Red Mountains. Then we turned up the mountain and I got a glimpse of some awesome red/orange colors in the distance. "Hurry," I cautiously directed, "I see the color! It's great. Let's get there!"

Having been there before, I knew where the pull-out on the road was. When we arrived, I quickly asked him to pull over. I excitedly grabbed my gear and started setting up. We were there just in time, but I knew it would not last long—impermanence. I had to work fast, but cautiously fast. I had to hold back my emotions so that I would carefully engage my right brain and then go through the steps I take in Phase I of this model.

The lighting was absolutely perfect. I had never seen the Red Mountains glow like that. All I had to do was move fast through my check list. Then, there it was! I had my image.

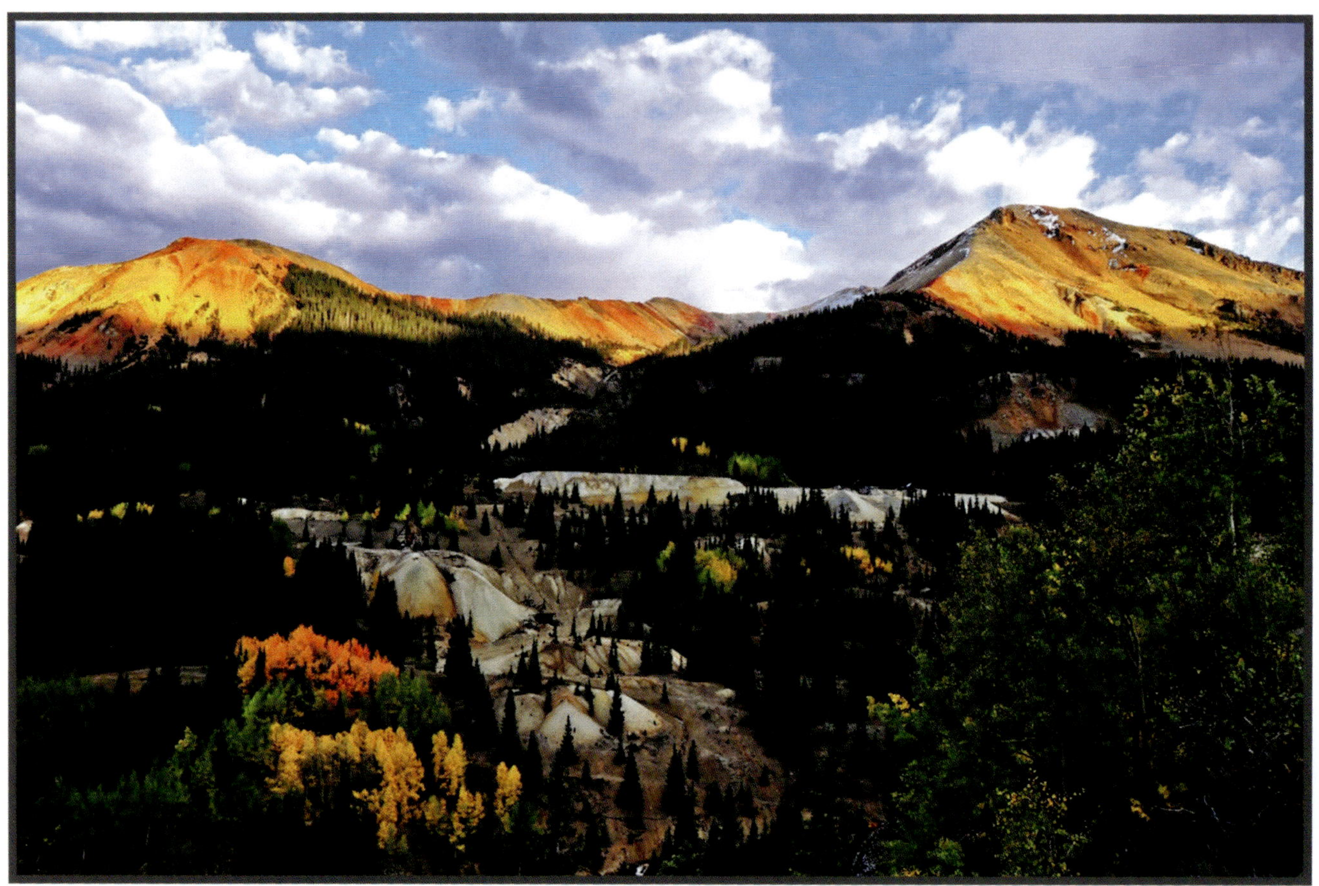

"Red Mountains at Sunset"

They really looked just like that! It was absolutely breathtaking. The autumn colors in the trees repeated the colors on the mountains. It was sad to see the colors dissolve as the sun set behind us just a few minutes later.

"Chance favors the prepared mind." Anonymous

This is a good segue into the next steps in the THINKING part of **Phase I.** I have the first letters in, Depth of Field, and Exposure highlighted in red. I did this to bring attention to the fact that these three steps, CDE, are of utmost importance to me. If the conditions are perfect for me to create an image, when I get my composition, depth of field, and exposure just the way I want them, I will guarantee myself a good image. **Perspective**, by the way, is part of composition.

I over stress this point when I offer my workshops and 1-on-1 field lessons, at the risk of my students getting tired of hearing me repeat it. "Don't forget to walk yourself slowly through CDE," they hear me repeat. As I go around checking in on each of my students, I often ask them to walk me through what they're thinking as they apply CDE. It is my way of reinforcing the thought process and to make sure they "get it."

I force my students to think about what they're saying. I ask them questions like, "What's your composition going to be? What f/stop do you think you're going to use, and why? What's your exposure going to be?" There are no correct answers; only right answers.

At the end of a class, workshop, or field lesson, I ask my students, "Tell me. What were your Take-Aways? What did you pick up today? What resonated with you?" The most frequent response I get is something along the lines of, "You made me realize that I need to slow down, take my time to think about what I'm doing."

I tell them that we are not just people with cameras. We are not taking pictures; we are creating images. Our goal should be, not to duplicate life, but to interpret it and translate our thoughts and feelings. That's what artists do.

I can tell if my students are still struggling with the concepts I teach. After a couple of hours of training, they will ask, "Okay, Eli. Like, for this scene, what f/stop should I use?" My quick comeback is always, "Never start with that question. Never ask yourself what f/stop, shutter speed, or exposure you should use. Always start with, 'What do I want this to look like?' Your answer to *that* question, will answer your left brain questions."

Let's say that I see a beautiful large butterfly that catches my attention. I see diffused sunlight on it, and the background is in the shade. I want the butterfly to "pop," i.e., really stand out. And, I want to convert my background to a backdrop. In that scenario, I will use a wide f/stop, in order to create my backdrop. Then, to make the butterfly pop, I will underexpose the image, using my exposure compensation dial. I call this image "Ethereal Silk."

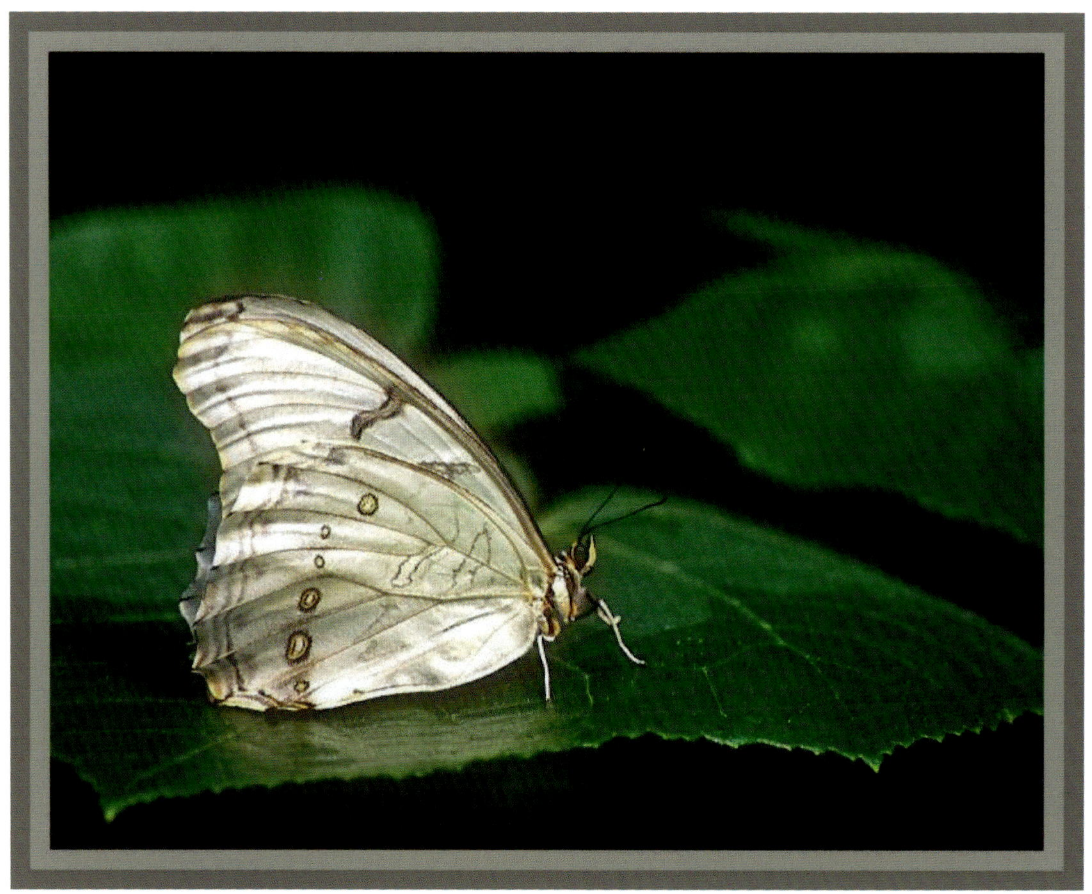

Now, let me get back to CDE. Composition is so, so critical to create the best images possible. Although I include it under this model, it is more of a right brain application in photography. I list it here because it is one of the steps I take in creating my images. I get so many questions about this subject that I devote an entire section on it later in the book.

For now, I will provide an overview of **C**omposition. For me, composition is about what I want to include or not include in my viewfinder, and *where* I want to place certain elements.

My decisions have to do with making my images more interesting, more appealing, or more dramatic—not stale or stagnant. For example, for the butterfly image, I placed the butterfly toward the lower left side, not in dead center, to add more interest. I chose to include the whole leaf under the butterfly. I also included a couple of leaves in the background to add interest and what I call "eye flow." The image is still about the butterfly, but it's not just a picture of a butterfly. Again, I will expand on this in my next section on composition.

Depth of Field (DOF). Although I will know in advance what I am going to do with my depth of field, after I place my camera on my tripod I will begin to fine tune my composition—to get it just right. Once I get the composition I want, I start working on my depth of field, my f/stops and focusing.

Depth of field, by my definition, is everything between my camera and the farthest element I see in my viewfinder. In the case of the butterfly, the closest element is the lower left tip of the leaf. The farthest element is the background behind the farthest leaf, which I could see at the time, but you cannot see in the image. F/stops control for depth of field, i.e., how much of my depth of field I want to have in sharp focus. Again, my choice of f/stop will be based on how I want my subject to look. Let's stay with that for a moment. Before you read the following, take a look at "Ethereal Silk" once more.

Imagine that you could actually see the depth of field you're getting, based on any hypothetical f/stop you choose. Your depth of field might look something like the diagram on the next page.

YOU **BUTTERFLY** **BACKGROUND**

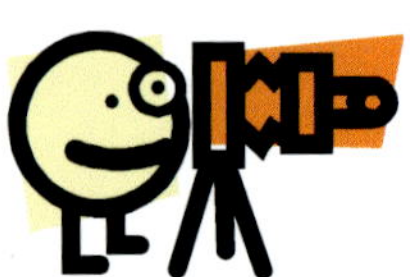

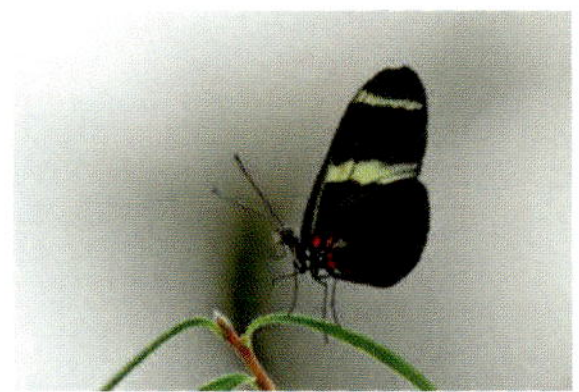

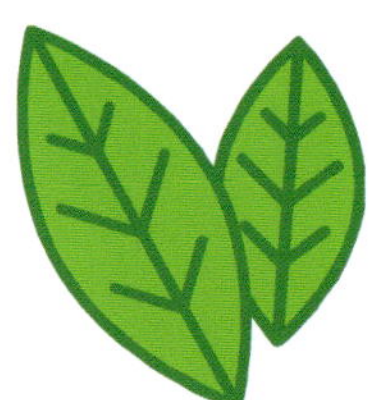

(Focus point is on the butterfly)

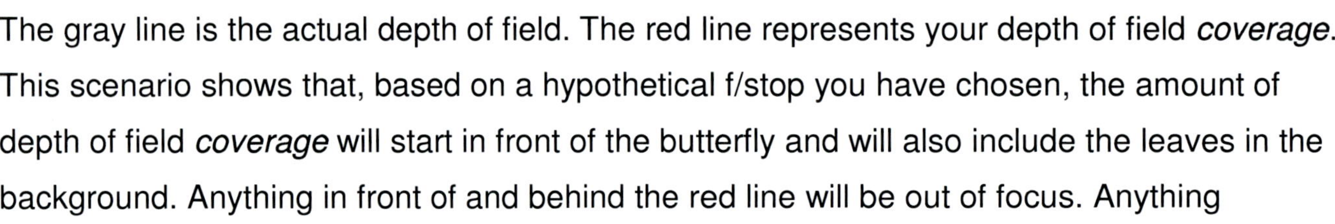

The gray line is the actual depth of field. The red line represents your depth of field *coverage*. This scenario shows that, based on a hypothetical f/stop you have chosen, the amount of depth of field *coverage* will start in front of the butterfly and will also include the leaves in the background. Anything in front of and behind the red line will be out of focus. Anything between you and that red line will be blurry, or out of focus.

Okay, so that explains the relationship between f/stops and depth of field, in a general sense. The f/stops determine how much of your depth of field will be in sharp focus.

How much of your depth of field will be in sharp focus depends on several factors, in addition to the size of the camera sensor—the smaller the sensor, the more inherent DOF. These are key variables to consider when depth of field coverage is critical to the final image.

1) Your distance from the subject. The closer you get, the less DOF you will get in sharp focus, sometimes even at f/22. The farther away you get, the more DOF you will get.

2) The distance of background from your subject. The closer it is to your subject, the more difficult it will be to blur it. The farther away, the better the chances of getting those nice blurred backgrounds.

3) The lens focal length. It's not just the f/stop used, but the *size* of the opening as well that determines the depth of field coverage. An f/8 on a 300mm lens will give less depth of field than an f/8 on a 24mm lens, all else being equal, because of the *size* of the opening.

4) Your selection of *focus point*. This is a factor some photographers overlook, ignore, or simply do not know. Let's re-do the butterfly diagram to illustrate this. Let's say that you really want to blur the background, but you're out of f/stops—that is the widest f/stop you can use, given your lens. No problem. Enter focusing point.

In this scenario, everything will be the same as before *except* your focus point, which will be closer to you than before.

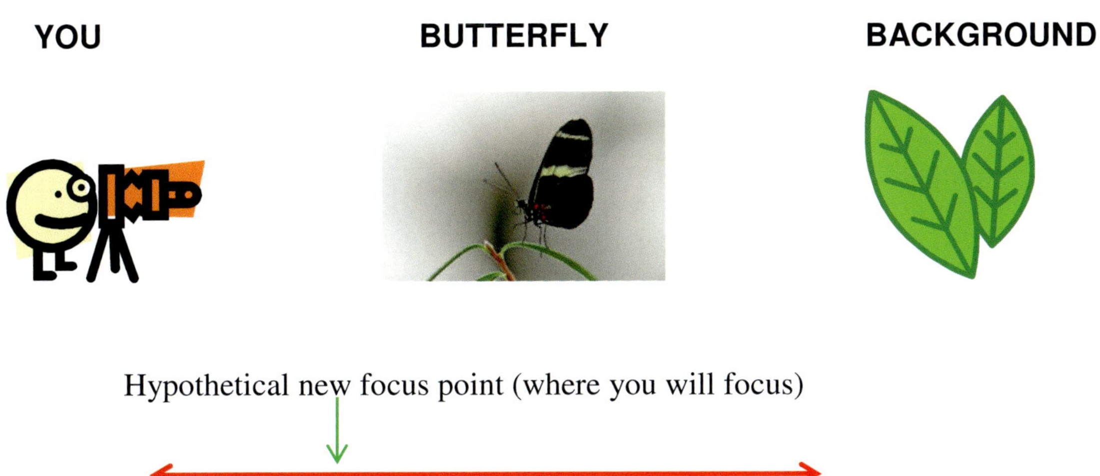

The red line, again, represents your DOF *coverage*, which is the same amount as before. However, if you move your *focus point* closer to you than before, you will *also* move the depth of field *coverage* along with it. Your butterfly will still be in focus, but the background will now be blurred because it is slightly outside the DOF coverage. The same identical depth of field coverage, with a different *focus point,* will give you an out of focus background. This selective focusing technique is especially useful when shooting with smaller sensors or when you don't own an expensive f/1.8 or f/2.8 lens.

Here is an example of where I had a lot of DOF to cover. When in doubt, I always cover as much depth of field as I can. I would rather have more DOF coverage than I need than not enough. For this image, Whatcom Falls in Bellingham, Washington, I used an f/32 to ensure as much DOF coverage as possible. My focusing point was on the waterfall.

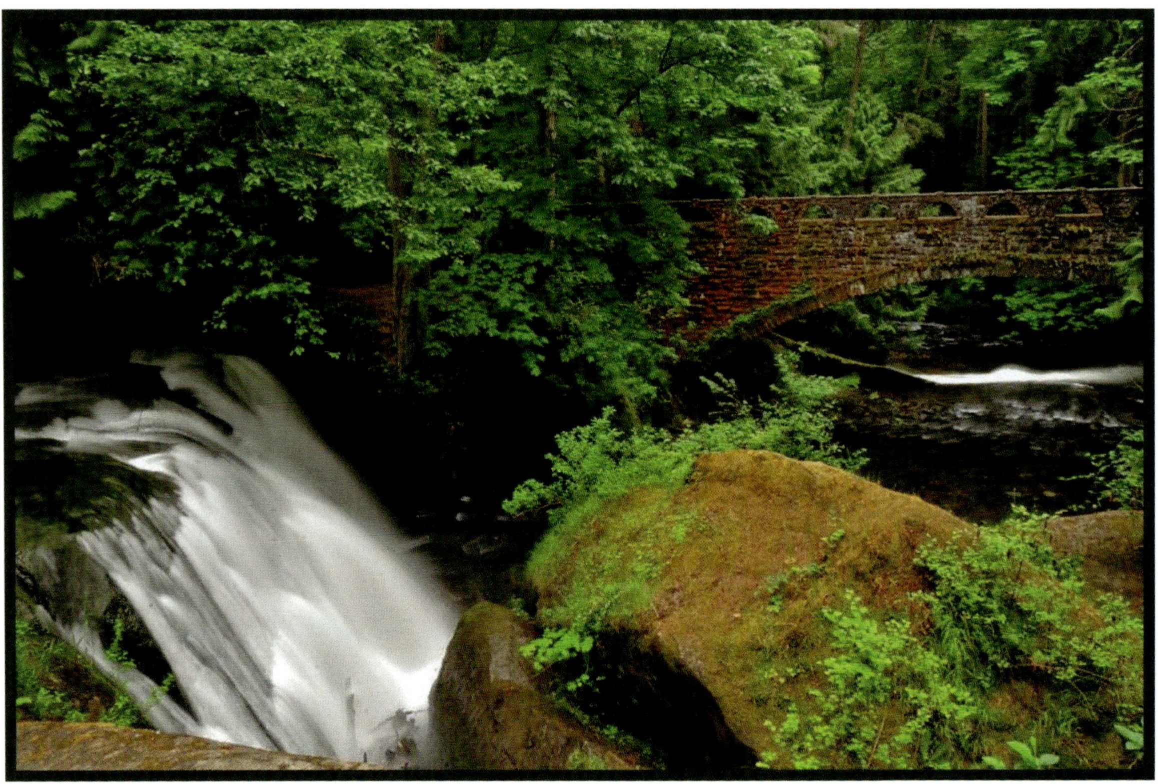

Exposure. The last piece of the CDE formula. This is the trickiest piece of the three. The reason for this is that, literally, every shot will require a different exposure. If we want our scene to look the way we want it to look, even a slight adjustment in exposure can make a big difference. Let me first give you my definition of what I mean by "exposure." This will not be a scientific explanation, but rather a practical, user friendly explanation to photographic exposure. There, I got that out of the way—for those who don't like left brain explanations, especially when it comes to the subject of exposure.

I'll give you the bad news first. The built-in exposure meter is designed to turn whites and blacks gray. Yeah, that's right! It will try to *darken* whites or bright colors, and *lighten* blacks or dark colors. In other words, it will under expose bright colors and over expose dark colors. That means that if I photograph a ski slope, with tiny colorful skiers on it, that ski slope will appear more gray than white. And the skiers, in turn, will virtually disappear into little dark objects in the gray snow. Sound familiar? The opposite happens with blacks or dark colors—the meter will try to lighten them, to turn them into gray subjects.

The meter will pick up all the bright or white, dark, and in-between colors that appear in the viewfinder when we aim our cameras at a scene. It is a reflective meter, which picks up light *reflected* from the scene, not the light falling on the scene. Why is this important to know? Light reflected from snow or white sand will be more intense, compared to light reflected from a more neutral scene—one which has a greater distribution of neutral colors like browns, dark greens, grays, and other less extreme colors. Additionally, the light *falling* on any scene can make a big difference in the way our photos "turn out." This is why, when it comes to flora, I prefer shooting under an overcast sky—it minimizes the meter's struggle to decide what it's going to do with very bright or very dark elements when seen in bright sunlight. Light reflections from subjects in overcast conditions are more evenly distributed and not as intense, more like when light *falls* on them.

The exposure light meter is the #1 problem in photography—it can really mess up your photos if you don't understand how it works. My #1 solution to that problem is the exposure compensation dial, mentioned earlier. Here is a simple way to remember how that great +/- exposure compensation dial works. If the image is too dark (underexposed), move the dial to the + side. Plus means more; more means more light; more light means a lighter image. If the image is too light (overexposed), move the dial to the – side. Minus means less; less means less light; less light means a darker image. When you make those adjustments, retake the photo. Voila!

The illustrations on the next page are typical examples of the kind of problems we can expect to encounter when we let the built-in meter do our thinking for us.

These two examples reflect, no pun intended, what the built-in meter does with a black subject. The image on the left is what the meter did to a black hat. The image on the right is what I did to correct for it—now it looks black. I intentionally converted these images to B&W to help stress this point.

THE PROBLEM

The meter did what it is designed to do: turn a black object gray, or over expose it.

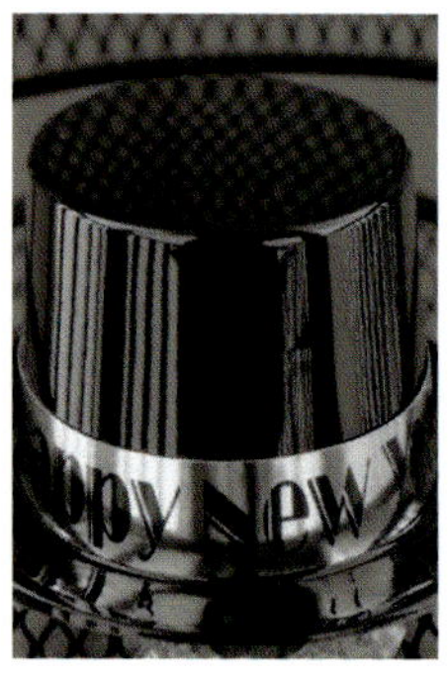

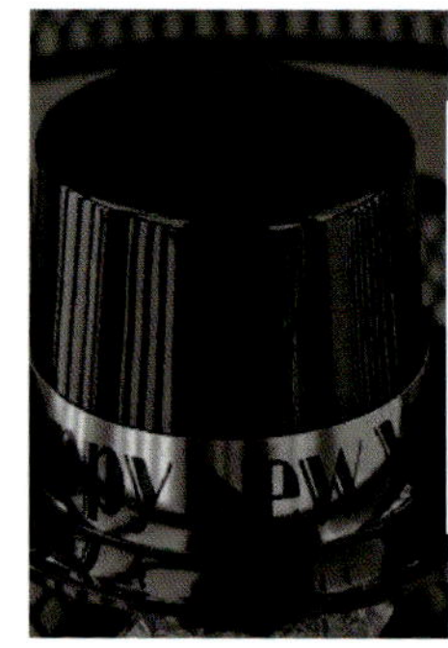

SOLUTION

Under exposed by 1 2/3 stops, to bring it back down to black.

The next examples show what the built-in meter does to a white subject, in this case, white aspens against white snow. The image on the left is what the meter did to the white aspens. It turned them "gray." The image on the right is what I did to correct for it—the aspens and snow now look white, as they should be. The built-in meter does not know what we want.

THE PROBLEM

The meter did what it is designed to do: turn a white object gray, or under expose it.

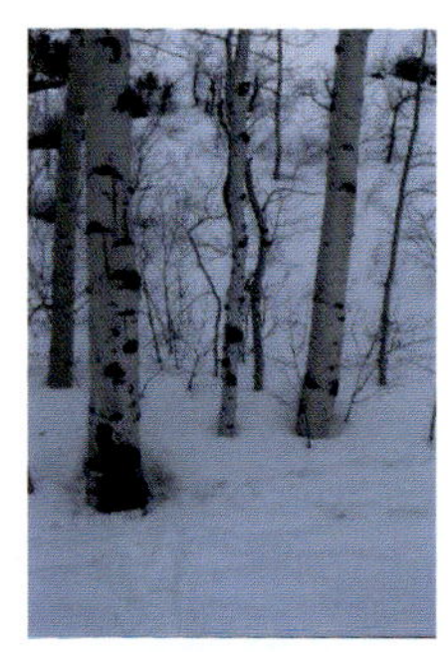

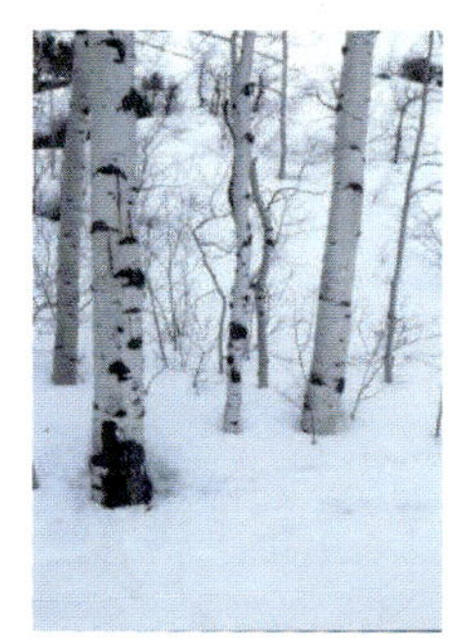

SOLUTION

Over exposed by 1 2/3 stops, to bring the aspens back to white.

In summary, the solution to these predictable exposure meter problems sounds counter intuitive: under expose black or dark objects, and over expose white or light objects, as I did with these examples. We need to make adjustments from where our meter *took* us.

Here is how I deal with that troublesome meter. When I walk myself through the CDE formula, I set my camera's +/- exposure compensation dial beforehand to where I estimate will give me the desired exposure. That is what I did when I created the image on page 77.

My next steps are as follows. I set up my tripod and fine-tune my **C**omposition. Knowing in advance what I want my subject to look like, I then manually focus and adjust both my f/stop and focusing point. I have a **D**epth of field *preview button*, so I can see what I'm getting as I change my focusing point and f/stops. It is one of my favorite tools in photography. My #1 tool is the exposure compensation dial. Once I have my composition and DOF the way I want them, I get my shot, knowing that I might have to make one final tweak to my **E**xposure, using my +/- exposure compensation dial. If all three look great, I smile with satisfaction. I've got my shot!

The image on the next page is an example of where the exposure was actually my Plan B. I have to work fast when I'm in the field. In this case, what I had in mind was to get some nice autumn colors in and around Oxbow Bend in Grand Tetons National Park in Wyoming. My timing was off that particular afternoon. The sun was already beginning to set over Mt. Moran. I was there too late to pick up the autumn colors. As I looked at the scene, I quickly went to Plan B. When I noticed the sun above Mt. Moran, I decided to turn this into a nighttime-looking spiritual scene. I did some extreme under exposure. In other words, rather than fight the late afternoon lighting, I flowed with the flow. Instead of complaining about what I did not have, I asked myself, "What *does* this moment give me?" I waited until the sun touched the top of Mt. Moran before I created my spiritual image. I shot this at a -2 1/3 exposure! I used an f/stop of f/32 to make sure I got a star burst from the large setting sun.

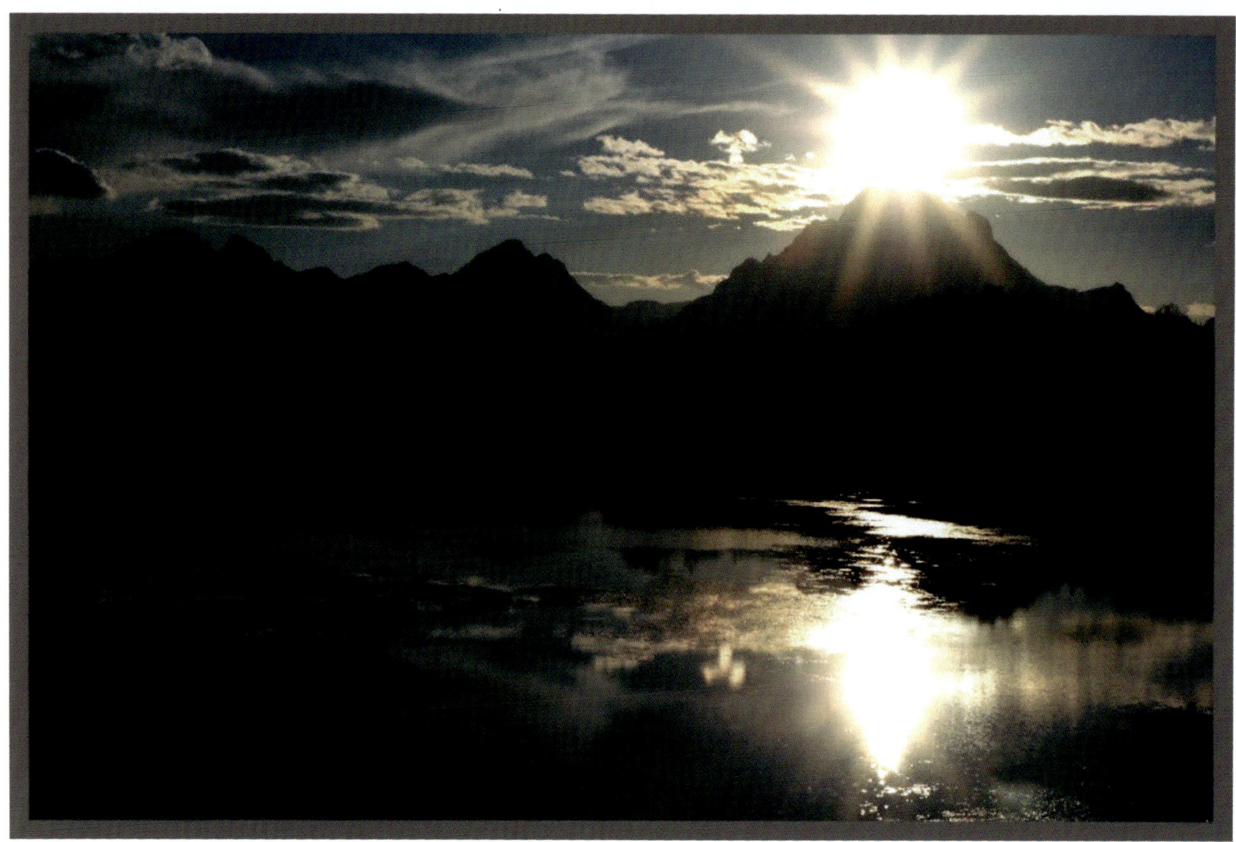

"The Spirit of Oxbow"

Shutter speed. I think you know what I'm going to say next. What do I want it to look like? Living in Colorado, and not being a wildlife photographer per se, I will talk about what to do with waterfalls, cascades, rivers, and creeks. Basically, for any type of photography, I'm talking about anything that has movement, is moving, or might move.

Throughout the years, I have grown to understand the inverse relationship between f/stops and shutter speeds. I understand that concept so well that I shoot in Aperture mode ninety-five percent of the time. The other five percent I shoot in Manual/Bulb, when I am shooting long exposures (more than 30 seconds), the moon, or fireworks. I instinctively know what to do with my f/stops to get fast or slow shutter speeds—depending on what I want. *Want* is the operative word here.

For this discussion I am going to use the example of a cascade, one that looks more like a waterfall in the final image. Remember that although I am talking about shutter speeds, everything else I have talked about up to this point also applies. I don't just think of the shutter speed I need to achieve certain results and ignore other crucial details. It is all cumulative; all part of a means to an end.

Here is the example I want to share. This is a cascade that is fed by a small glacier in Colorado called St. Mary's Glacier. I will talk primarily about my shutter speed selection for this particular shot. When I saw the glacier area and started scanning, it led me to this small but interesting cascade. I knew the cascade would look more like a waterfall if I got a "tighter" shot of the scene.

What I wanted to get from the scene was more of an ethereal, soothing, and peaceful feel. That is what I wanted it to look like. I knew that I was going to use slow shutter speeds in order to create that feeling. Photography is more art than science, so please don't ask, "So what shutter speed did you use?" I chose the one that gave me the best results, based on what I wanted. I bracketed, not my exposures, but my shutter speeds until I got what I wanted.

How slow of a shutter speed I will need, in any given scenario, depends on the results I want. A strong, full flowing waterfall in June during snow melt, for example, is going to give me fast gushing water. I might not need an extremely slow shutter speed to get what I want, because the water is rushing down so fast.

For the cascade scenario on the next page, the water wasn't flowing very fast, so I knew I had to use a very slow shutter speed. I tried several, between 1/4 and 1/10 of a second. I didn't want a 1-2 second exposure because I wanted to show some semblance of water flowing, not a cloud-like look to it. After reviewing my images, I favored the 1/4 of a second shutter speed.

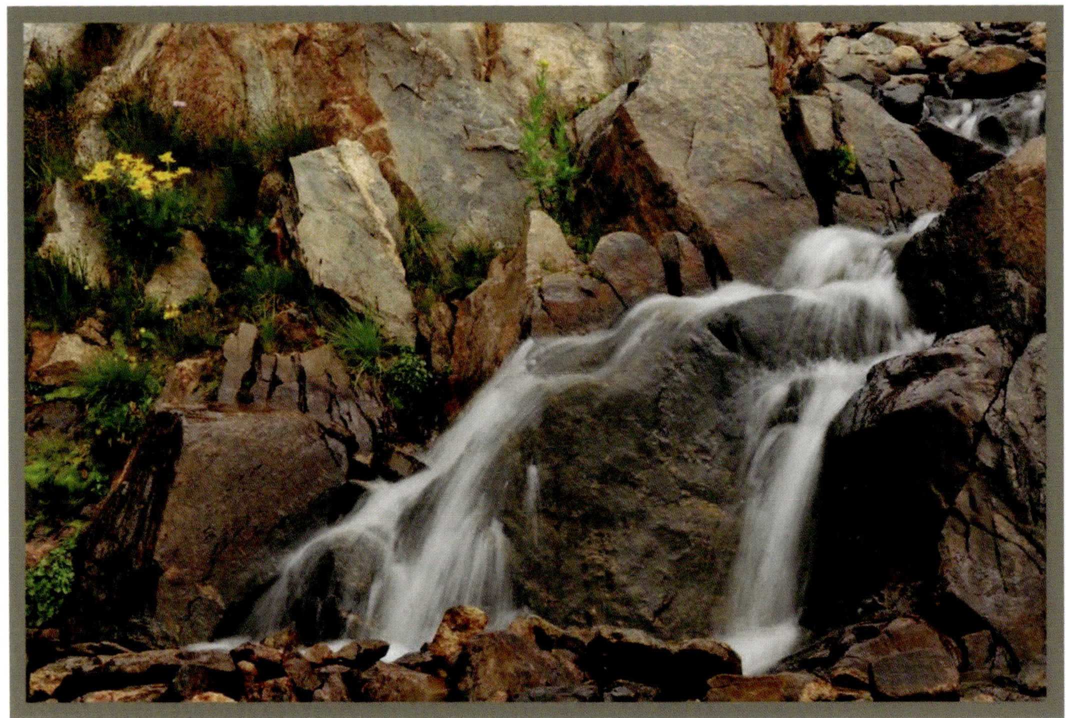

1/4 second shutter speed

Do you remember that inverse relationship I mentioned earlier? In order to get a slow shutter speed, I knew I would need a high number, or smaller, f/stop. Although I did not need f/32 for this scene for my DOF coverage, I used it only to get me to the shutter speeds I wanted. This image was at f/32 and 1/4 second. I used a warming filter (81B) to warm up the colors of a very cool gray day.

Compare the image above with the one on the next page, of the same scene. This one, with a different composition, is at f/11 and 1/640th of a second, without a filter. The "feel" is totally different with a faster shutter speed and no filter—more like what it looked like to the naked eye. As you can see, I didn't need f/32 to get sufficient depth of field coverage.

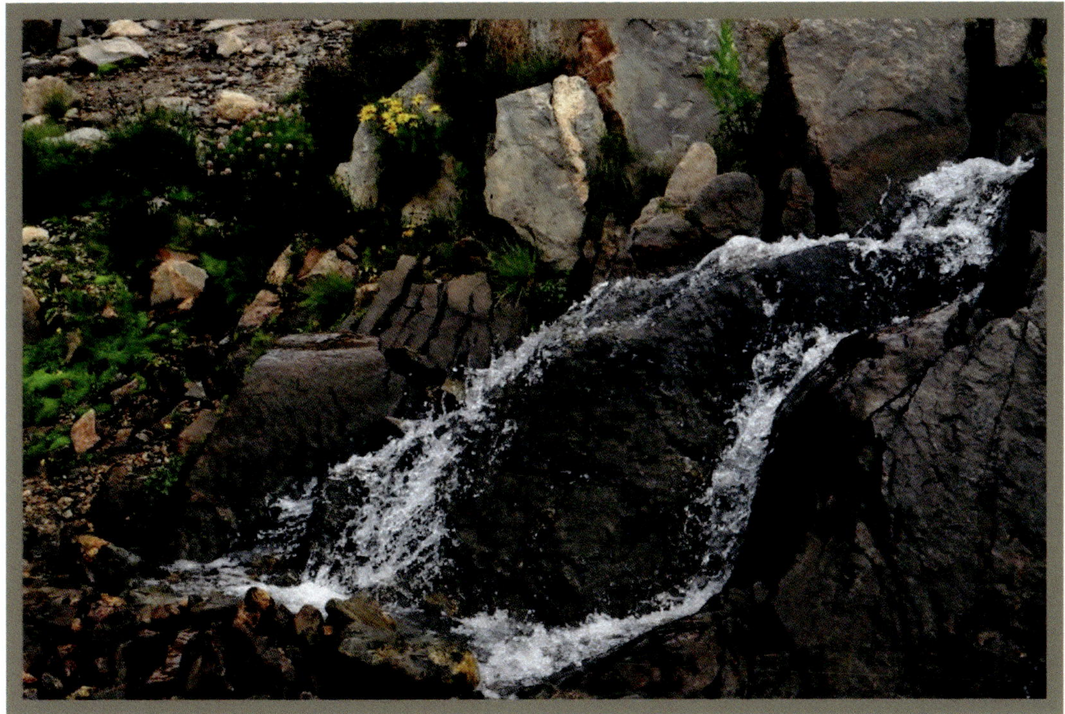

My goal is always to get, not an accurate, the best, or a better duplicate of what my eyes see, but the best interpretation based on what I want it to look and feel like, much like artists do with their paintings. I am an artist first, photographer second.

This next point is extremely important to keep in mind when trying to interpret a scene. In real life, when we see a beautiful and peaceful scene, like the cascade image, the feeling we get from it comes from a combination of sight and emotion. We *see* a cascade, rocks, flowers, and other elements. Psychologically, we are also emotionally overwhelmed. We say, "Oh wow, how beautiful," then just stand, or sit, preferably on a dry boulder, and take it all in. We are instantly emotionally connected to where we are. We are wowed! The problem is that a photograph, whether it's a slide, projected image, digital file, or print, has no emotions. It is just a two dimensional emotion-free object. In order to retain that emotion, that "wow" factor, we might have to create an image that is not exactly the same as what our eyes see.

The first image of the cascade, with the warming filter and shot at 1/4 second, came from this larger life picture. When I was there, even from a distance, I was getting that emotional “wow” factor. However, that “wow” factor is totally gone from this perspective---it’s just a picture.

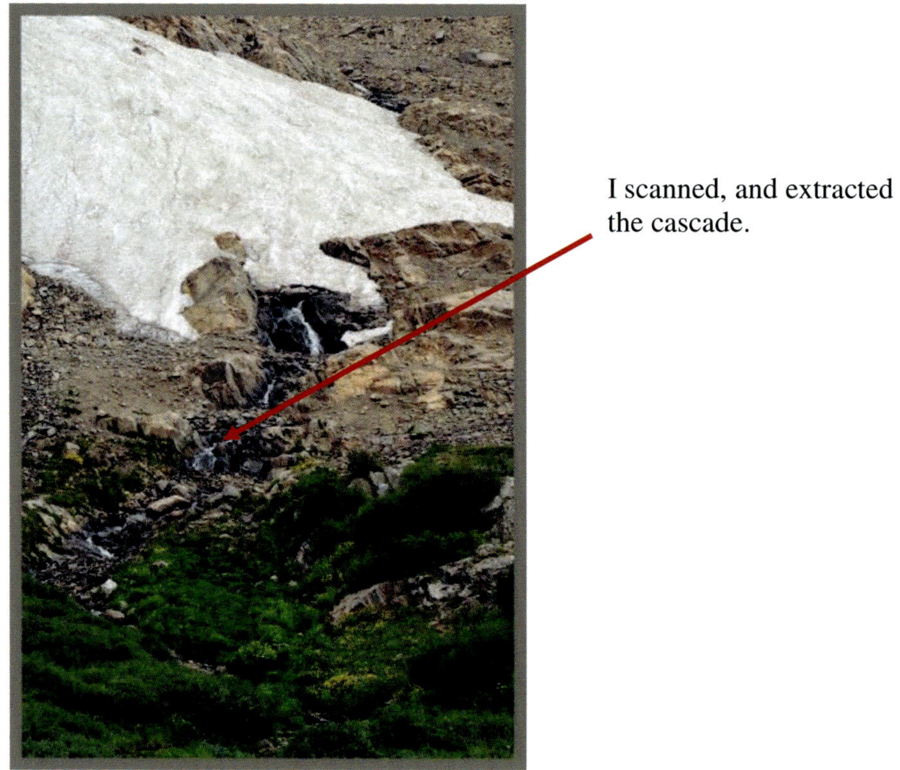

As you can see from the first image, in order to retain as much of the life “wow” factor as possible, we need a different translation of what we see. The mistake we often make is that we see something, not realizing that our emotions are a big part of the moment, and then say, “Wow. Isn’t that beautiful?” Then we stand there and go “click.” We look at our photo when we get back home, then proclaim in disappointment, “It looked much better when I was there.” Sound familiar?

Well, we certainly didn’t speed through the topic of shutter speeds. I think we can now weave our way to the subject of ISO.

ISO. Since this not a basic how-to book on left brain stuff, I will make this simple. Let's go back to the cascade. I shot that at ISO 100 because I was trying to get as slow a shutter speed as possible. I still favor using lower ISOs. Admittedly, some cameras can hold up very well, if not extremely well, at ISOs of 1600, 3200, or even higher. However, for most of my scenarios, I rarely need more than an ISO of 800. I would rather shoot at 100, 200, or 400, with longer exposures. Occasionally, I might go higher, but only if it meets my criteria of what I want it to look like. I have gone as high as 1250, but that's extremely rare.

My most applicable use of ISOs higher than 100 or 200 is when I have a scenario where I want to have my cake and eat it too. There are times when I need an f/16 or higher f/stop to get the DOF coverage I want, but the corresponding shutter speed is too slow to get a sharp image. My depth of field coverage might be what I want, but I also need a faster shutter speed for everything to look as I envision. In those situations, I will pump up my ISO to 400 or higher in order to get a faster shutter speed and still keep my desired DOF.

I encountered exactly that situation when I was at the Royal Gorge in Colorado. I had to shoot without a tripod, since I was in mid-air inside a gondola, which was swaying in a light breeze. It was cloudy and dark, so I knew I was going to get a slow shutter speed when I went down to f/20. I did. So, in order to have my cake (a lot of depth of field) and eat it too (get a fast enough shutter speed to prevent movement blur), I pumped up my ISO. The following image was shot at ISO 500, which allowed me to shoot at 1/320 shutter speed.

Please see my diagram on page 190. It shows the relationship between f/stops, shutter speeds, and ISO—for those "have my cake and eat it too" situations. It explains how you can solve tricky problems like this one on the next page.

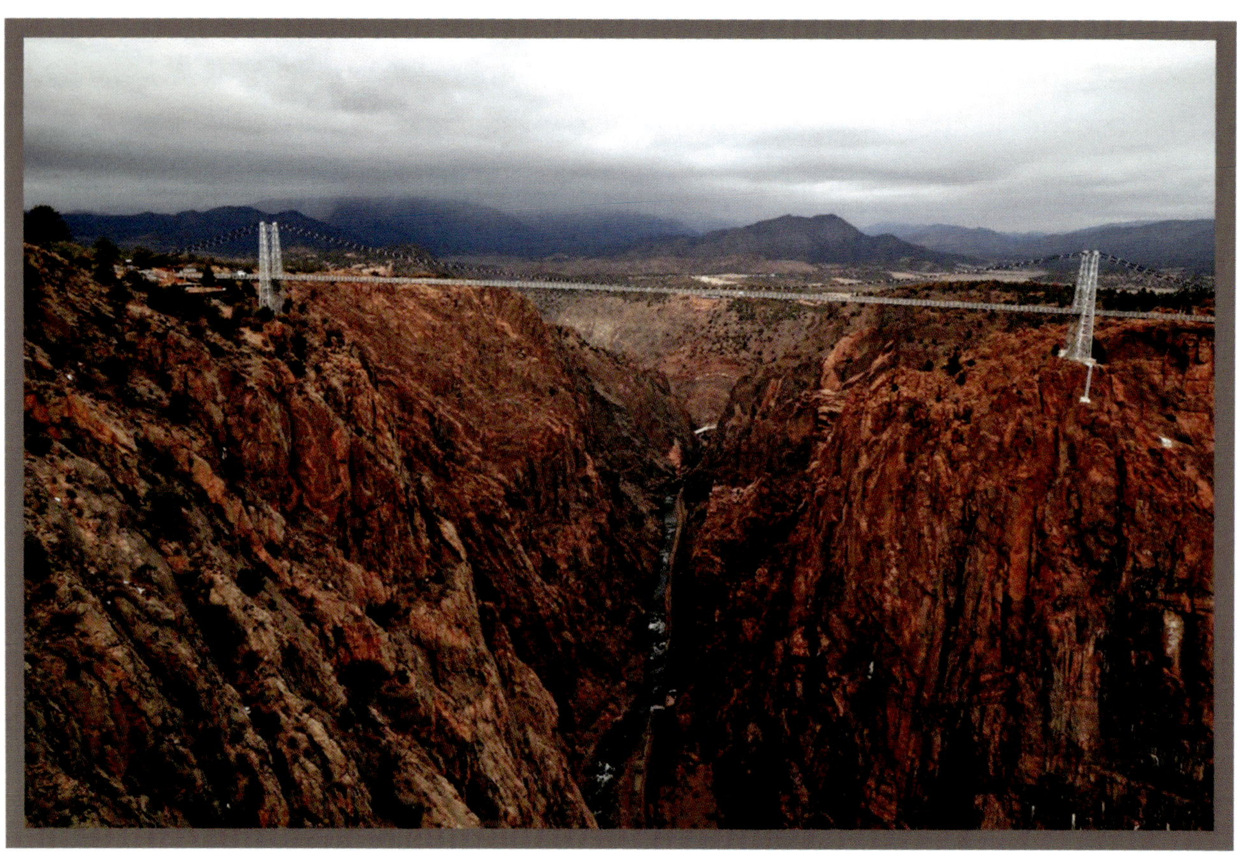

"Royal Gorge From The Air"

Tripod or no tripod? For me, 95% of the time it's a no brainer—always a tripod. It's easier to talk about the times I do *not* use one. I shoot without a tripod in places where they do not allow them or when the results I want just cannot be achieved with my camera on it. Sometimes I want to make my subjects move, rotate, or swirl. I do not use my tripod for those shots—I just simply move or swirl my camera. I will keep my camera on the tripod, but loosen the head so I can move or pan my camera. In order to get the best, sharpest, no-blur images *without* a tripod, I use this simple rule of thumb: make sure my shutter speed is equal to, or greater than, the focal length I'm using. For example, if I am using a 70mm-300mm lens and I have the focal length set at 200mm, my shutter speed should be equal to or greater than $1/200^{th}$ of a second—the higher the better. The reason this rule of thumb works so well is because as we increase the focal length of our lens (e.g., 200mm, 300mm, 400mm), not only is our subject magnified, but--read my lips—so is the movement, the shake, in our hand! So, please watch out for that.

I prefer to use my tripod the majority of the time. When I have to shoot with slow shutter speeds (e.g., 1/3 or 1 second) I can still get that shot perfectly, and tack sharp, with my tripod. Composition is my top criteria for creating great photography. I can fine-tune, and therefore improve my compositions when I use my tripod. It is next to impossible to hand-hold my camera and get the exact composition I want, especially if to do so will require a slow shutter speed. There is, by the way, no "composition" tool in photo editing software.

Lens. Zooms have come a long way since the 1980s, though some photographers still prefer prime lenses. My clients have never asked me if I shoot with prime or zoom lenses. Quality is the most important factor. I would rather use a high-end lens than a high-end camera. To me, quality optics are more important than extra bells and whistles on a camera.

Today, my workhorse is my 24mm-70mm lens. It covers a large percentage of the type of scenarios I prefer to photograph. My second favorite is my 17mm-50mm lens. Both are f/2.8 lenses. I will resort to my 70mm-300mm telephoto lens when I cannot get close enough to my subjects, which helps me get those tight, sometimes macro-looking images.

I have my favorite lens characteristics, and they all have unique attributes. For example, when I want to create the illusion of compression, subjects seeming to be closer to each other than they really are, I will back away and use a 200mm-300mm range. That telephoto compression principle works great for landscapes, where I can make mountains look much closer than they really are, or make layers of mountains seem much closer to each other than they really are.

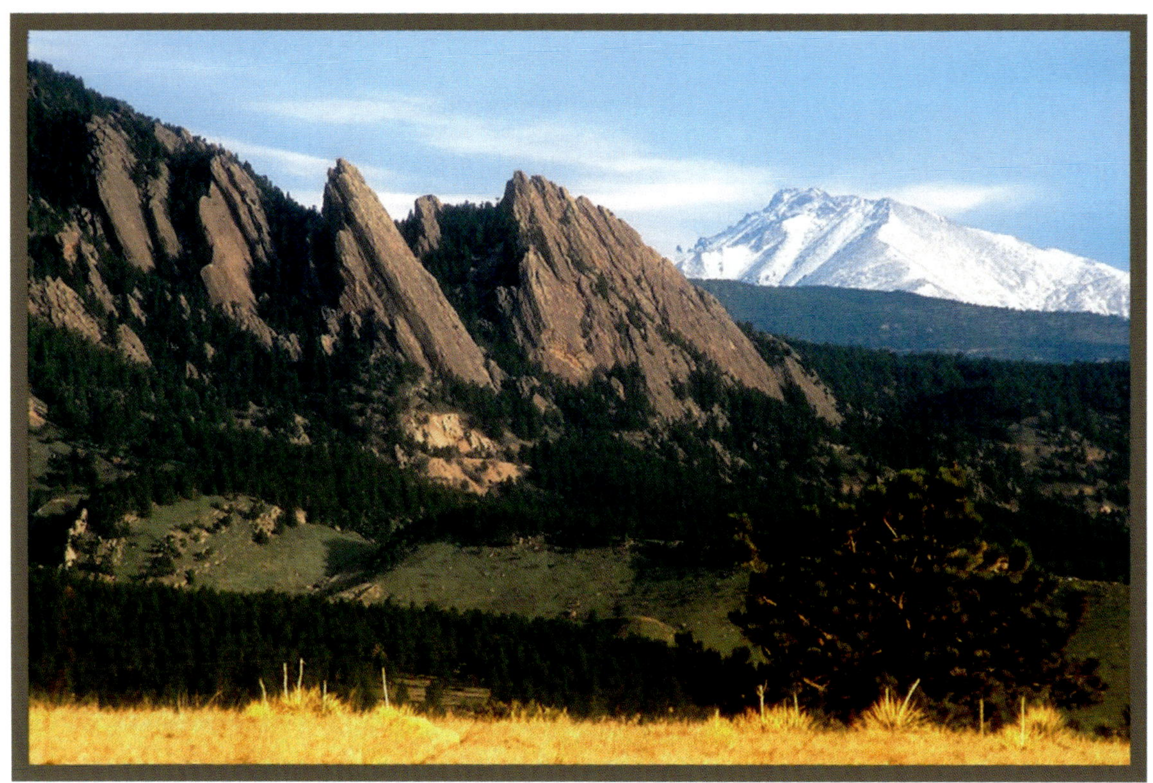

This is a good example of the illusion of compression. The diagonal peaks, called the Flatirons, serve as the backdrop to Boulder, Colorado. Approximately 40-50 miles away, are Mt. Meeker and Longs Peak—still snowcapped in April. They look, and are, much farther away in real life. Photographed with a telephoto lens, they look much closer.

I need to leave you with a caveat about wide angle lenses. Whenever you have one of those "Oh wow" scenarios, please be careful. Wide angle lenses can easily take away the "wow" factor. They can sometimes cover too much ground, if you will. For example, if you are looking up at three awesome jagged peaks, you might just need a 22mm to 24mm range to keep the "wow" factor. A 17mm lens might include too much needless landscape on each side of the peaks, too much foreground, too much sky, and the peaks will look small. Those are the times when you go home and say, "They looked more amazing when I was there." So, careful with that.

Filtration. The use of filters is simply subjective. There is no magic formula that dictates exactly when a filter is needed. The decisions are based on effect and personal taste. Although some filtration can be done with photo editing software, I still prefer to do it in the field whenever applicable. I do have my favorite filters. I already mentioned my FLD filter, which I used on "Hard Hats & Concrete."

I like to use my circular polarizing filter when I want to enrich blue skies and white clouds, cut through glare, enhance colors on a sunny day, or if I want to slow down my shutter speed for special effects. I use it sparingly though—only as needed. Here are examples of the same image—one without, and the other with a polarizing filter. Note the overall color saturation, greens in the trees, the mountain hues, and the deep blue polarized sky.

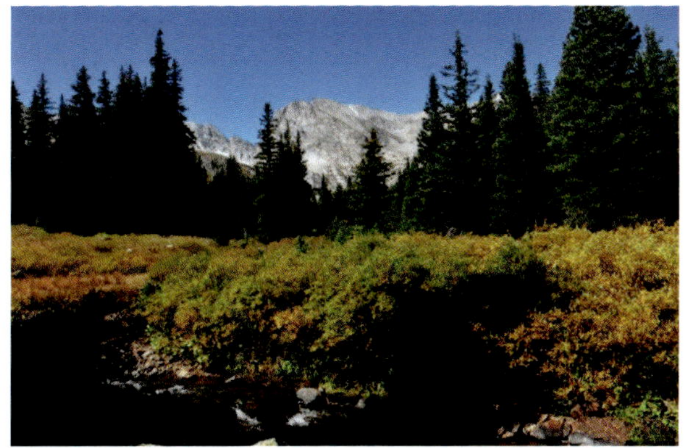

Without polarizer

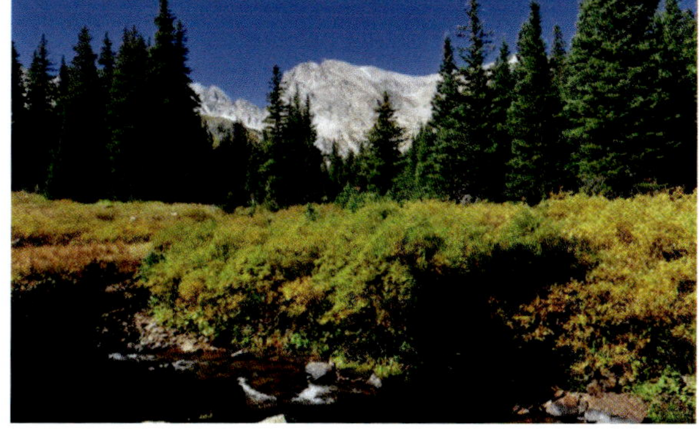

With polarizer

My other favorite, which I don't use as often as the polarizer, is my 81B filter, also known as a warming filter. You saw one example already of the cascade at St. Mary's Glacier. My other favorite, especially for landscapes, is my 2-stop GND filter—graduated neutral density filter, which I usually use to minimize the exposure range between land and sky. The image on the next page illustrates the use of a GND filter in a morning landscape setting.

Without a GND filter, either the sky would have been blown out (overexposed) and the rest of the scene properly exposed, or the sky would have been properly exposed, but the bottom half of the scene would have been under-exposed. A GND filter helps solve those frustrating dilemmas. It is rectangular in shape and slides in front of the lens. Be careful where you place it as you slide it into view.

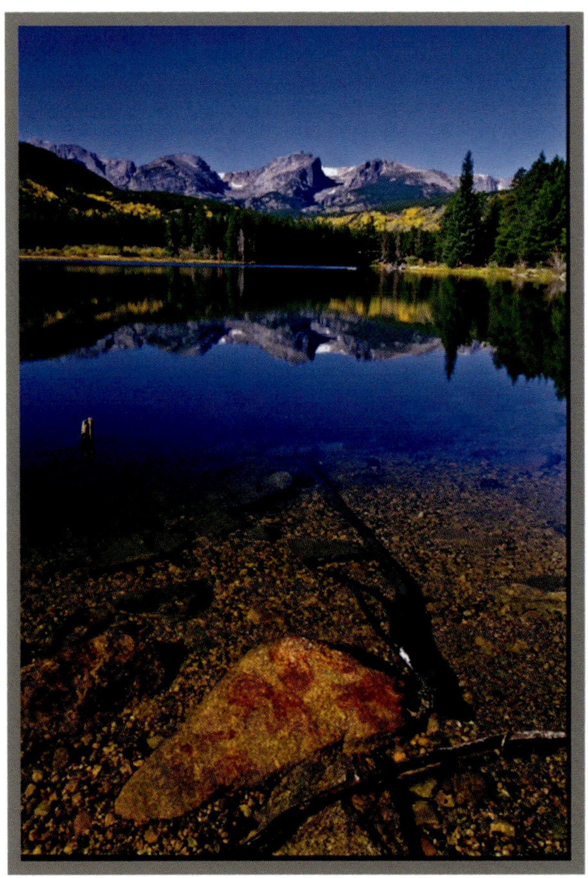

The GND filter came in handy here, where I wanted to hold back, or decrease, the exposure on the sky, to bring it closer to the exposure on the landscape. The result is a nice blue sky, as opposed to a washed out, over exposed sky we often get in similar landscape photos.

I also use filters in conjunction with a low ISO, for the sole purpose of slowing down the shutter speed on a sunny day. If I combine filters, I can really slow down the shutter, sometimes by as much as 2-4 stops or more.

Menu settings. This one is so strongly based on personal taste and preference that I will spend minimal time on it. It is important to go through all your menus and sub menus before you start shooting. That will set the tone for the "look" of your images, unless you prefer to shoot exclusively in Raw format.

I used to shoot with Fuji Velvia 50 film. I loved the look of that film. Today, I activate my menu settings to approximate the look I got with my favorite film. Then, I can fine-tune my images later with my photo editing software if necessary.

There are a few settings which I change only as needed. I change my White Balance, especially when shooting indoors without flash. That change might include fluorescent, incandescent, or sometimes even the Auto setting. Again, there is nothing magical about these settings. I take test shots before my projects and decide what will work best, given the lighting conditions. As mentioned earlier, I will change my ISO as needed. I usually shoot on Aperture Priority, but sometimes switch to Bulb for really long exposures, fireworks and moon shots—adjusting f/stops and shutter speeds as needed.

Exposure metering is usually set at matrix metering. Sometimes, depending on the desired effect, I will switch to spot or center-weighted metering. When shooting with spot metering, I will sometimes bracket from the spot metering exposure if necessary. The following image is one where I did not have to do that. I liked what I had done, without having to make any needed adjustments from the spot metering exposure.

Some of my favorite images have been created through the application of spot metering. It is yet another photographic "paint brush" at my disposal. I use it to "paint" a scene, the same way artists paint on canvas.

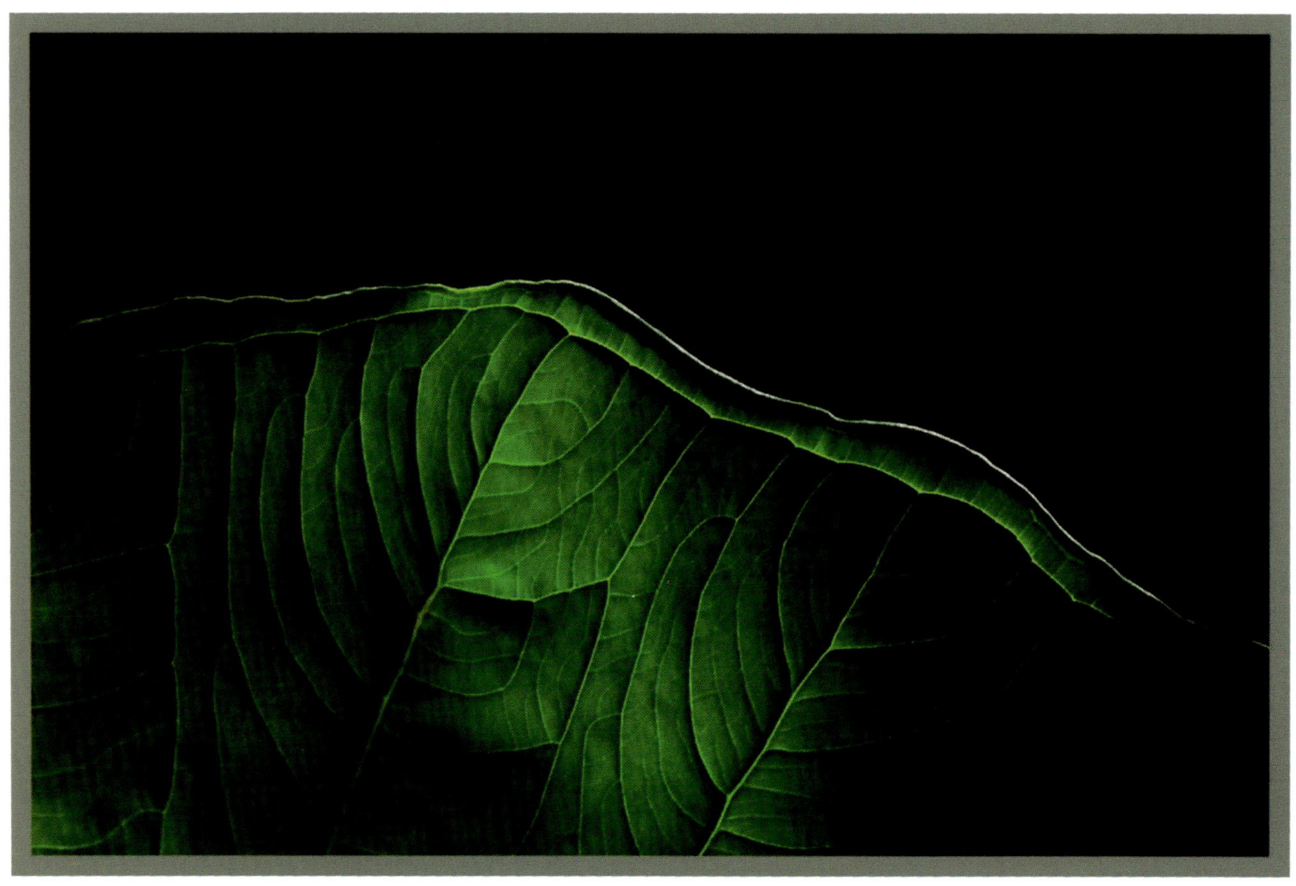

"Lit Within"

These leaves were receiving great lighting, while the background was subdued under dark shade. I knew that if I spot metered on them I would create some artistic high contrast in the image, including contrast between the leaves and the shaded background. This scene, as others I've shown, did not have this much contrast to the naked eye. It did *not* look like this. I had to imagine what I could make it look like, if....

Vertical/Horizontal. This one is simple. For me, in most cases, if my subject or scene is horizontal, it goes horizontal. If it is vertical, it goes vertical. If I want to make a specific statement, sometimes I will shoot horizontal subjects vertical or vertical subjects horizontal. On the next page is a vertical subject, a tree, which I photographed horizontally to emphasize this one single lone tree in the middle of an expansive high desert. The surrealism comes from the desert-like foreground against the huge snow-capped mountains in the wide San Luis Valley in Colorado.

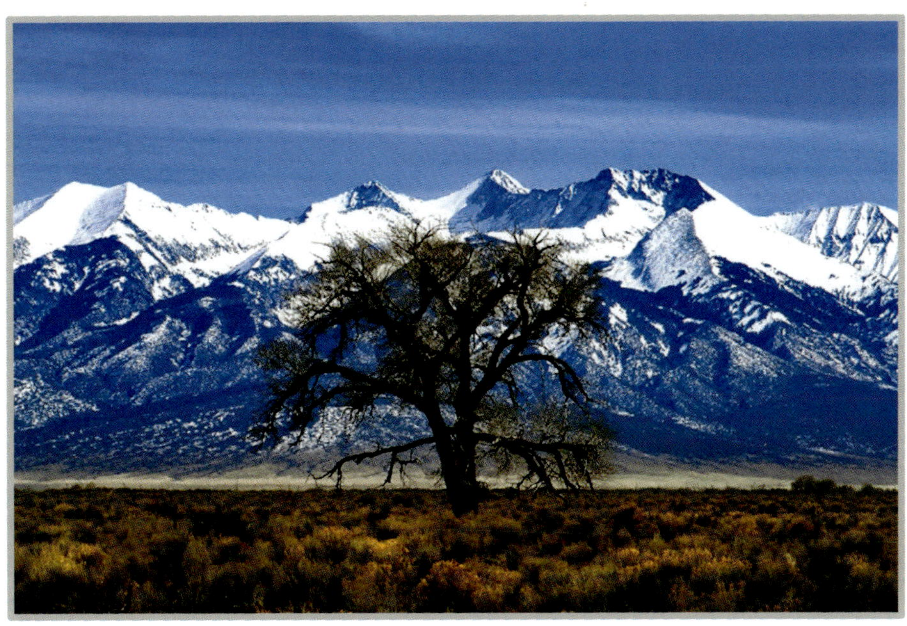

The message I got was, "What is this tree doing in the middle of the desert?"

Cropping. We are all stuck with a rectangular viewfinder or camera screen, but sometimes the best images do not fit perfectly in that rectangle, or those rectangle dimensions. Most of the time, because of careful in-camera compositions, I can place everything I want to place within that prescribed rectangle. I do my own image cropping in the field, although some images might need additional cropping later. Sometimes I will get my shot, knowing that I am going to crop it later to eliminate what I call "dead space," or wasted space that doesn't contribute to the image, as in the following cropped image of flying sandhill cranes along the San Luis Valley at sunrise. A note of caution here, for those of you who sell your images or think you might want to eventually start licensing your images: always keep the original non-cropped version. Buyers often like the extra space for adding text, captions, etc.

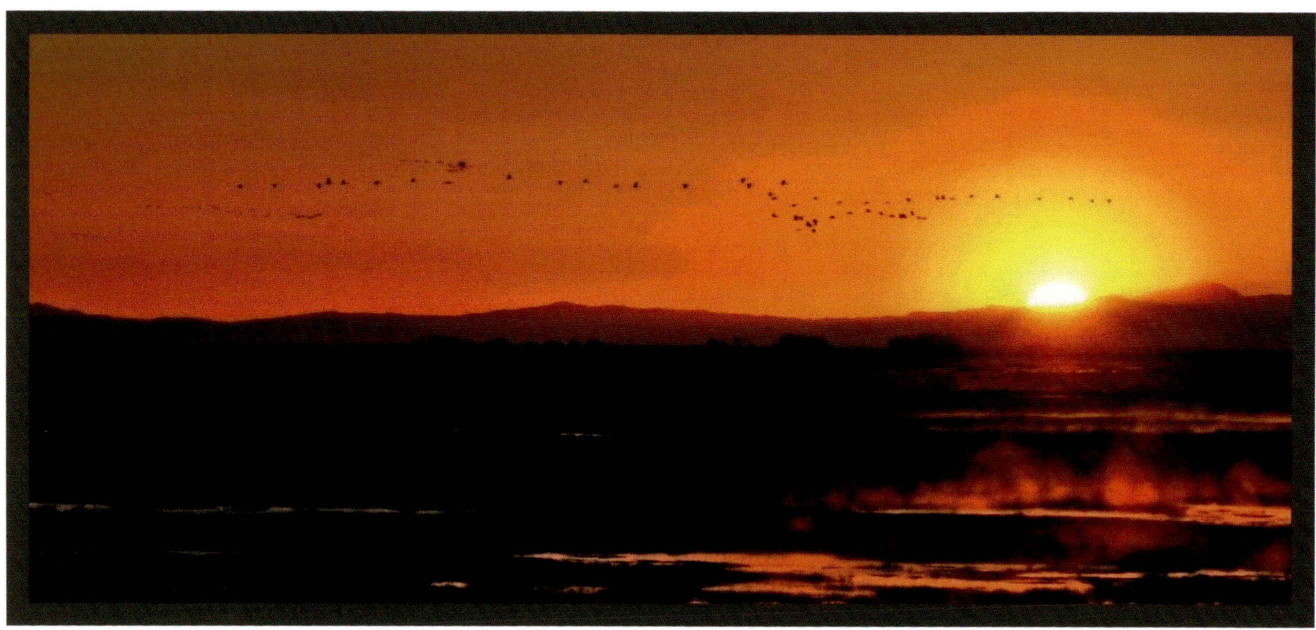

PREVIEW & TWEAK. This is the part where I preview my image and fine-tune if necessary. After I go through my check list under the THINKING part and look at my monitor, I might decide to make one or two more adjustments to the image. Those adjustments can include bracketing my f/stops or shutter speeds to get totally different results, bracketing exposures, creating two images using two different metering modes, or creating one image that is a multiple exposure and one that is not. Often, if I know that everything will be identical except for one or two adjustments I have made, I will delete the first image so I won't get confused later as to which one is my final in-camera image. Sometimes, an image looks good as two or three different renditions. They all look good for different reasons, so I'll keep them all.

The following are examples of when my subject worked well as two different renditions. "Radiance Flare" is a double exposure; "Radiance," a -2 stop under exposure, is not. Art is subjective. Photography is art. Viewers will favor one or the other, or both.

Same scene; different look. Which rendition resonates with you?

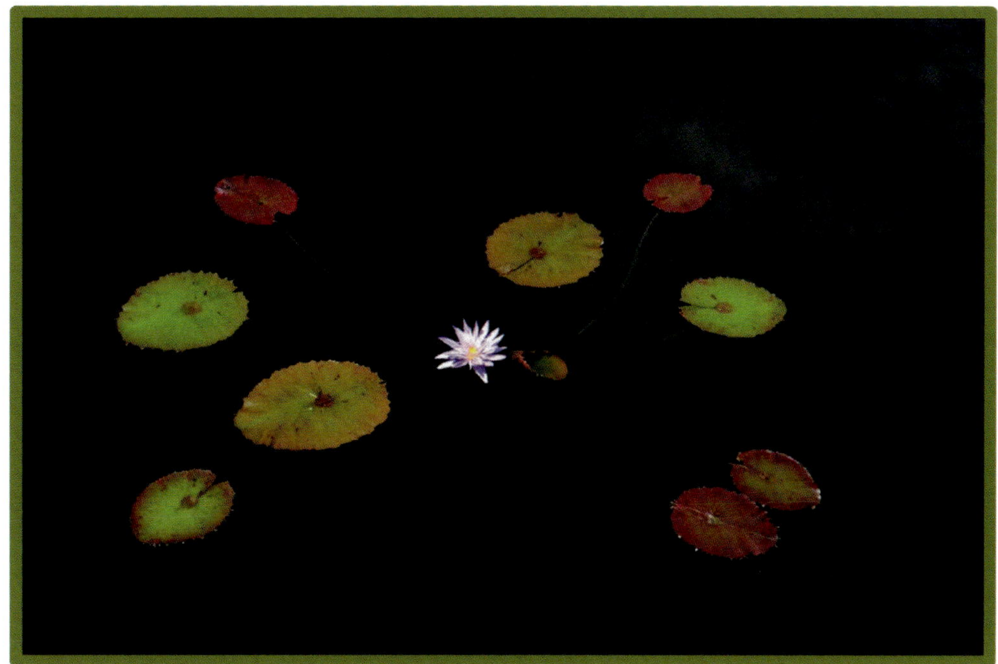

"Radiance"

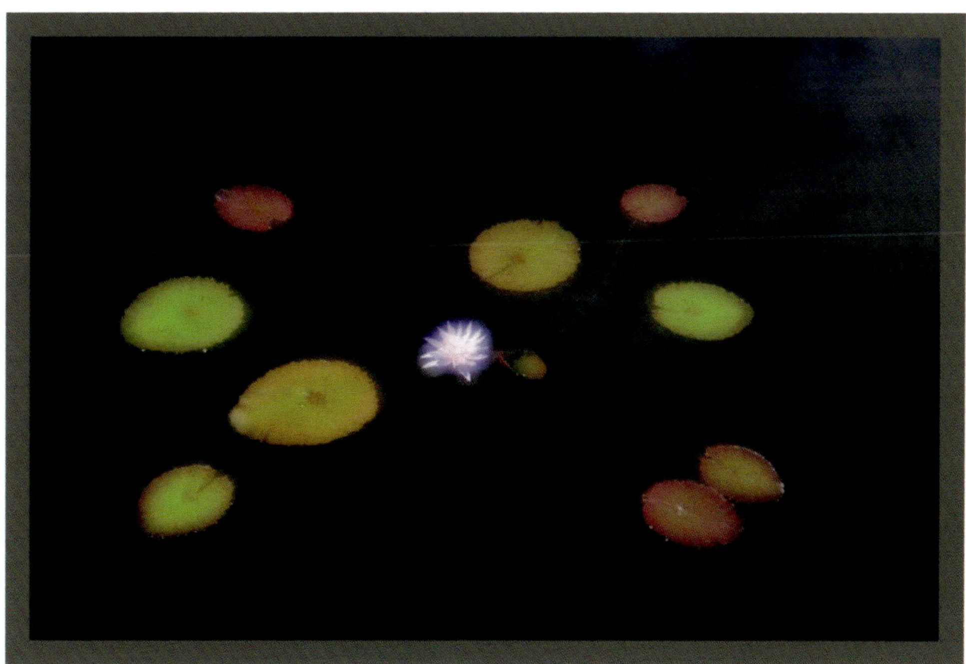

"Radiance Flare"

It took a lot of time to share and discuss both parts of **Phase I**, but it was extremely important to do so. This is repetition, but it is important to repeat: I wanted to take you into my left brain so you can see what happens when my right brain shakes hands with my left brain and says, "I've got an idea, and this is what I need from you."

PHASE II

FINE TUNING IN DIGITAL LAB. I mentioned before that, on the average, 80%-90% of my image results are done in camera. The other 10%-20% are done by fine-tuning with photo editing software. I do some fine-tuning for many of my images, though not all.

I have offered slide show presentations for several photo clubs in Colorado and Arkansas. The theme of one of my slide shows is "Be An Artist First, Photographer Second." At the end of one of those presentations, a participant in Colorado asked me, "If you don't do HDR, what do you do?" HDR, in a nutshell, is a photo editing process whereby you take several photos of the same scene, at 3-7 (or more) different exposures. Through the use of software peripherals, you can then combine all three or seven images into one, therefore reducing the lighting exposure range (also called dynamic range) between the darkest and the lightest parts of the scene.

I told that participant what I tell everyone else. I have my favorite photo editing tools which I like and use. I prefer the term "fine tuning" to "post processing." The latter sounds like it's something we do after we "take" a picture. Fine tuning, to me, means that it is part of the photo image creation process. It is an extension, a continuation, and thus part of the entire process of creating an image. For me, though, it is a small percentage of that process, not the primary process.

So, if I don't do HDR, what do I do? I started using photo editing software before the advent of digital cameras. Fine tuning with editing software is not a new process for me. The following are my most commonly used tools.

REVIEW & ADJUST. If you look at the THE PHOTO IMAGE CREATION PROCESS illustration on page 114, you will notice that most of what I do, in terms of my process, is done in camera. I don't even touch some images—I like them just the way I created them in camera. One example is "Wet Cubism," introduced in Section III.

When I do some fine tuning, I might adjust brightness and contrast, and maybe a little cropping. I rarely add saturation, but have on rare occasions. I prefer the Vibrance tool. Dodging and burning I use as needed. No film, sensor, or light meter can record every possible light range in a scene equally well. There might be an area in the image that is a bit dark. If it is, and it's not important to the essence of the image, I won't dodge it, or try to lighten it. I apply the same decision-making to burning, or darkening. If an area in the image is too light, bright, or washed out, it might compete for attention, that is, it might take away from the center of interest. In those cases, I might burn, or darken, that area a bit.

Ansel Adams, by the way, did tons of dodging and burning. He was doing photo editing, or post processing, way before we had heard of terms like "digital photography" and "digital lab." The general public knows him for his photography; photographers know him for his lab work. You might say that his real strength was really in the lab. For one of his most famous prints, "Moonrise Over Hernandez," he literally took out some clouds in the sky which he didn't like. Now, that's what I call post processing. Some people would say that he manipulated the photograph.

Oftentimes, all I need to do is click on Auto Tone or Auto Color in my photo editing program and that's all I need to get the results I want. Sometimes, I may not like the results when I brighten the image, but like the results by adjusting Curves a little or working with Shadows/Highlights. Sometimes, I might like the image both in color and as a black and white image. In those few cases, I will convert it to a black and white, then make needed adjustments to get my blacks, whites, and grays the way I want them. There are times when I keep the original color image, a black and white rendition, and a sepia rendition as well. Converting images to sepia, by the way, is very easy. The technique I use is to simply convert the image to a black and white first, then add a little red from the Color Balance tool.

I like Fill Light a lot, especially for landscapes and scenics where some areas are in the shadows or in the shade. If those lost areas are important to the results I want, I will fill the shadows with Fill Light, which will add a little more light to them in order to bring out some of the hidden details not recorded properly by the film, sensor, or light meter. I like it because the results don't look edited. That is my bottom line when I fine tune my images—I want them to look like a photograph, not a different medium. Similar to Fill Light, sometimes I may increase or decrease shadows or decrease highlights, which also do not look edited.

I do, on rare occasions, play around with some of my images to create a non-photograph piece, but, that is done as a different version of the original. It is my artistic philosophy that if I do something severe to the image with my software, to the point where it no longer looks like a photograph, I don't call it a photograph—it is now another rendition of the original, in a different medium. It's perfectly okay to do so, that is art too, but I will call it what it is and not try to pass it off as one of my photo images. Here is an example of where I did just that by using photo editing software to convert a perfectly fine photo image to another medium. In this case, I took an already nice image of an abandoned fire truck and added what is called a Solarized filter to it. This looks more like a painting than a photograph. And, in a sense, it is—a digital, computerized painting, not a photo image. The medium used is what I call "digital mixed media" or "hybrid photo art." It is a different kind of digital playground. I was playing in that playground when I created the next piece.

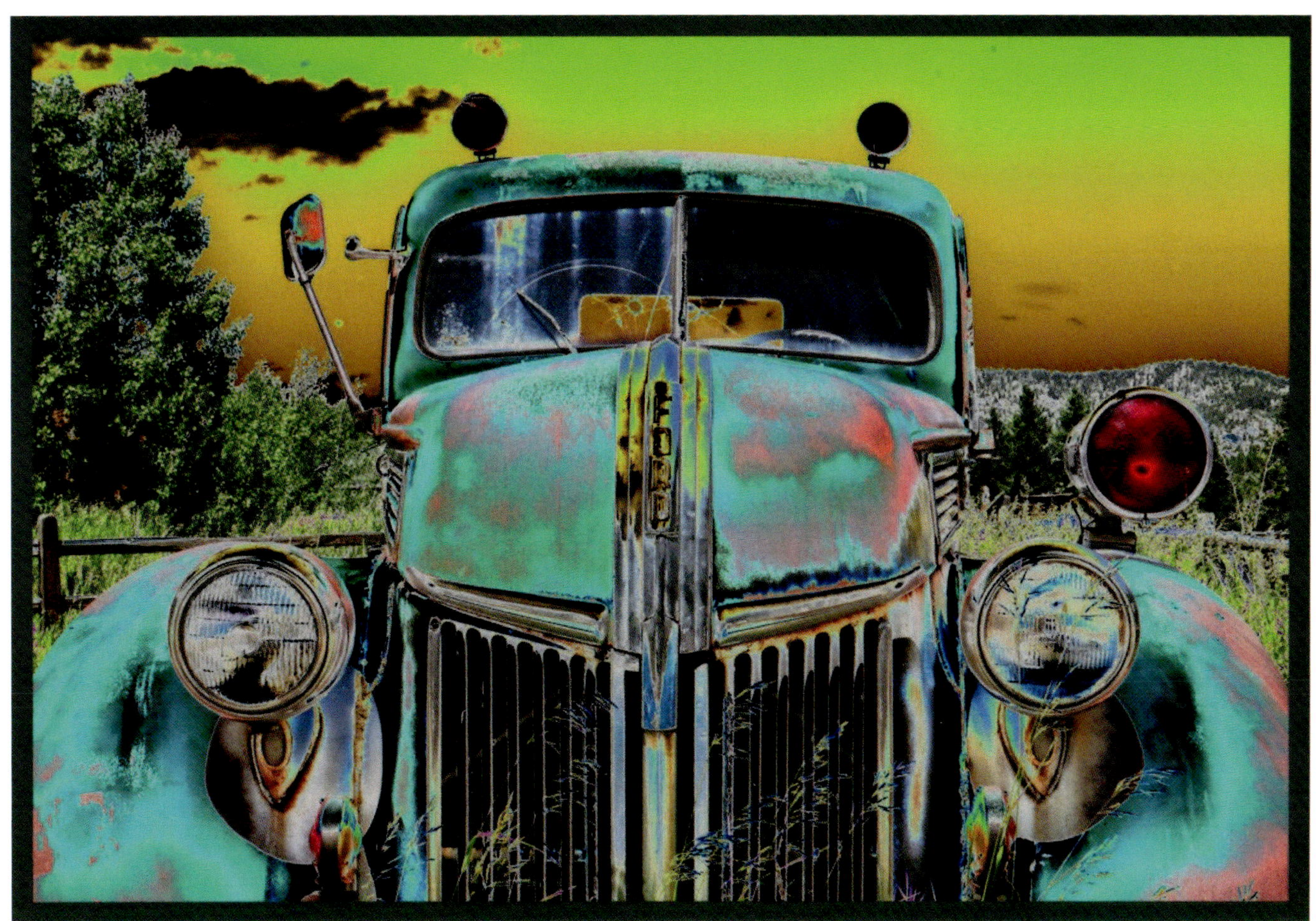

As you noticed, I spent a lot more time talking about PHASE I than I did about PHASE II. That should tell you something. I spend more time with in-camera photography than in after-the-fact fine tuning with photo editing software.

I alluded to my one page overview, The Photo Image Creation Process, at the beginning of this section. That overview, on the next page, coupled with the last part to this section, will give you a good summary of my photo image creation process.

THE PHOTO IMAGE CREATION PROCESS™

The photo image creation process begins with the realization that nothing we use is perfect.

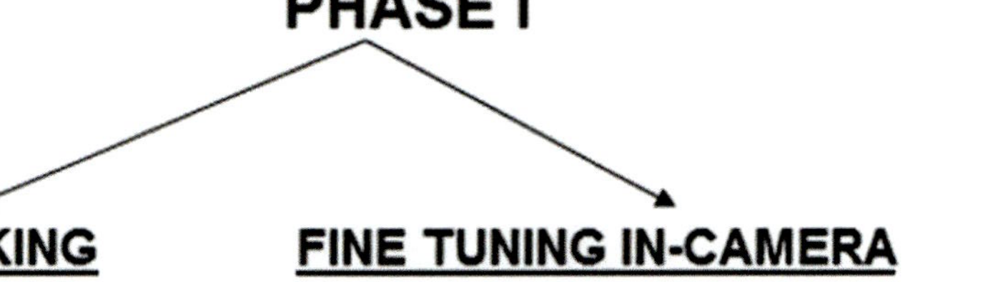

PHASE I

THINKING — **FINE TUNING IN-CAMERA**

(Pre Processing)

DETERMINE

- See with imagination
- Interpretation
- Detachment
- Un-labeling
- Timing
- Lighting
- Composition
- Perspective
- Depth of Field
- Exposure
- Shutter speed
- ISO
- Tripod/no tripod
- Lens
- Filtration
- Menu settings
- Vertical/Horizontal
- Cropping
- Other factors

PREVIEW & TWEAK

- Fine tune all "thinking" points
- Bracketing
- Exposure compensation
- Metering mode

PHASE II

FINE-TUNING IN DIGITAL LAB

(Post Processing)

REVIEW & ADJUST

- Brightness/Contrast
- Dodging/Burning
- Auto tone/color
- Curves
- Black & White
- Fill light
- Shadows/Highlights
- Other tools

= **Final Image**

MY THREE MODELS—OVERVIEW

Let me now summarize and give you an overview of my three photography models and what I do to incorporate them into my art. I have spent a lot of time talking about them separately, but it would help to give you a short re-cap.

It all begins with my right brain ***visualizing***, ***imagining*** what I could create through my photographic tools—my camera, lenses, and filters. My right brain is interdependent with my left brain, just like a traditional canvas artist relies on her brushes, palette, and palette knives. However, it is the artist, not her tools, that creates the final piece of art. I wonder how many admirers ever said to Georgia O'Keeffe, "Beautiful work! You must use high end expensive brushes."

With any given scenario, my ***intuition*** leads me to begin ***scanning***. My scanning then leads me to ***see something***, which leads me to ***extract*** something from the big picture. I then focus on my extraction and ***eliminate*** everything around me –tune it out. Remember, for photography purposes, the eyes see too much.

I consider myself lucky to have a vivid imagination. It is that inherent ***imagination*** that gets me to my end results. It is with that imagination that I can see something before I see it.

I was on Pearl Street Mall in downtown Boulder, Colorado, a public place where you see some of the most eclectic gatherings of human beings. It is a magnet for street performers. I saw an interesting street performer playing the banjo. He played John Denver-like music, but looked more like John Lennon. My imagination started doing its thing. I watched him for several minutes, noticing his personality, instrument, music, and the colors around him. I glanced up to the second floor of a nearby building. There was a balcony-like railing on the second floor. I imagined that maybe it used to be an upstairs apartment, or someone's home many years ago. The residents would open the New Orleans style louvered windows and step out onto the small balcony for fresh air. I then imagined the banjo player having been one of the historic residents. Going one step further, I could see the ghost of the banjo player as he played on that balcony.

The obvious right brain step needed to satisfy my imagination was to combine both the banjo player and the balcony in my camera.

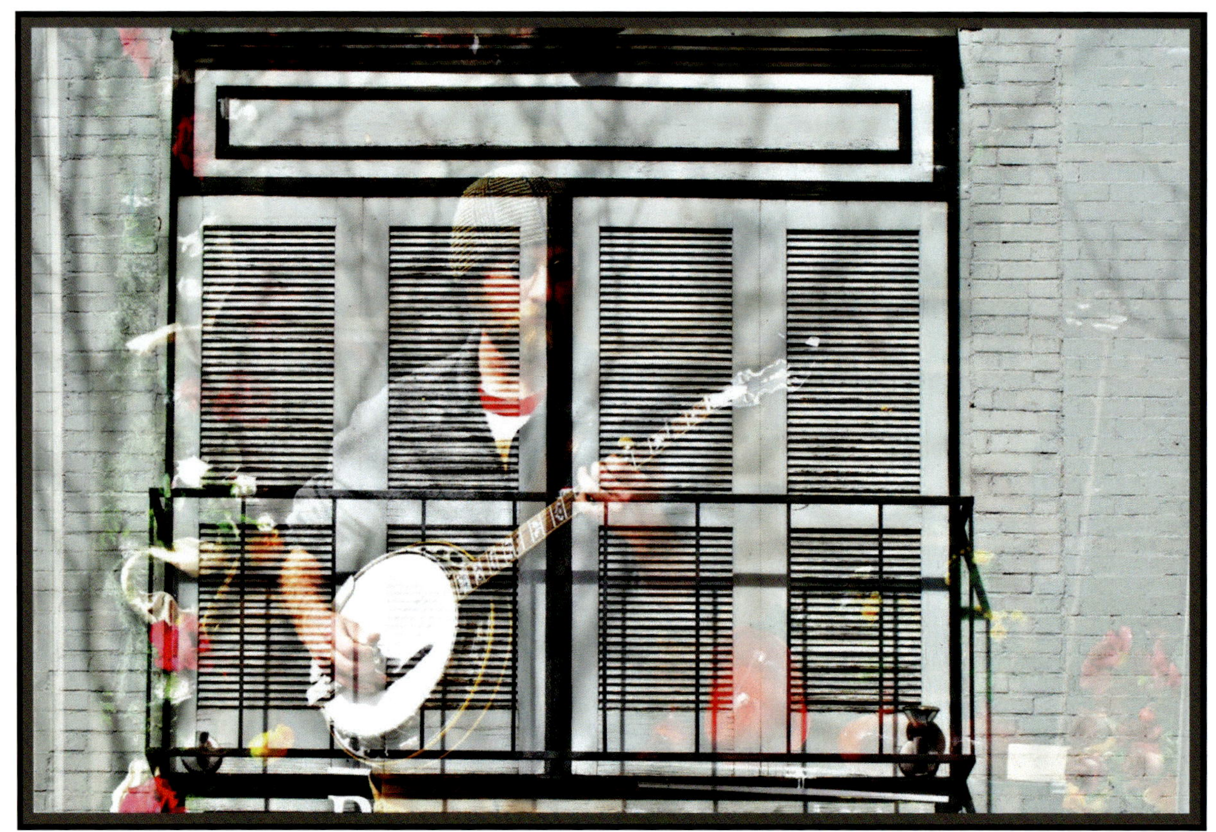

"Ghost of Pearl"

My imagination also helps me decide whether a particular scene can be further enhanced with a touch of ***Impressionism***. That is exactly what happened when I created this next image. The flowers were beautiful enough on their own, but I decided they needed an extra artistic touch.

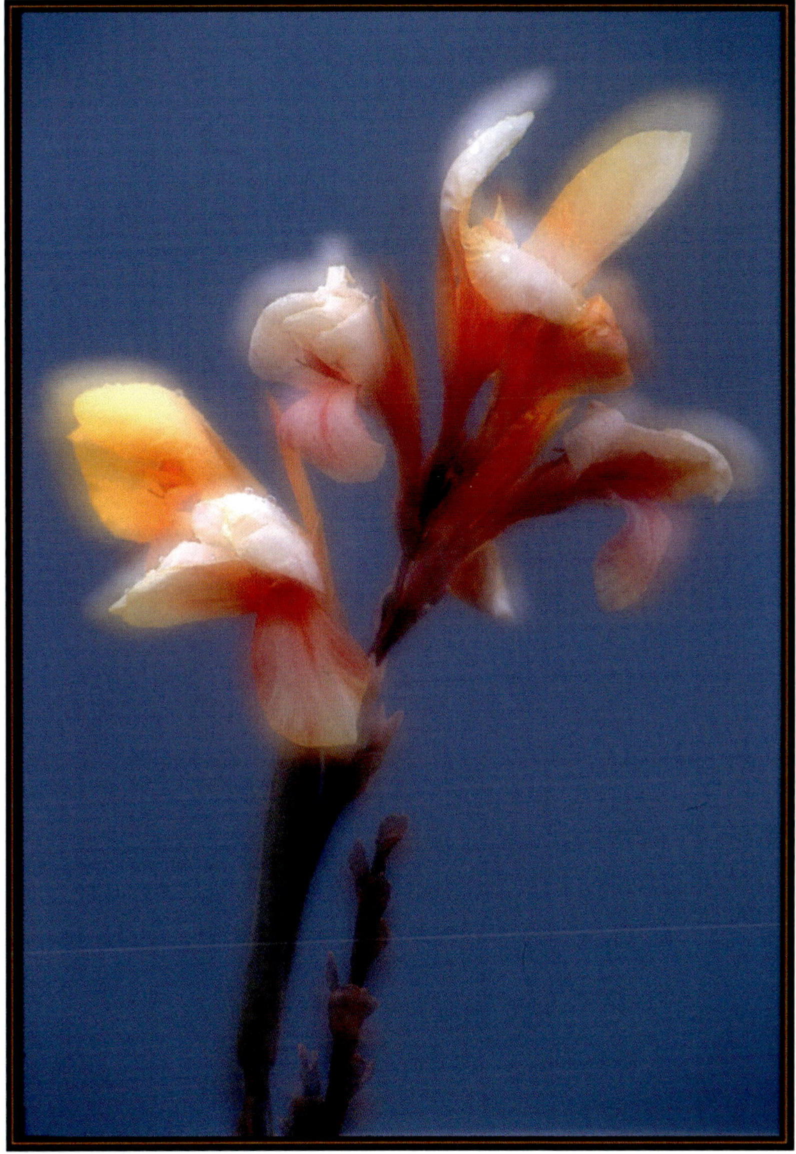

Pool Dreamin'

I was working out in the fitness center of my complex. As I looked out toward the pool, I saw these colorful flowers in a huge decorative vase. I saw what my naked eyes did not. After my workout, I went home and came back with my camera in tow. When I studied them at close range, I knew I had to do a double exposure, which resulted in the flower pedals having a halo effect. The background blue is the sky reflected from a nearby fitness center window.

As you can imagine, it takes a lot of imagination to apply a touch of ***Surrealism*** to my images. I have shared some examples already, but here is another one where the surrealism was already there---I just had to record it. Here's the scene. Steamboat Springs, Colorado. There used to be a really cool coffee shop there called Mocha Mollie's. Sad to say, it no longer exists. ***Impermanence***. It was a popular place with the locals, including me. During my first visit, I ordered my favorite and much loved soy chai tea. Soon after, I had to go to the restroom. The instant I opened the door I knew I had to photograph, yes, the restroom! It was irresistible. Luckily, I had my camera and tripod with me. I quickly locked the door behind me and started setting up. I was so mesmerized by what I saw that I went blank for a minute, forgetting where I was and why I was there. I got my shot though, and then took care of business. I got a release from the artist, knowing that I might use or sell this image someday.

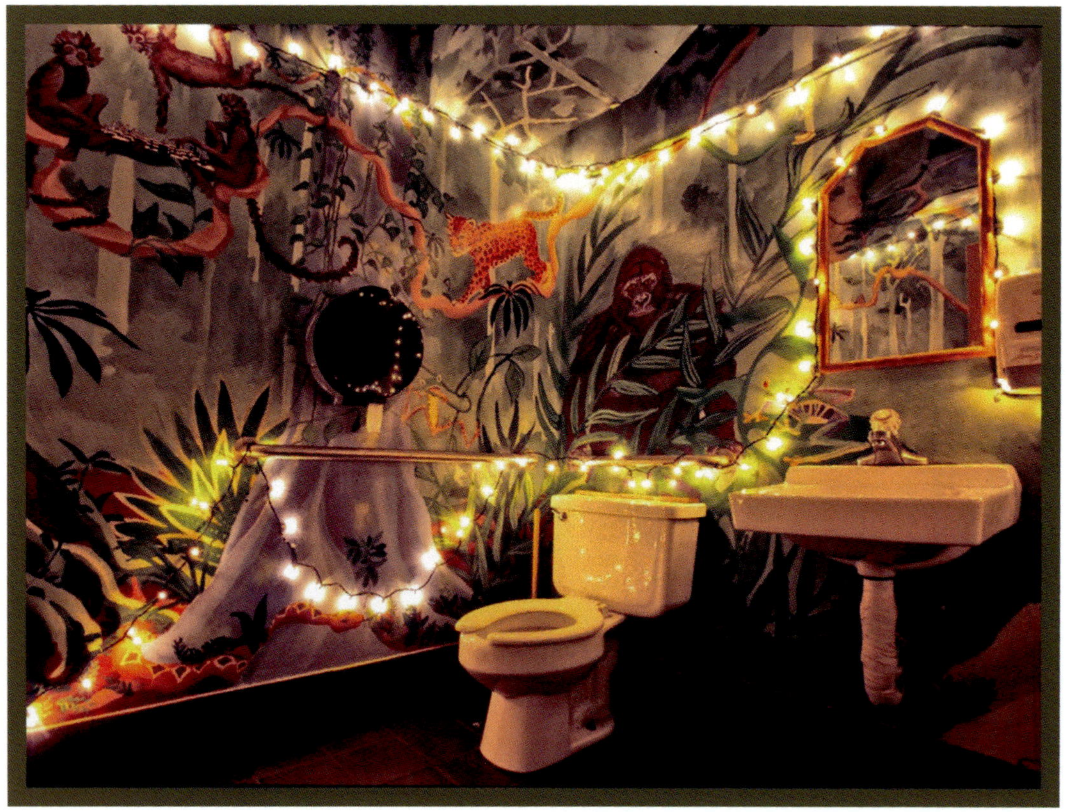

"It's A Jungle In There"

The artist, Chula Walker-Griffith, titled her mural art "Rain Forest of Gabon."

Eastern philosophy was the last piece of my ELI'S 5-POINT PHOTO ART MODEL. I talked about ***detachment***, ***un-labeling***, ***impermanence***, and **interdependence**. Of the four concepts, the ones I apply almost always are detachment, un-labeling and the principle of impermanence. I apply interdependence when I see it happening.

The concept of detachment was difficult for me at first. After several years of practice, I have been able to detach myself from situations, problems, issues, etc. Detachment has helped me solve life problems quicker and more efficiently, and to see solutions more clearly. That same concept has also helped me with my photography. When I *detach* myself from labels, I can see photographic opportunities more clearly, as if I can peel reality off a wall and see what is really behind it. That is what I was able to do with "Hard Hats & Concrete."

Here is an example that combines detachment, un-labeling, impermanence and the concept of interdependence. I saw a grove of lodge pole pines along Guanela Pass, not too far from where I live. My eyes saw autumn flora and trees. When I subconsciously applied eastern philosophy, I saw a sense of mystery; a sense that I could see where I was going, but not really. This is roughly what the scene looked like through my eyes.

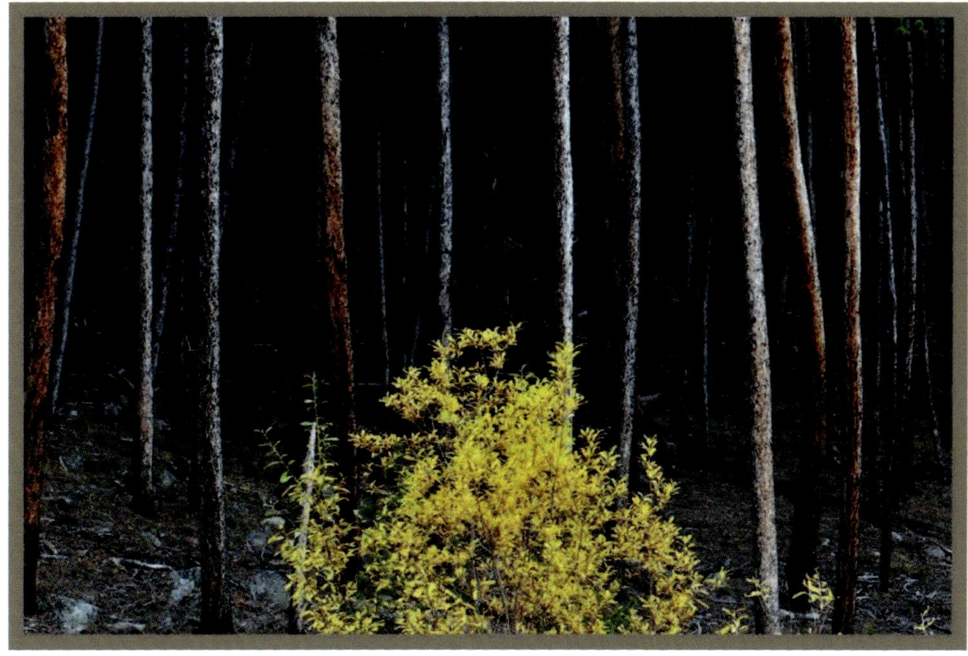

To add to the mystery and to what I "saw" and felt, my right brain told my left brain, "I need this to be about two stops underexposed." It was then that I saw what I imagined. I like both renditions. This second image adds more mystery to "What's out there?" The trees quickly fade into the mysteriously dark woods.

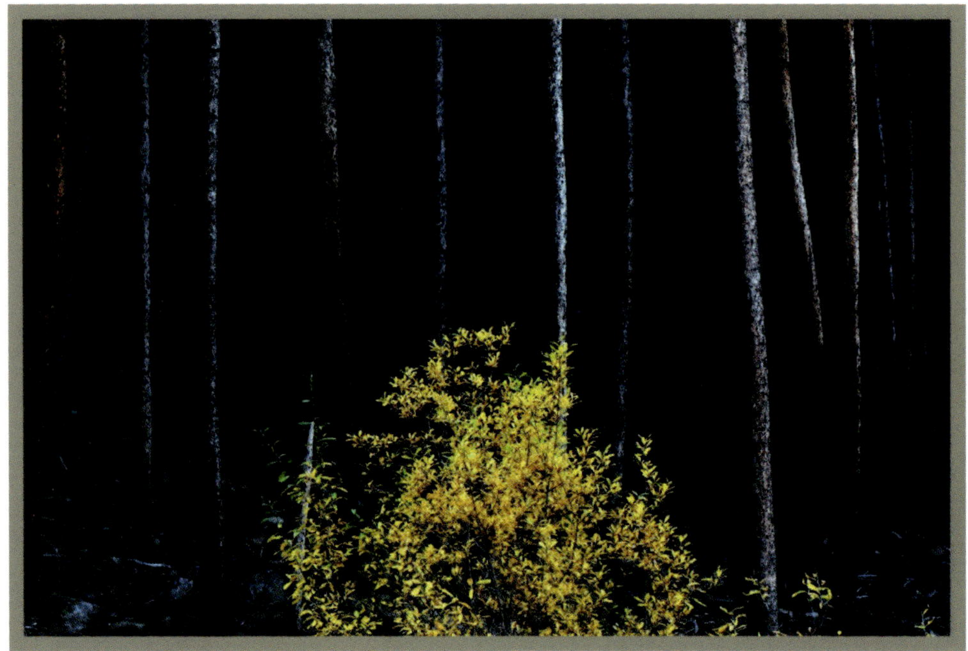

The photo image creation process was the last of my three paradigms. As mentioned before, people ask me, "Do you have a check list you go through before you take your pictures?" Well, although I don't "take pictures," I do have a checklist—found in my Photo Image Creation Process. After I put my right brain to work and decide how I want my image to look, including my composition, I go through my mostly left brain list under the THINKING process in my model.

Today's digital advantage of getting a preview of what I got allows me to *fine tune in camera*, i.e., *preview and tweak*. This, by the way, is not a totally new advantage. Before digital cameras, photographers, especially studio photographers, had Polaroid backs that gave them a preview of their shots. They then made their adjustments based on those Polaroid previews, then got their final shots.

Nothing we use in photography is perfect. It never has been. This is why an important part in photography is to know when to shoot, and when not to shoot. When I do decide to shoot, no matter what I do in camera, most images will need at least some minor *fine tuning*. This, also, is not totally new. A lot of photographers, especially beginning photographers, think that to fine tune an image in the digital lab is cheating. What they don't realize is that slide photographers before the digital age would take their slides to the lab for "fine tuning." They would instruct the lab technician to "crop a little here," or "burn this corner a bit." *We* have now replaced the lab technician, in a significant way.

I still prefer, though, to do most of my photography in camera, and then do some fine tuning later if needed. At the same time, though, I do not want to get sloppy and just "click," hoping that I can fix it later in the digital lab.

My message to you, from a right brain photography perspective, is simple. Create your images in your mind, and then tell your camera what you need to get what you want. This, for me, is preferable to creating something after the fact, in the digital lab. I use my digital lab to fine tune my images, not to create them. There is a big difference.

This takes me to the next section in the book, which I promised you. Composition is part of the CDE formula which I have applied for years. All else being equal, if I get all three parts of the formula right, I will get a good image. Composition takes us back to the right brain. It is one of the primary ingredients artists use when deciding how they want their paintings to look. Many artists will sketch out the main elements of their compositions on the canvas before they start painting.

SECTION VI

COMPOSITION

I have done a lot of photography judging during the last twenty years. Of all the key and important photographic principles, composition remains the weakest in many photographs I have judged. I don't know if some photographers never studied composition or if they forget to apply it, but I see it as a weakness among many photographers, even advanced and professional photographers.

I was lucky in that I had to study composition in college during my art days. I learned the concepts and applied them to my watercolors, oils, and acrylic works. I also studied paintings by the masters.

For this section, I will discuss composition and all the components related to the subject. After that discussion, I will show several images and point out which composition principles are present in them, and why I chose to include them as part of my final image. I will use the terms "components" and "principles" interchangeably.

Composition, unlike colors and subjects, is not something that art admirers necessarily notice or identify instantly. Most people will comment on the colors used, the subject itself, or maybe the lighting. If I hear them say something like, "I like the way she used this leading line to draw attention to the subject," I know they have studied composition.

When I visit art exhibits, it is evident to me that painters, unlike a lot of photographers, have an understanding of this critical art component. When I see the principles applied, they jump out at me. I can spot them in paintings and photographs, even from afar.

As I have said throughout this book, photography is more art than science. Additionally, art is subjective. Composition is part of the artistic endeavor, therefore also subjective. I will talk about various principles which I have learned and apply today, but they are not principles that can be perfectly applied every time. Artists have an advantage in that they can add a tree to fill in some empty space on their canvasses, add a bush on the lower left hand corner to contain the eye within the scene, or include a brick road to lead the viewer's eye to the main subject or an important part of the painting. We as photographers don't have that advantage, unless we want to spend hours with editing software combining several images into one composite, which would require skills other than photography.

Okay, I have already given you a hint as to what we're talking about when it comes to composition. Now let me give you my definition of composition, its components, and how I apply them to my photography.

Composition is about what I want to include or not include in my viewfinder, and *where* I want to place certain elements. My goal is always to make my images more interesting, more appealing, or more dramatic—not stale or stagnant. By "elements" I mean anything I see in the scene I am photographing, whether it's a broad landscape or a close-up. My discussion will concentrate mostly around subjects or scenes other than portraits.

We are all stuck with that rectangle called a view finder—everything we see will go inside those four corners. We need to carefully decide what elements we are going to include in that viewfinder, even if we might need to crop a particular image later.

Let me spend more time on defining elements. When I look out at any scene, I might see rocks, trees, creeks, tables, people, equipment, benches, storefronts, or signs. Those, and other examples I did not list, are my elements. The question for me is always, "What do I want this to look like?" The answers to that question can include a certain mood, a message, impact, storyline, a feeling, and so on. I slow down and get in touch with what I'm seeing, feeling, or sensing. I ask myself, "Why did I stop? What made me stop?" It's important to get in touch with that, in order to translate that into the final image.

I then move on to what I want to do with the elements I see—where I can best place them, or position myself in relationship to them. I am seeking my interpretation; my translation of the scene.

I study the scene slowly and carefully. I usually spend more time at this phase than actually getting my shot. Oftentimes, getting the shot per se is the easiest part of the process. Like a quarter mile runner at a track and field meet, the act of crossing the finish line is the easy part—it's getting there that requires more work.

Composition principles are not rules; they are guidelines. If they enhance my intended purpose, I will introduce them into my images. Sometimes my intended purpose is best met by not incorporating some of those same principles. My intended message, statement, or the feeling I want to convey will lead to my decisions regarding composition.

So, what are the composition principles which I so carefully spend time thinking about? As I walk you through them, keep in mind that I rarely find them in their most perfect form, and sometimes I find more usable principles than others. Bottom line: I will look for, and include, as many of these components that are present, and introduce them in the best way I can to achieve my mission, to answer my trademark question. You know what question that is…"What do I…..?"

"**CENTER OF INTEREST**." Let's start with this principle. Notice I used quotation marks around center of interest. For me, there is usually a center of interest—that main interest toward which the eye is drawn. The center of interest does not always have to be a single subject, like a person, a unique building, or flower. It can also be a group of elements---flowers, doorways, a row of trees that draw attention, and so on. Sometimes the entire scene is the subject, like some landscapes, abstracts, abandoned buildings, or cityscapes.

If all we are doing is "taking pictures," that activity is based on emotion, as I mentioned before. When we get so excited about what the eyes see, that visual is transferred to the brain as an "Oh wow" message, and then we click that little shutter button. We have to detach ourselves from that "wow" in order to go beyond taking pictures. The emotional "wow" and the final image "wow" are not the same. Please be careful to separate those two factors, sight and emotion. Sight is what we rely on to see. However, emotion can easily give us selective sight—we honestly do not see that busy background or that out of focus foreground.

I have seen prints where the photographer had a certain center of interest in mind, but it got lost in the translation—the translation between the initial emotional "wow" and the final image. I remember one evening when I gave feedback on a print. I made a lot of comments regarding room for improvement. In talking to the photographer later, he told me that what struck him about the scene was the creek. Honestly, when I saw his print, I did not see the creek. The center of interest got lost in his translation.

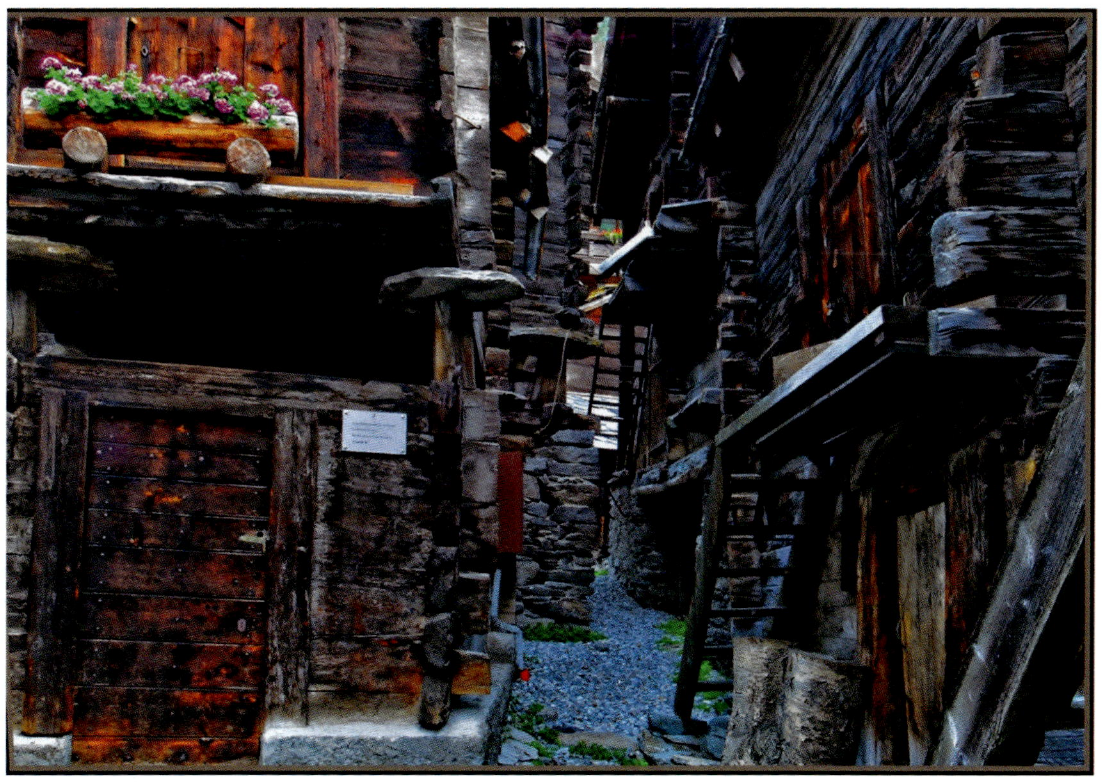

In this composition, the entire scene, the old historic structures clustered together in Zermatt, Switzerland, is the center of interest.

EYE FLOW. This is sometimes called "eye movement." In addition to having a center of interest, I usually add other elements in order for the eye to flow, to move throughout the image, as opposed to getting stuck in one place. My intent in adding other elements is to complement my main subject and add interest to the entire image. Even when my center of interest is, for example, a historic building facade, I will see if I can add a touch of eye flow. Whenever I include eye flow, I make sure it complements, not distract from, the center of interest.

I cannot leave this part without a helpful caveat. I'm always careful to make sure that any attempt at creating eye flow does not end up with elements that "compete" with my main subject. It's one thing to have some eye flow; it's another to include an element or elements that will compete with the center of interest. *Competing for attention* is what I am talking about. That can happen in a couple of ways. I might include an element in my image that is so big or colorful that it draws the eye away from my main subject. Another way this can happen is when there is a hot spot in the image—something that is so overexposed, "hot," that it draws attention to itself. I am always extremely careful with that. Sometimes, if what I see is perfect, except for that little hot spot, I will go ahead and get my shot, knowing that I will subdue that a bit in PHASE II of my earlier model—fine tuning in the digital lab.

BALANCE. It is important to achieve a sense of balance in our images. It is easier to begin the discussion on *balance* by talking about what creates a *lack* of balance. Imagine a scale on which you place items on one side or the other to achieve balance. If we have too many elements in the foreground, the image will feel like it's tilting toward us. The opposite also holds—if we have too many elements in the background, and not much in the foreground, it will feel like it's tilting backward. The same applies if we have too much on the left or right sides. If we cut the top part, lower part, right side, or left side of any image without losing its impact, that image did not have a good sense of balance. In order to counteract the sense of imbalance, we need to do careful cropping in the field.

I often see too much dead space, usually in the form of too much foreground or too much sky, which can often add to imbalance. Including unnecessary dead space does not contribute anything to the photograph. It does not add impact, interest, or appeal—it's just "there." If I cut that big chunk of sky from the image, the image will still look great, often even better than before. The idea is to fill the frame, but be careful with this too. You don't want the image to look too busy, with too much going on that the viewer gets lost in it.

The approach I use most to achieve a sense of balance is *size*. For example, I might introduce a large element in my scene that will serve as my center of interest, such as a beautiful and imposing cathedral. If I include other smaller elements throughout the image, such as a chapel and nuns walking toward the cathedral, they might give the overall scene a sense of balance. If I place the cathedral and the other smaller elements on opposite sides of the scale, they might balance each other out. The image does not have to be perfectly balanced. The idea is to reduce the negative impact caused my heavily lopsided images. I still remember my college art instructors warning me, "It's too top heavy."

In addition to size, sometimes I will look for color to create a sense of balance. Reds and yellows are the most arresting colors on the color wheel. They are also two of the three primary colors, blue being the third. Walk down the dish detergent and similar aisles in any super market and notice how many bottles and containers are red or yellow. Companies know that yellows and reds are eye-catching. When it comes to my photography, I will sometimes include a hint of red or yellow to add a sense of balance. A little bit of yellow or red on the scale can balance out a lot of grays, greens, or deep purples. If my main subject doesn't fill the image, but it's yellow, the eye will still be drawn to it—the yellow will pull the eye in, despite its relative size.

To summarize, the most important point to remember is this: do not end up with an image that is lopsided. I don't want too much empty, dead space in any part of my image—unless, to do so answers my question, "What do I want this to look like?" If drama, mystery, or a message is conveyed by including some dead space, I will do so, with intent in mind.

LEADING LINES. Put quotation marks around "leading lines." They are not lines per se, but anything that *leads* the eye to the subject, into the scene, or to an important part of the scene. They help to create eye flow. I use fences, roads, twigs, creeks, hiking trails, and other elements to serve as leading lines. I have even used negative space, like the space between clouds, to lead the eye into, not away from, the image.

My use of leading lines is usually intentional and well planned, but, I always say that photography requires a lot of skill, some planning, and a little luck. Sometimes it just all comes together, as if the composition gods talked to me, saying, "Eli, you've been a good person in your life. We'll throw them in for you."

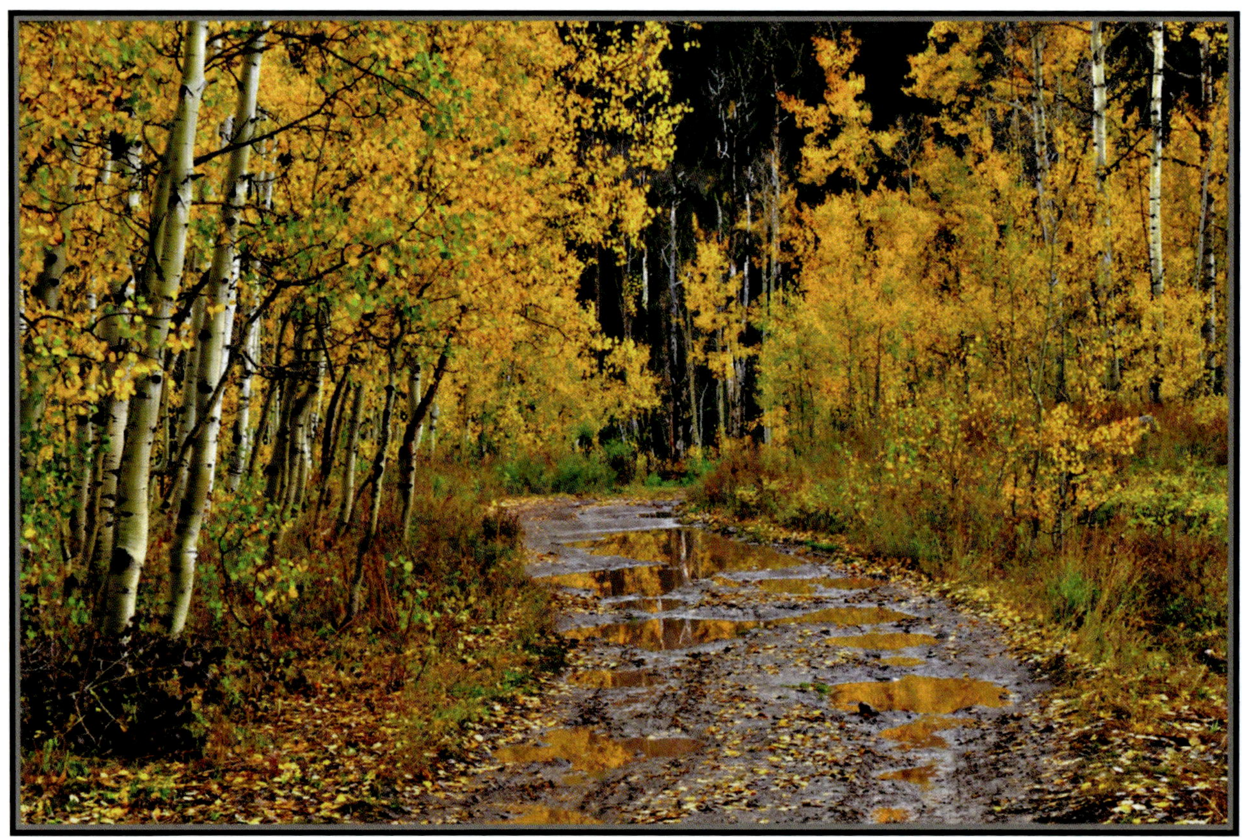

I found this spot by scanning while driving along Kebler Pass near Crested Butte, Colorado. I saw the puddles at a quick glance and just had to go back and take a closer look. As you can see, the road itself ***leads*** the eye into the scene.

CONTAINMENT. This principle is at least a partial solution to dead space. If it will enhance my composition, I will include an element or elements somewhere near the four corners, or anywhere toward the top or bottom, to *contain* the eye within the image and keep it from dropping off the edges. This includes any main subject that is moving. I will usually place a moving subject facing, or moving toward the inside of the frame. Sometimes the element I use as a *leading line* will also serve as containment, in that it helps to lead the eye into the image. We want to *contain* the viewer's eye within the frame and not let it drift outside the image. The exception would be if we want to make a statement, like adding mystery to the scene. If that works, it works. Again, what do we want the scene to look like, to convey, or to say?

Containment is not the same as "framing," which you might have heard or read about. To add a frame around the image can often look obvious and disturbing. A typical weak framing approach I have seen with landscapes is to place a pronounced tree on the left side and another on the right side of the image. They might "frame" the image, but they distract from the center of interest and often appear to be *the* center of interest.

This is a good place to talk about the idea of creating a sense of three dimensions in photography. What we often hear on the subject is that we should include something in the foreground, in the middle, and toward the back of the image. I have two caveats regarding the attempt to create a sense of three dimensions in a two dimensional image. First, it doesn't have to be obvious. It can be as subtle as a few stones or rocks in the foreground, which might also *lead* the eye into the image. Anytime an element *leads* the eye *into* the image, it is creating a sense of three dimensions, moving the eye *into* a two dimensional object. My second caveat is closely related. In my attempt to create depth, I don't want something like a large boulder in the foreground to take center stage. It will compete for attention with the center of interest. The viewer's eye will vacillate between the main subject and the boulder.

Containment is achieved when the image is self-contained. It stands alone, without feeling like something is missing or left out.

PERSPECTIVE. There is a tendency to shoot everything we see at eye level, standing up. Whether we are 5'5" or 6'5," if all we do is stand there and put our camera to our eyes, everything will look the same. I have seen photos of children and pets taken from an adult's eye level, looking down at the child or pet. Getting down to their level and getting that eye-to-eye connection is much more powerful and appealing. So, before you click, ask yourself if there is a different, better, perspective that will make your composition stronger.

I have placed my camera right on the floor, or just eighteen inches from the floor, on my tripod, aimed straight up. I have even stood on top of my car to get my shot. Whatever it takes—that is the message here.

Altering my perspective also adds more interest, mystery, intrigue, or drama to my images. Before I put my camera to my eye, before I place my camera on the tripod, I decide from what perspective I will create my image. I will walk around my intended center of interest, crouch, move to my left, move to my right, or maybe even look down at my subject, if feasible, before I put the camera to my eye. This is only one reason why I choose my tripods carefully--I want as many options as possible so I can alter my perspective, and that includes shooting straight down or straight up at my center of interest.

RULE OF THIRDS. This topic and the first principle covered, c*enter of Interest*, serve as good bookends for my discussion on the topic of composition. A few artists refer to the Golden Mean, a related concept, but I will stick to the Rule of Thirds for this book. They are related.

Take a look at the grid on the following page. Notice it is divided into equal thirds, both horizontally and vertically. This is where this principle gets its name.

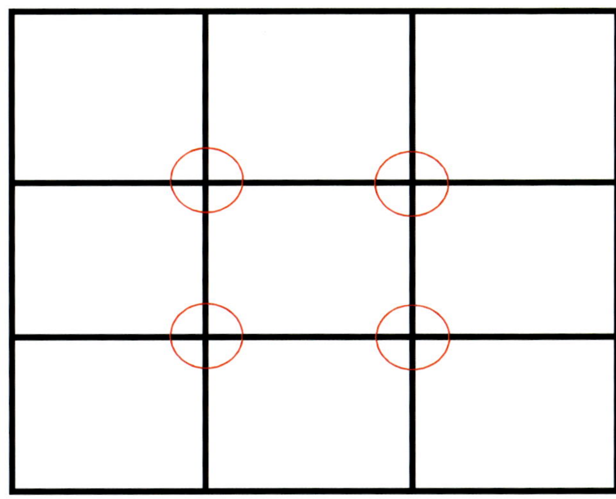

Imagine that this grid is your viewfinder. In fact, some cameras can display a similar grid in the viewfinder. I use mine to fine-tune my compositions and also to make adjustments to keystoning, i.e., to reduce the effect of parallel lines converging inward when I tilt my camera upward. The location of the red circles on the grid is where the Rule of Thirds comes into play. Although the principle has the word *rule* in it, it really isn't a rule; it's not set in stone. It is, however, an effective artistic tool, a rule of thumb that helps us improve our compositions.

I've covered *center of interest* already. As a reminder, I define it as the main interest toward which the eye is drawn. I placed the principle in quotation marks. I'll repeat why I did that. In most cases, I can enhance my compositions--make them more interesting, intriguing, and appealing by *not* placing my main subject in the center. The main subject usually looks better in the image if it is placed somewhere in the vicinity of any of those red circles, as opposed to dead center. The reason for this is that if it is right in dead center, it will look stale, stagnant, and forces the viewer to get stuck there—in the center. By placing the main subject off center, it gives me more room throughout the image to apply the other key composition components---balance, eye flow, leading lines, and containment. The end result is an image that is more appealing.

There are times when placing a subject in dead center works. However, if it does work it is because it meets my criteria of, "What do I want it to look like? What mood, message, impact, feeling, or story do I want to convey?" I integrate all of that by slowly inhaling the scene before me, letting it whisper to me. And I listen carefully.

I have applied these composition principles ever since I picked up my first camera. They were a carry-over from my art days and have worked aesthetically well for me.

Before I show you several examples of how I apply composition to my images, keep in mind that I will not always find all seven components. My goal is to find and incorporate as many as possible. Simplicity is also important, as an overriding goal. I don't have to cover every inch of the image with all these principles. I can include some or most of them without ending up with an image that is too busy, crammed with too many elements that can make the image confusing or chaotic.

I will first share a few images I shared earlier. My reasoning is that those images contain more than one or two composition principles and are therefore worth looking at again, this time from a composition perspective. Let me start with those first.

"One can live in the shadow of an idea without grasping it." Elizabeth Bowen

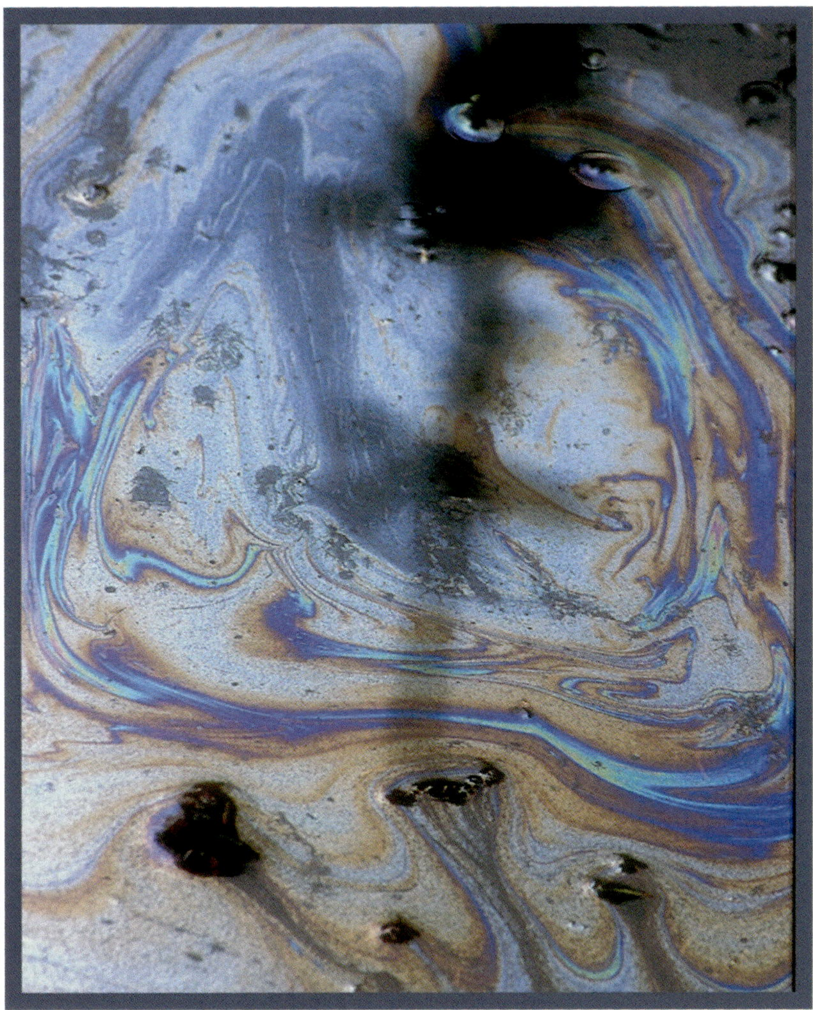

"On The Right Path"

I talked about this image in the I.S.E.E. SOMETHING section. It was just a simple puddle. I integrated several composition principles here. Let me list them.

That dark larger area in the upper right hand corner, which my sister said looks like a fox, is where ***my eye was drawn to*** first because it was so different than the other shapes and colors. I placed it in the ***rule of thirds***. That part of the image also forms a triangle shape that ***leads*** the eye into the image. This image also has a lot of ***eye flow*** throughout. Can you see that?

There is an interesting curved blue line toward the bottom, which one of my students said looks like a blue eel. What I saw was another ***leading line*** that led the eye into the image. I also saw several small rocks, or pebbles, which I included to add ***containment.*** There is no dead space in this image, which keeps it from being off ***balance***.

The ***perspective*** from which I created the puddle image in the previous page was crucial to the final effect. I placed my tripod approximately two feet from the ground, in order to get that interesting view and lighting.

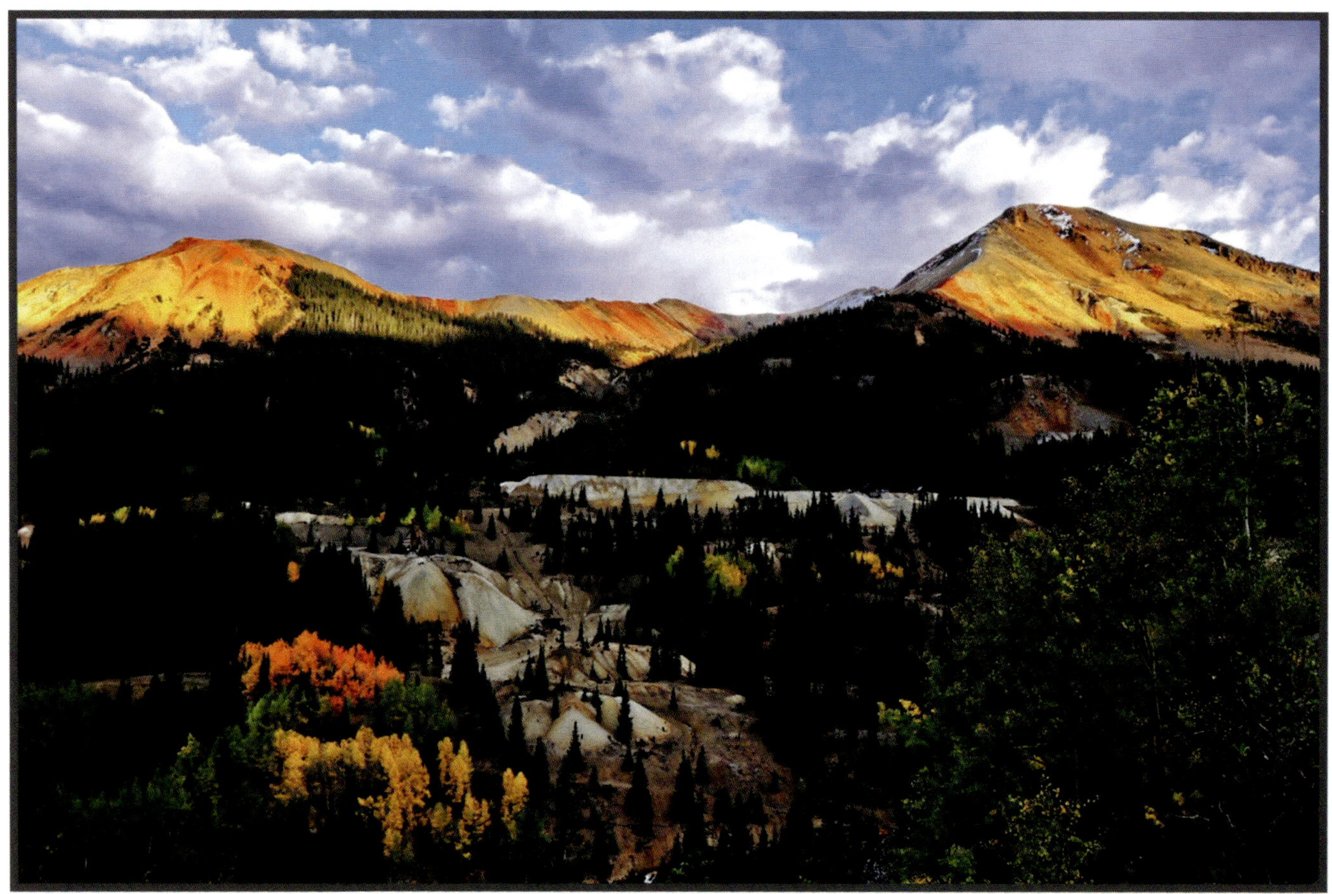

"Red Mountains at Sunset"

There is no question here as to what the ***center of interest*** is—the red mountains. Your eyes can't help but see them first. I placed both peaks near the ***rule of thirds;*** not in dead center. I also placed the horizon line roughly one-third from the top. I use the top third or bottom third "rule" for landscapes, usually. Doing so gives me more space to introduce other complementary principles. In this case, ***balance***—the yellows and oranges of the trees help balance out the red mountains, plus they repeat the colors. The shades of green, neutral tones, and grays, also help ***balance out*** the red mountains. The yellow and orange trees on the lower left, the trees in the lower right, and the clouds help to add ***containment***.

There is also a lot of ***eye flow*** throughout the image—it's not stagnant. When this image is viewed at a larger size, you can also see remnants of an old mining structure and tailings from the historic Colorado mining processes.

The awesome red mountains did not need ***leading lines*** to draw attention to them. However, as luck would have it, there is a swath of tans, browns, and grays that stand out from the rest of the scene, which subliminally lead the eye toward the left peak.

My ***perspective*** was simply serendipitous. These mountains are along the Million Dollar Highway, and although there are several great pull-offs along the road, I still had to decide on the specific spot that would help me pull all the elements together to give me the best composition possible.

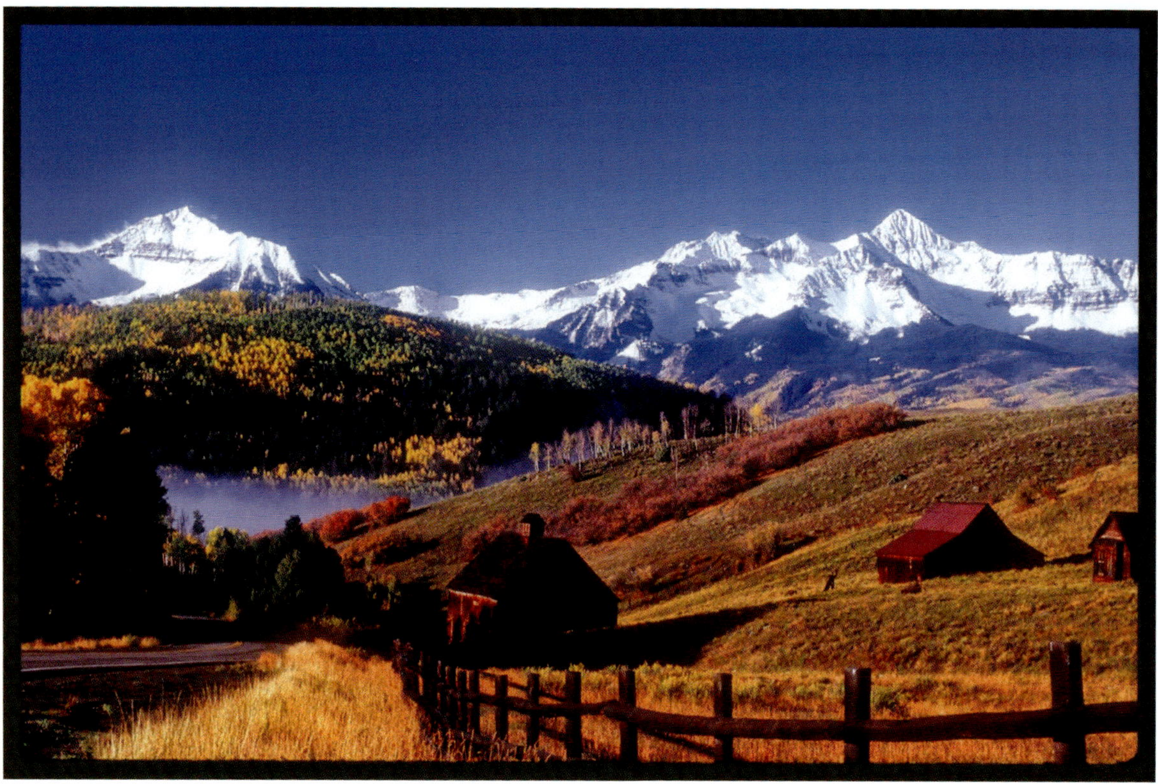

Talk about being at the right place at the right time! This scene is a couple of miles north of Telluride, my favorite place in Colorado. On this particular day, my goal was to photograph Wilson Peak, that huge and awesome 14,000 foot peak on the right. I went up the road toward the airport that morning and photographed it from up there, but, it wasn't until I drove back down that I saw this. There were two other photographers nearby. After I talked to them and asked them if I was in their way, one of them said, "No, you're fine. It don't get much better than this." I agreed.

This was one of those scenes where you pinch yourself to make sure you're not dreaming. All the components of good composition were there—I just had to find the best ***perspective*** that would take advantage of what was already there for me.

As I studied the scene, it quickly came together for me. I saw the fence—***containment*** and ***leading line.*** The road on the lower left also served that role, but not as much. The ranch structures on the right added to **containment** and **eye flow**. I placed the horizon line roughly around the upper third of the image. The peaks are what standout, because of their size, bright snow and placement—they are the primary ***center of interest***. They are ***balanced*** by all the other more subdued elements—smaller mountains, trees, fog in the distance, hillsides, and structures. Those same elements also add ***eye flow*** throughout the image. This composition placed the peaks and some of the structures near the ***rule of thirds.*** They are not in dead center. The ***perspective*** for this shot was very important. After a few seconds of studying the scene, I decided to get down to fence level to add more interest to the image. I was approximately three feet from the ground.

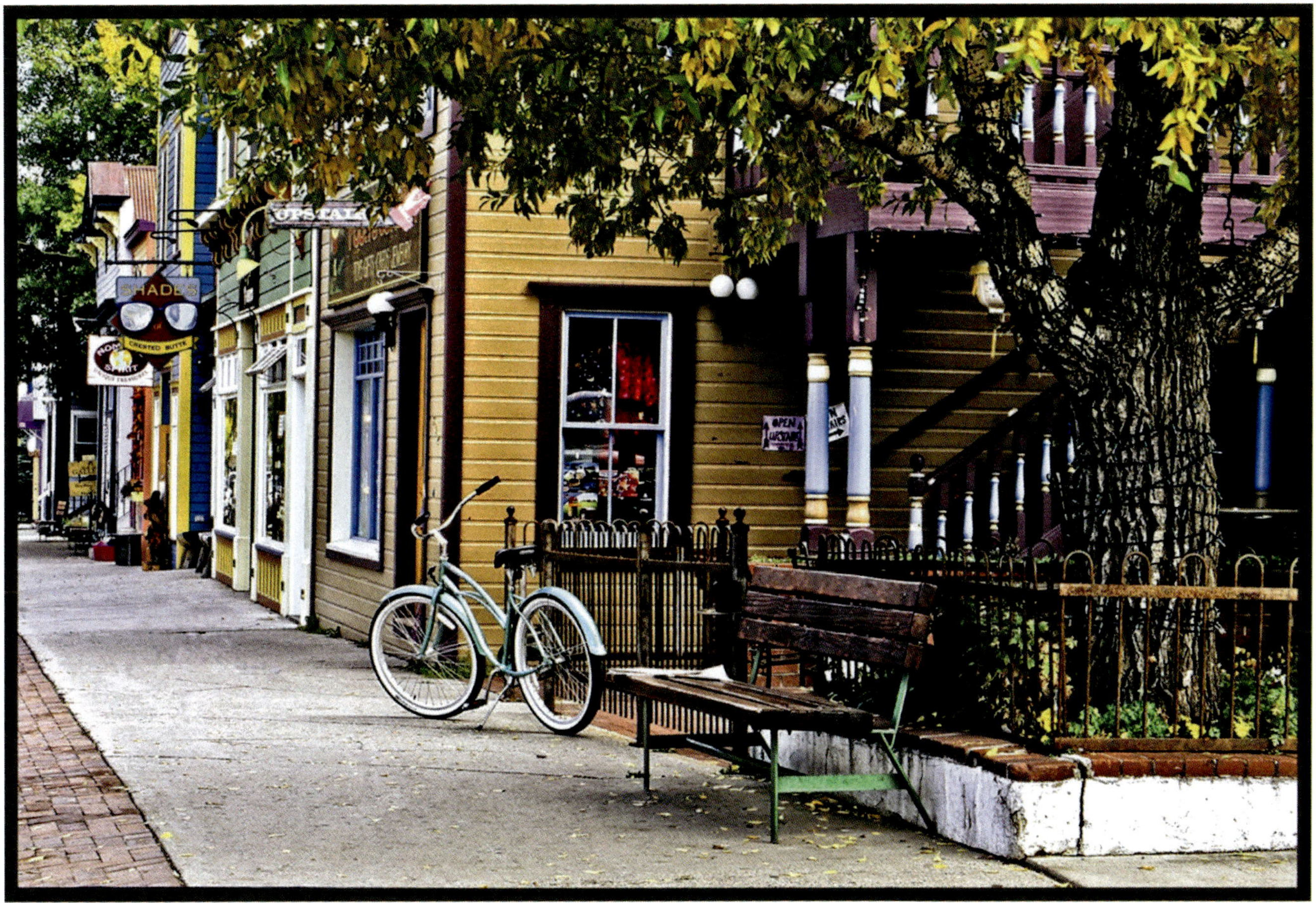

"The Slow Life"

"The Slow Life" is yet another example of where composition principles apply. This is a section of quaint and historic Crested Butte, Colorado, near the south central part of the state. I did not set this up. All I did was to ask permission from one of the shop owners to close the door so I could get my shot. I decided to keep the newspaper on the bench to add interest. The reason for no people? It was an early Saturday morning.

Although the entire scene, a cross section of downtown, is the ***center of interest***, your eye can't help but quickly move toward the unique 1950s style bicycle. Depending on your visual perspective, either the entire scene, or the bicycle, is the center of interest.

There are several ***leading lines*** in this scene—lines that lead to certain parts of the image. The bench leads the eye to the bicycle, which in turns leads the eye along the street. The sidewalk itself serves as a leading line. The stairs on the right lead the eye inward. The tree and its branches serve a dual purpose: ***containment*** and ***leading line***. There is a good sense of ***balance*** throughout—no heavy areas or dead space. There is definitely a lot of ***eye flow*** here—the bench, bike, stairs, the tree, windows, flowers, and signs.

It is important to stress that the position of the photographer, in relationship to the scene, is extremely critical when looking for the right composition. It doesn't just happen. I shot this scene from just below eye level, standing across the street. I have been to Crested Butte many times, but this was the only time everything just came together for me—the autumn colors, the bicycle, the newspaper, and no people. I cannot reproduce this scene again. Impermanence.

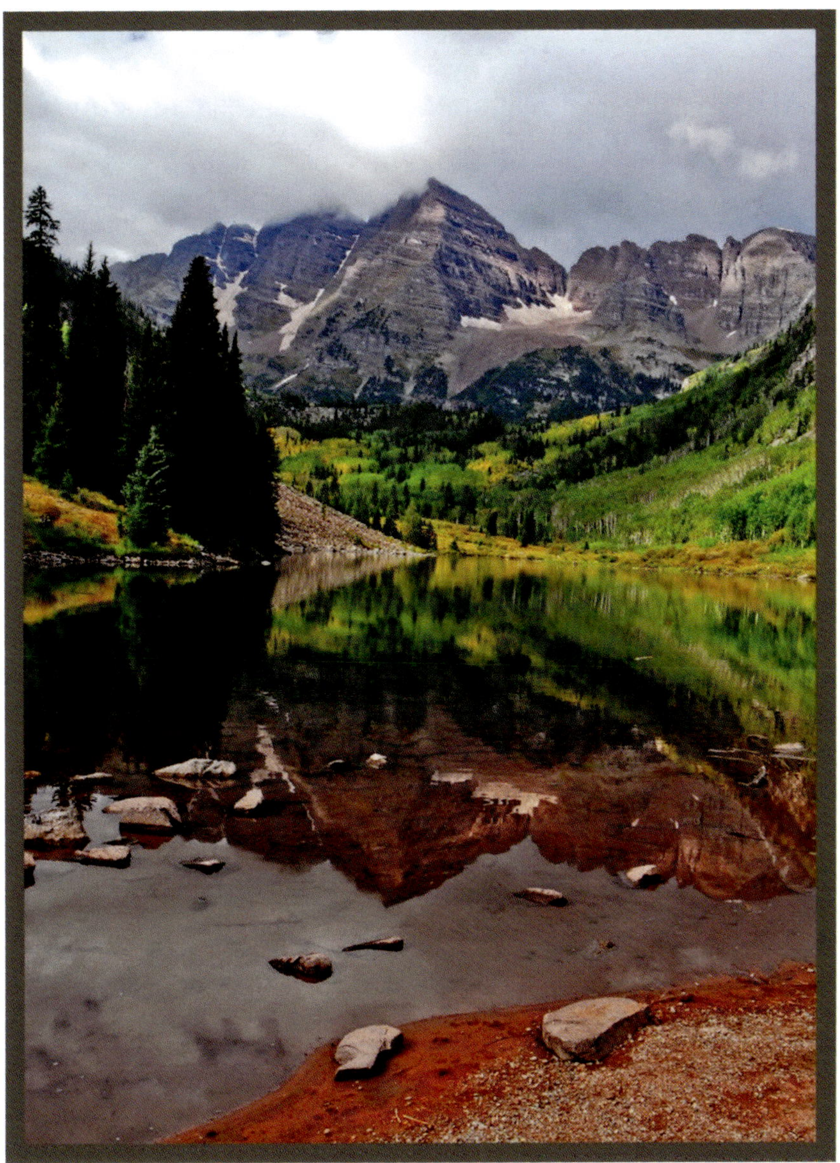

"Maroon Bells Morning"

It is said that this is the most photographed scene in the state. Maroon Bells, near Aspen. The two peaks, the Maroon Bells, are over 14,000 feet in elevation. I waited about forty-five minutes for the lighting to be just right. I created other images during that wait.

This is a cropped rendition of the original image. The original had some dead space toward the bottom. This cropped version helps to enhance the ***containment*** served by the rocks at the bottom of the image.

The reflections add to the ***balance*** in the image. The rocks, reflection, and trees create ***eye flow*** throughout. In the landscape itself, there are two triangular shapes on each side of the image that serve as ***leading lines***. This composition is effective, even though I did not follow the ***rule of thirds***. To have done so would have minimized the "wow" factor these peaks evoke.

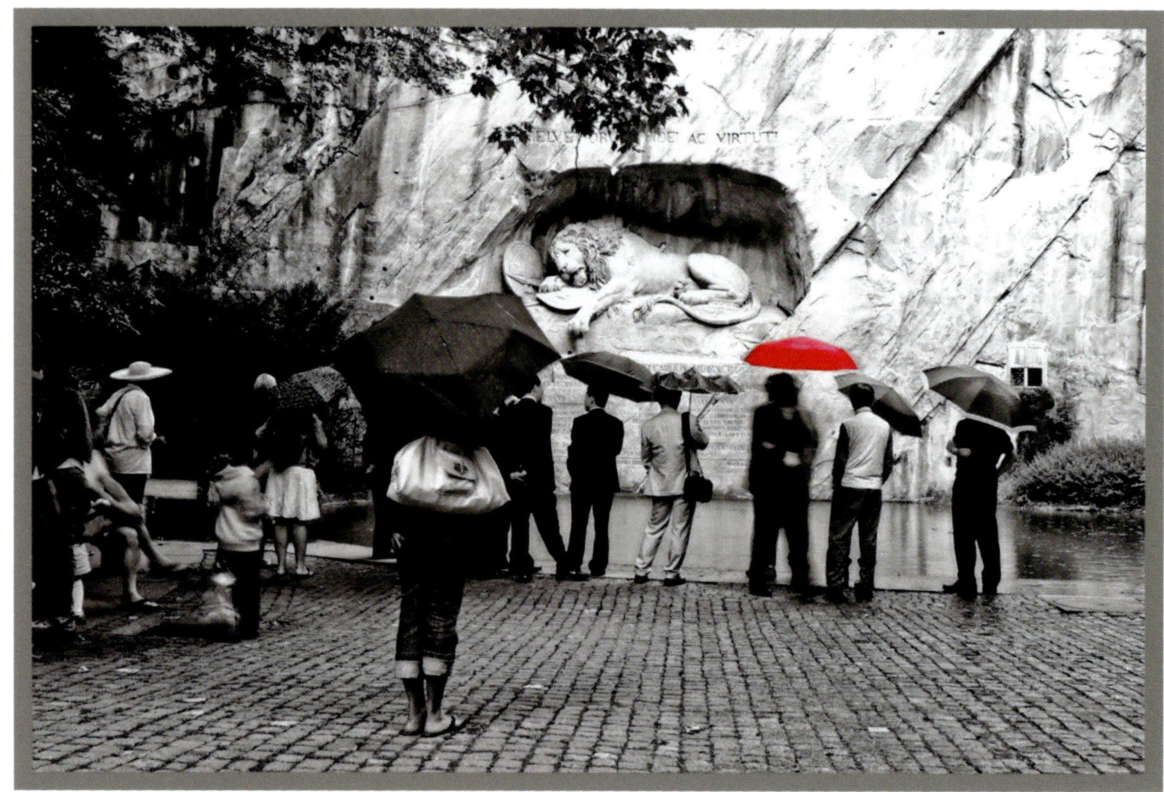

"Lion Monument"

This image was created in Luzern, Switzerland. This is different from all other images presented in this book. The original is in color. There wasn't much color in this scene on that damp and cloudy day. Everything was in mostly grays, dark blues, and greens—except for one red umbrella. Through the use of photo editing software, I converted the original to a black and white image, except for the red umbrella.

Let me mention ***perspective*** first. I wanted to look up toward the monument, the ***center of interest***, so I placed my tripod roughly two feet from the ground. The low perspective allowed me to use the cobblestones as ***leading*** lines. Your eyes can't help but flow inward. The lion itself is near the middle, but not in dead center.

There is a lot of ***eye flow*** in this image—people, stones, umbrellas, the pond, and, of course, the lion carved out of the mountain. When I converted the image as you see it, I was okay with the red umbrella possibly ***competing*** with the lion. What helped to counterbalance the red umbrella was the strong presence of that young lady with the giant purse, and her umbrella ***leading*** the eye toward the lion. Also, notice that there are several elements that seem to ***lead the eye*** toward the lion monument—stones, umbrellas, the man's hat on the left, and the sharply carved line on the mountain.

If the artist's sharp diagonal lines in the upper right corner were not there, I might have ended up with some uncomfortable ***dead space*** in that part of the image. Instead, they serve as **containment** and **leading lines**.

As I indicated before, finding composition components is not perfect. We will not always find everything we're looking for, nor will we find them exactly where we would like them to be. The only thing we can do is to find as many as we can, and do the best we can with what we've got. We will, however, end up with improved compositions when we look for and incorporate as many as possible. This scene is a good example. There is a bit of ***dead space*** toward the bottom right side. The cobble stones help offset that by leading the eye back into the image.

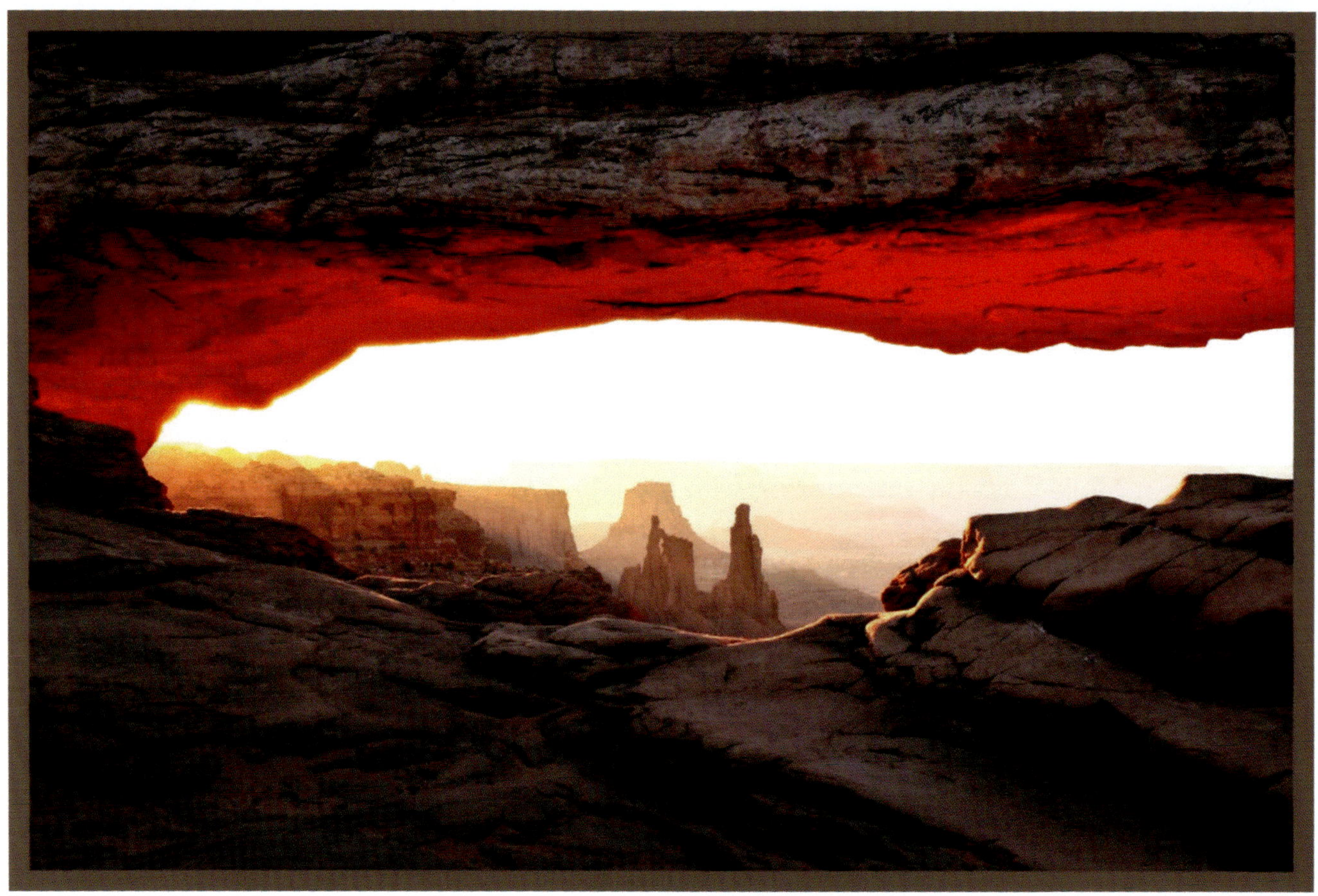

"Mesa Arch"

By the time I arrived at this arch in Canyonlands, Utah, at 6:00 a.m., there were nine other photographers already there. Luckily, the spot I had scoped out the day before was still available. I just squeezed in between two polite photographers.

I went there the day before. I did that so I could make several decisions before show time the morning after. I had decided the day before that I would shoot the scene at f/32, where my focusing point was going to be--between the arch and the next layer of cliffs, that I would use manual focusing, and I was going to use a warming filter to enhance the vibrant colors. Oh, and I also determined my composition the day before.

This image, like "Maroon Bells Morning," is still effective without following the ***rule of thirds***. For me, ***the center of interest*** was the arch itself. The formations in the distance serve as "supporting actors" and add to the ***eye flow***. One of the formations in the distance is named

“The Washer Woman.” When I was there, with at least nine other photographers, everyone looked so serious. I thought I’d loosen things up a bit by looking up from my camera and commenting, “If I were that formation, I would be insulted knowing that someone had named me Washer Woman.” No one seemed amused.

My ***perspective*** for this image was almost at eye level. I wanted to see over the bottom part of the foreground to expose the distant formations. As for ***balance***, notice the red glow of the arch. The early morning sun is reflecting light up to it from nearby walls. Although it covers no more than approximately one-fifth of the entire image, the vibrant ***red*** color balances out the rest of the scene. There are other colors and elements in the image, but we can’t help but see the arch first. And, even though the foreground is larger than the actual arch, it doesn’t feel heavy, again, because its size cannot compete with the bright redness of the arch.

The scene did not have nicely tucked away elements for me to add as ***containment.*** At the same time, there weren’t any large areas of ***dead space*** to which the eye could escape.

I just have to include the following image as a lesson on how to scan for images. The day before I created the Mesa Arch image, my intuition told me to scan the entire area around the arch. I noticed that about twenty yards to the right of the famous arch, there was a great view of the canyon below. There were no natural arches down there, and the view did not look all that impressive, but I went beyond what my eyes could see. I saw something. After I scanned the scene, the message I was getting from my imagination was that the canyon would look different with early morning lighting. I knew that I had to get that shot too the next morning. I would have to work fast, so I could get both the arch and the canyon during the same early morning light.

Approximately three minutes after I started photographing Mesa Arch, I could tell by looking at my screen that I had what I wanted. I was the first photographer to move away from the arch. I quickly walked to my right to check out the canyon below. I wasn’t disappointed—it looked awesome alright.

Only one photographer noticed me. She picked up her tripod and walked slowly toward me. She didn't walk very far before shouting out to me, "Is there any color over there?" I said, "No, that's why I like it." She turned around and walked back. She, and the others, missed out on these opportunities.

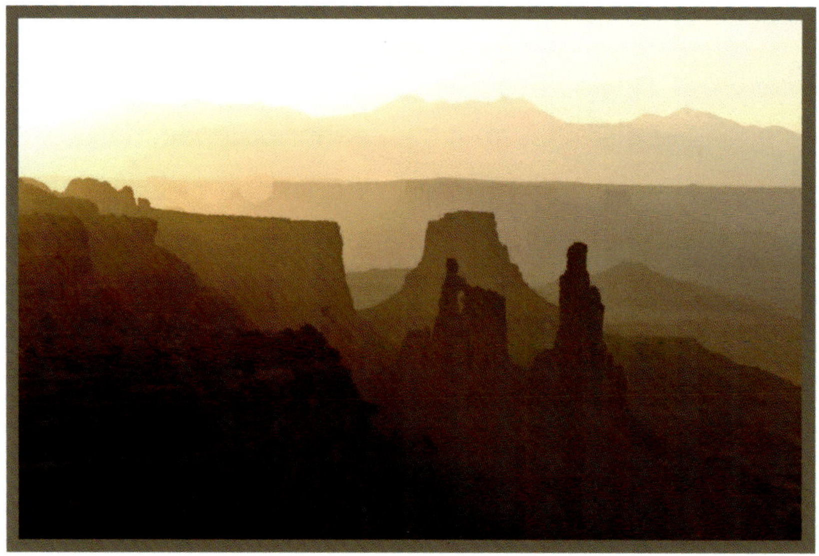

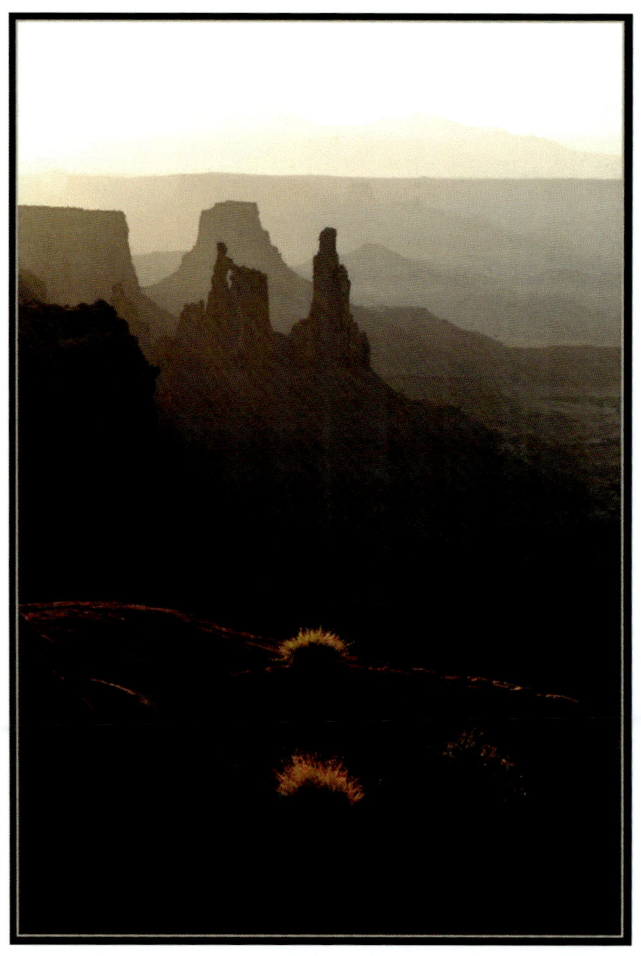

In addition to reds, yellow also draws attention in art. It can take up a small percentage of space in an image, yet ***balance*** out larger areas of darker colors. Here is an example of how powerful the color yellow can be.

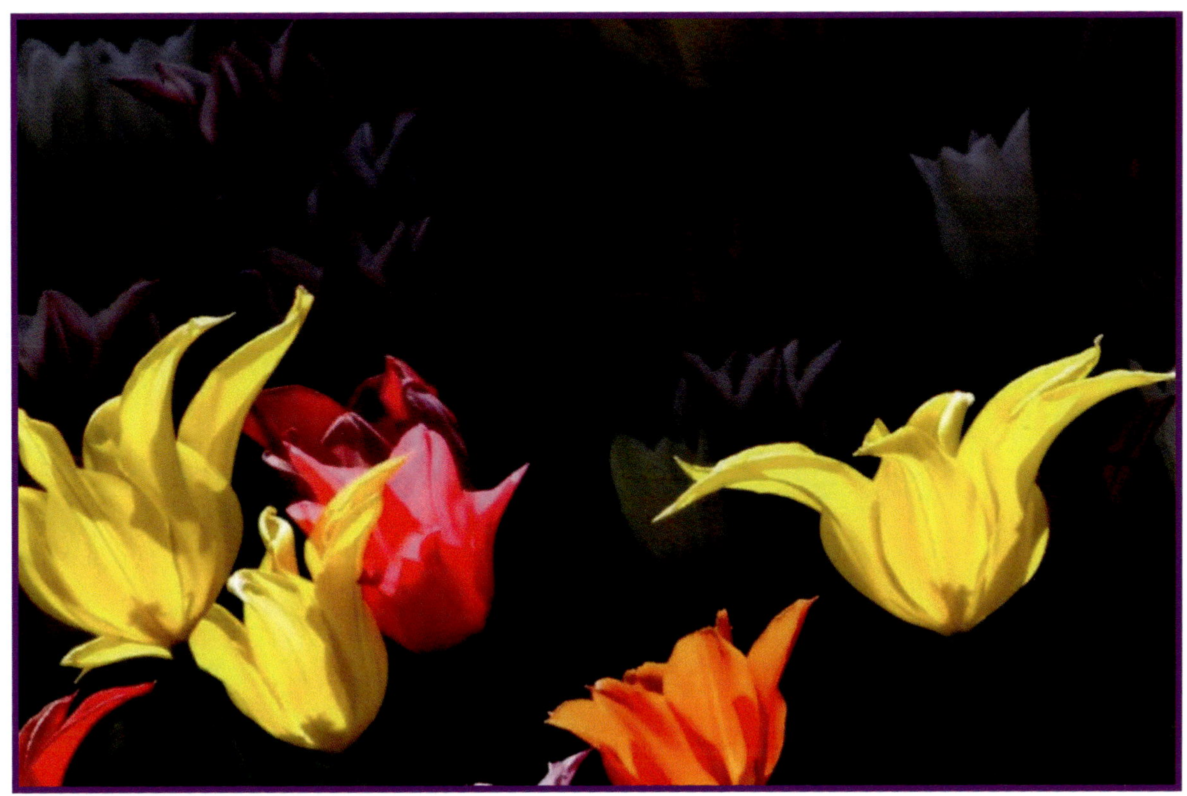

"Out of the Shadows"

As you can see, it doesn't take the eyes much time to land on the yellows before they start ***flowing*** throughout the rest of this image. Although the flowers actually occupy a small percentage of the frame, in comparison to all other elements combined, they hold their own in terms of balance and attention.

Notice also that I placed the yellow flowers in the ***rule of thirds***, which also serve as ***containment***. They also ***lead*** you into the rest of the image because they face or point toward the inside.

This image was created with spot metering. I took my spot reading from the yellow flowers, then bracketed around that spot metering exposure.

I shared several examples of what constitutes good composition. As you saw, incorporating the principles of good composition works for me in many situations and scenarios. However, we don't have to include all, or even most, of the principles to create a good image. Here is one image where the center of interest is almost in dead center—but it commands center stage.

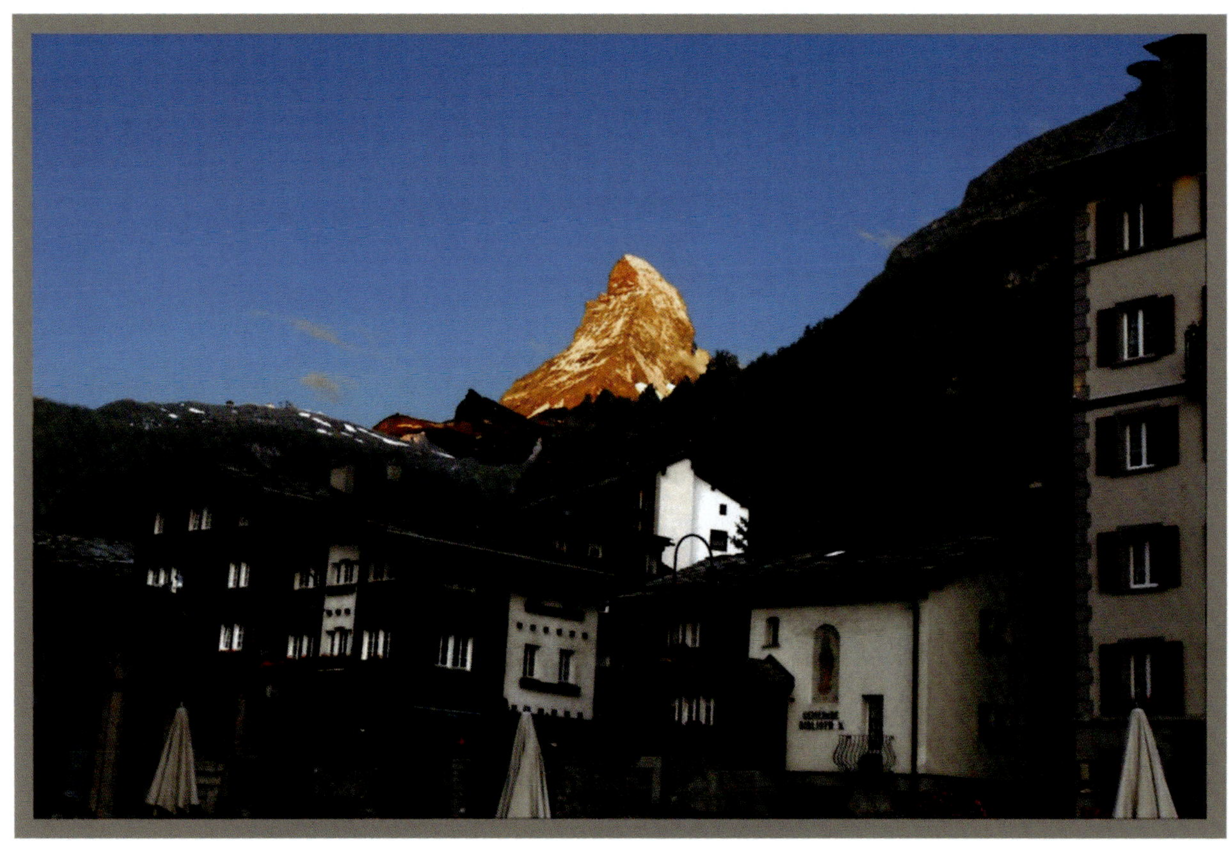

"The Matterhorn"

Before I went to Switzerland, I did my research. I saw a lot of images of the Matterhorn, but none with alpenglow colors. I figured that if it works in Colorado, it should work there too. I paid the price in order to get that alpenglow—sleep, for one, but it was worth the sacrifice.

As you can see, the Matterhorn is almost in dead center, but it still works well for this scene. It is, after all, the ***center of interest***. The only other composition principles at play here are ***eye flow***, ***perspective***, and ***balance***—can you see them?

I will now show you a couple of composition examples, of the same scene, where one is less effective than the other. This is a very typical photo-taking scenario.

I went to Zapata Falls in Colorado, near Great Sand Dunes National Park. You can see the falls only during winter, when you can actually walk up to them over a frozen creek. The next examples are from late September. There was a hint of early autumn in the air.

Okay, here is what we typically do. We come up to this secluded scene and the first thing that grabs our attention, from several yards away, is the peacefully rushing sounds of the creek in the distance. When we arrive, that emotional "wow" factor hits us. The soothing sounds of the creek echo from the surrounding canyon walls. We just want to sit there in a timeless vacuum and enjoy the sense of peace that surrounds us. Then we decide to "take a picture." Emotion takes over. We are so overwhelmed by the moment, from the soothing sounds of the creek. We pick up our camera and take a common horizontal photo of the creek. Click.

Take a look at the images on the next two pages. Look at what happens when we just go "click" without thinking about it, then compare that image to what we can get if we just take a deep breath, slow down, and detach our emotions from our eyes.

Click.

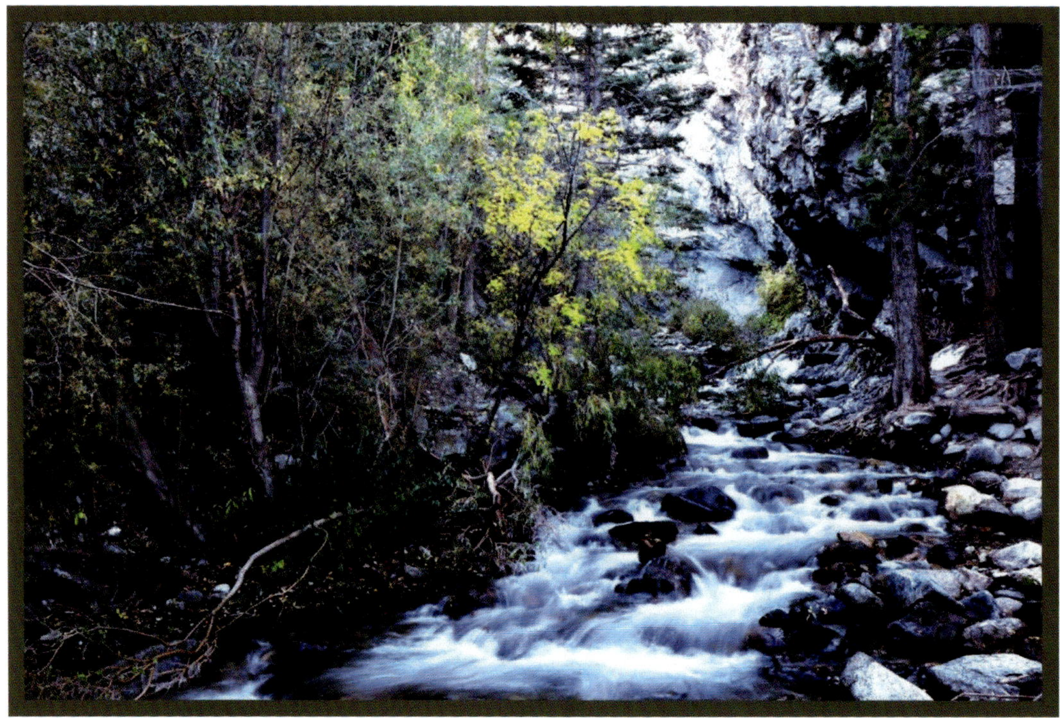

The resulting picture has no emotion. If you look carefully, there are at least a couple of composition weaknesses in this photo. There is a tree, in dead center, to which our eyes are drawn because of its bright early autumn yellows. Also notice that the left half of the picture is very unappealing. It is filled with a bunch of bland-looking trees that add nothing of value to the photo. In fact, they distract from the image by adding weight to that side of the photo. If we cut this photo just to the left of the yellow tree in the middle, we will lose nothing of significance. Oh, and by the way, there is also a creek in the photo, the subject that first drew our attention to the scene.

Now, let's redo this one again. The idea is to capitalize on the most interesting elements and compositional components in the scene. Additionally, although we see the scene horizontally with our eyes, who says it needs to be horizontal?

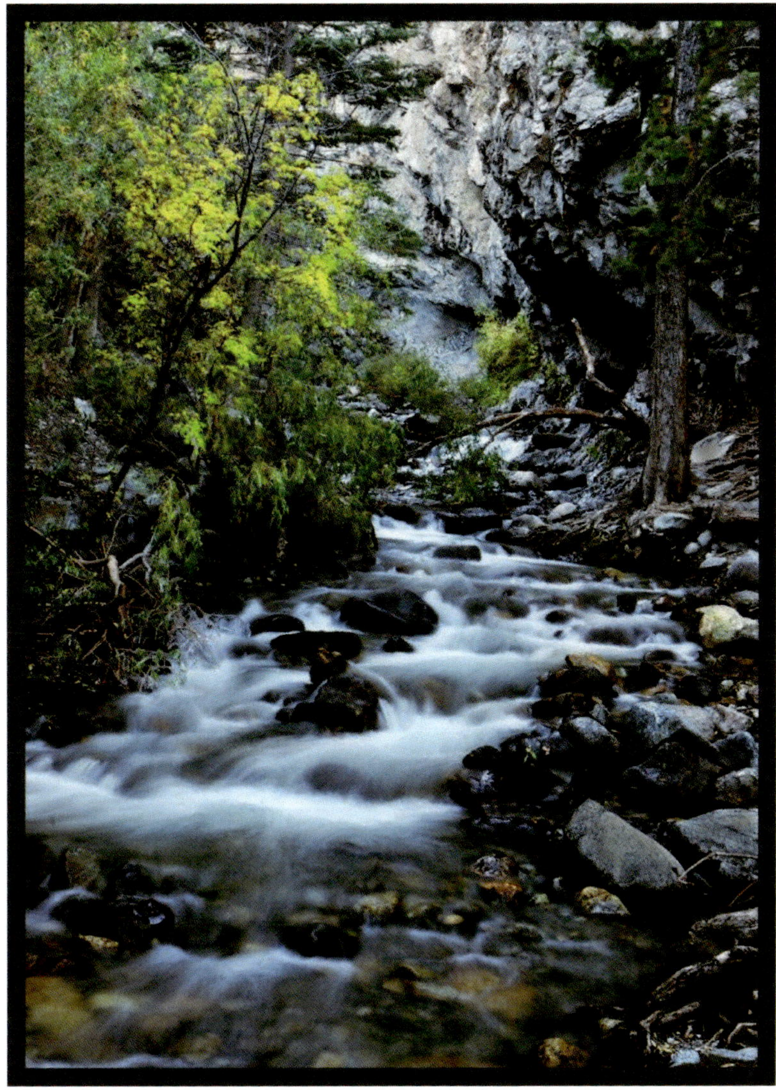

I wanted to create the sense of peace and tranquility I got from this isolated place. As for elements, I saw, of course, the creek, but I wanted to complement it with other "supporting characters," i.e., other elements that complemented the creek. The rock wall in the back adds mystery. The yellowing tree is leaning inward, ***leading*** the eye into the image, and ***balances*** the creek. The tree in the upper right creates ***eye flow*** and also serves as ***containment***. There is also a smaller tree in the upper right hand corner that is leaning inward, ***leading*** the eye toward the creek. The rocks toward the bottom, as subtle as they are, also serve as ***containment***. My ***perspective*** was at eye level, to pick up all the breaks in the creek as it flowed over the rocks. I wanted the creek to lead its flow toward me, and for it to take up more space in the image, for more interest and attention. The entire scene is the real subject. However, because the creek occupies a significant amount of the image, and because of its color contrast against its surroundings, we can't help but be drawn to it. A 1/2 second shutter speed blurred the water, adding to the sense of peacefulness. A shutter speed of, say, 1/800, would have distracted from the sense of tranquility I felt at the time. The creek would have looked too dramatic. I cropped the image slightly from the top, to eliminate unnecessary, non-contributing parts of the scene. I also chose to use a warming filter for the vertical rendition to warm up the colors.

You might ask, "Do you see all that at the time you're there?" You bet. I look for it.

Now, you might be saying, "Well, composition principles are fine for most scenes, but what about tight close-ups? Can I incorporate these same principles to those images?" The answer is, "Yes." Even when I am creating my tight close-ups, I am still cognizant of how to arrange the elements in the scene, and still try to find as many principles as I can. The elements in such images are different, but they still play the same key roles in creating the best compositions possible.

I was with a student during one of my 1-on-1 photo field lessons. We walked along a path as I was sharing some key points to remember. I suddenly interrupted myself when I saw a grouping of colorful leaves to my left—plants that were in transition between summer and autumn.

Before I tell you what I told her during her field lesson, let me first show you the image on the next page. Please note that the same composition principles apply to much smaller subjects and scenarios.

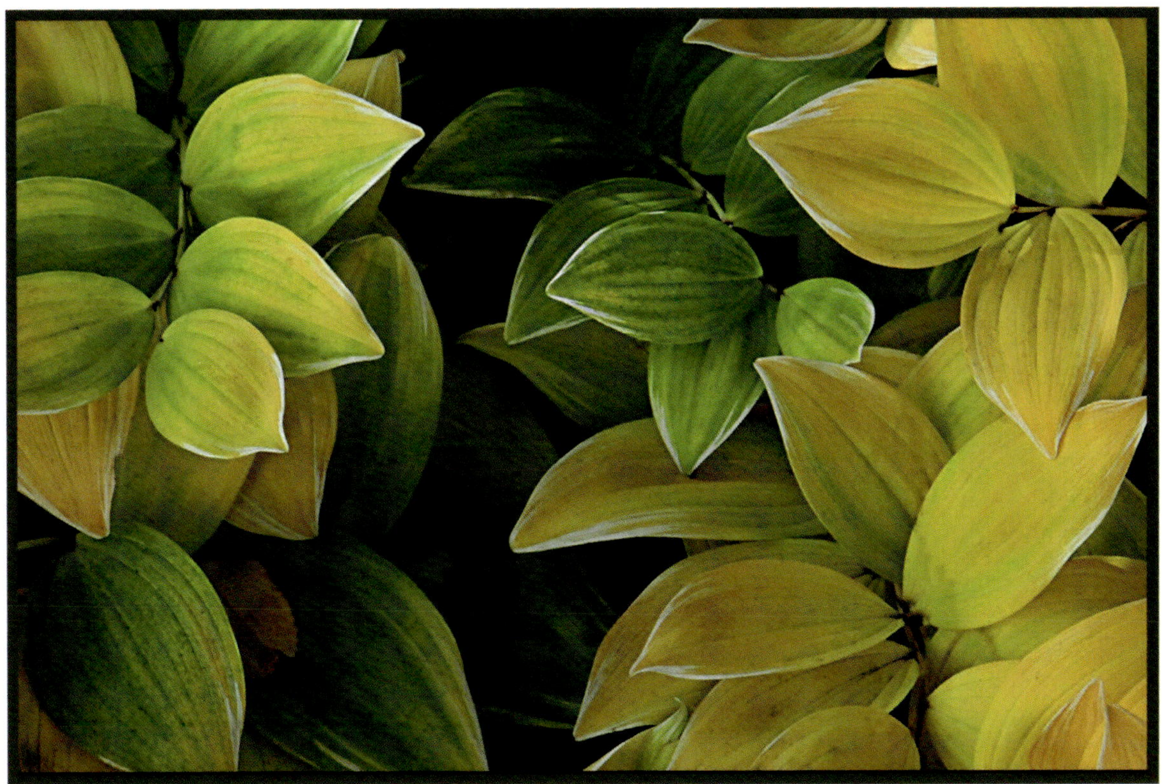

As we walked along the path, we saw several large plants in the area with striking yellowing leaves. I stopped walking, stopped talking, and redirected our attention to the leaves. Almost simultaneously, Kendra said, "I was looking at those…." Then I walked her through the CDE formula. I will focus here primarily on the C part of our instructional discussion.

As I directed Kendra's attention to the leaves in front of us, I said, "Okay, before you set up, before you even get your camera, look at this carefully. There are a lot of leaves here, so the idea is to find the ones that give us the best composition. I am looking at these right over here (I pointed to the grouping of leaves in this image). I can already imagine what will be in my viewfinder. These three leaves (I pointed to the three on the upper left) will be in the upper left corner of my viewfinder, pointing inward. I also see those two leaves (I pointed to the two yellow leaves on the upper right) pointing toward the inside of the viewfinder. I also like the dark background—it will make the leaves pop." Do you see the eye flow in this image?

Later, during that 3-hour field lesson, Kendra admitted that of the three (CDE), she had more trouble with composition, adding that I saw things she didn't. We kept working on that during the field lesson.

As a final thought on composition, I include these last two images. They illustrate how timing alone can affect the feel of a composition, even when two compositions are virtually the same. The smallest of changes can make a big difference in photography. This applies, not just to composition, but to everything we do with each image.

I was with another student during a one-day photo lesson in Idaho Springs, Colorado. We photographed an interesting water wheel in the morning, as I coached her, and then went back again later that afternoon. The morning shot was around 8:30. The afternoon shot was around 4:00. I used a warming filter both times.

These examples also serve to remind us of another important lesson. Sometimes we see a subject worth photographing, but maybe the timing is not quite right for it.

This is the morning image.

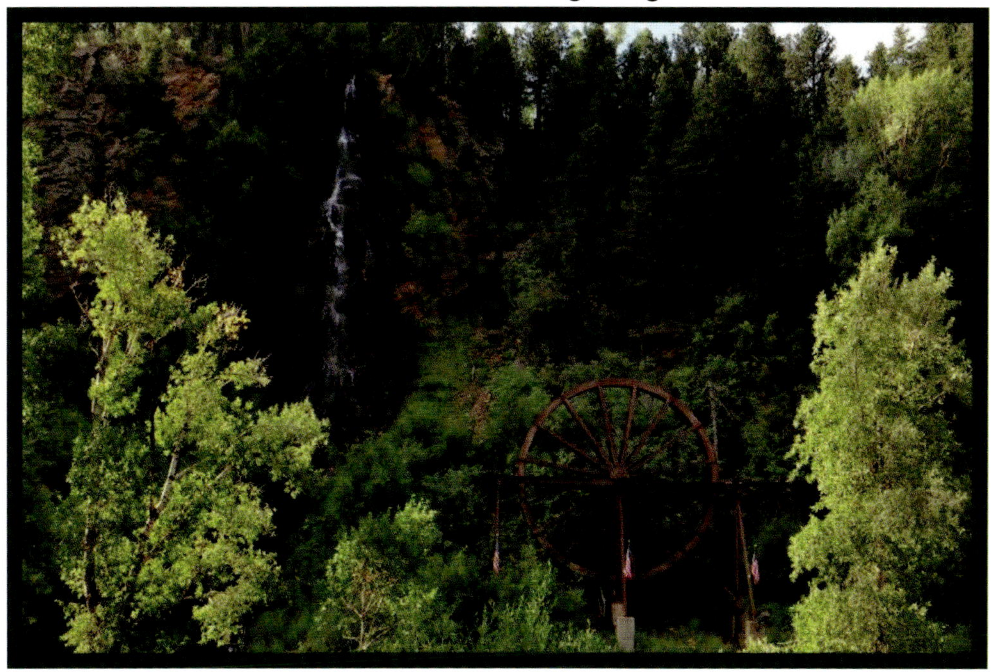

This is the afternoon image. Big difference, right?

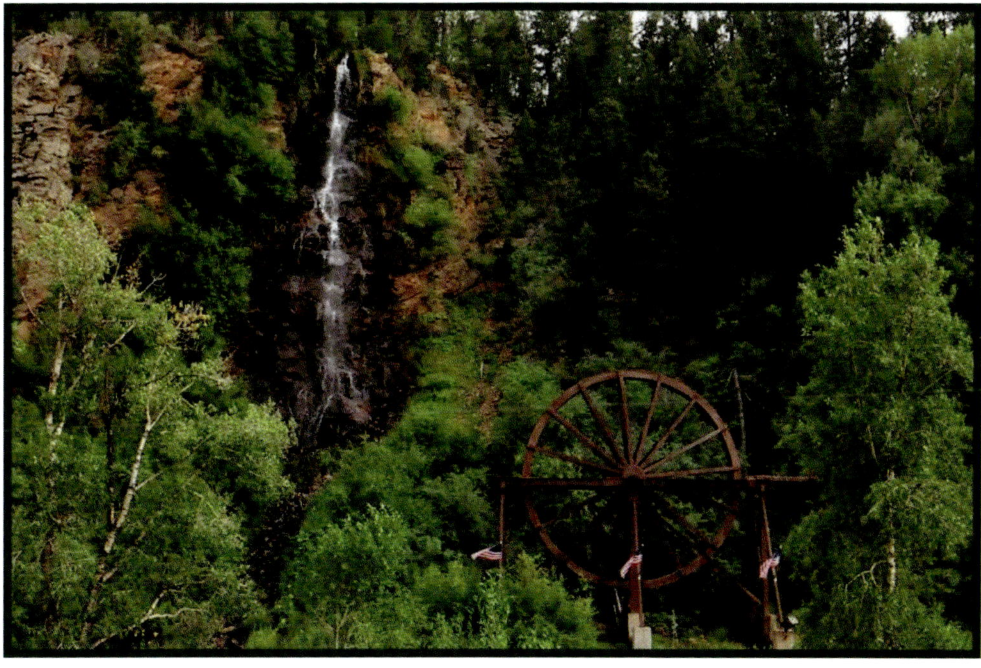

I placed both the waterwheel and the waterfall roughly within the ***rule of thirds***. Notice that both got lost in the early morning image. Additionally, the sun was striking the two trees in the foreground, bringing more attention to them than the water wheel or waterfall. The afternoon lighting, on the other hand, lit the entire scene more evenly, leading the eye more easily to the primary and secondary subjects. Notice the two aspen trees in the lower left. They serve as ***containment*** and ***lead*** the eye toward the waterfall--no accident or coincidence.

COMPOSITION--IN CONCLUSION

I have provided you with a lot of discussion on the subject and have also shared several instructional examples. I hope you now have a better understanding of how important and critical composition is to photography. It is part of right brain thinking in that it is an important artistic piece that goes into the creation of an image. It is an extremely vital part of the triad CDE formula—Composition, Depth of Field, and Exposure. I repeat: all else being equal, if you get all three right, you'll get a good shot.

After more than twenty years in the field of photography, composition and its fundamental principles have become second nature to me. It's more at an intuitive level than on a highly conscious level. I don't have to take a lot of time analyzing a scene to find all the components I need to get a good composition. I can take a quick glance at the scene, determine my ***center of interest***, and then quickly see ***rule of thirds***, ***leading lines***, ***eye flow***, ***balance***, ***perspective***, and ***containment***. I do it so quickly that I sometimes surprise myself when I see my images on the computer.

Throughout this discussion on composition, the tips and suggestions I have made were in reference to the creative aesthetics side of photography. Sometimes, the opposite of some of these principles, like dead space, can be a plus in the context of commercial use.

Are you ready for your composition assignment?

CHALLENGE ASSIGNMENT Test Yourself

Go back and review all the images presented in this book, except those which I already helped you with in this section on composition. Spend time with each one and see how many composition principles, components, you can find. As you do that, remember that they weren't accidents-- they were placed there intentionally to improve my compositions. Don't feel that you have to find all of them in each image--simply see how many there are, and why they work to enhance the composition. If you see some images that only have a few of the composition principles, ask yourself why that composition is still effective. It is possible to have just one or two of the principles and still have a good image. If it works, it is probably because, absent other composition principles, the image is not stale or stagnant-it is still dynamic and powerful.

As you go through this assignment, ask yourself whether you would have spotted those composition components if you had not read this section.

Make yourself a grid like this as you study each image, and fill in the blanks.

COMPOSITION PRINCIPLE	**Is it present in this image? Why does it work?** (review the section on composition if not sure)
Center of Interest	
Eye Flow	
Balance	
Leading Lines	
Containment	
Perspective	
Rule of Thirds	

You can also make a copy of this grid as a guide when you're out in the field. It takes some practice and time before it all begins to come together. Please don't kick yourself in the butt as you do this. Give yourself time. Most importantly, be patient with yourself.

SECTION VII

BEHIND THE CAMERA

Like in *The Wizard of Oz*, I am going to take you behind the curtain. I am not a wizard, but you will get to see what I do behind the mysterious curtain.

It was toward the end of one of my Right Brain Photography classes when a student said, "I bet you can create something out of nothing." I laughed and responded with, "No. I'm not a magician, but I can usually find something." I share this story to point out that I usually find something by seeing with my imagination. My tools are useless without my imagination. Everything I will share in this section has to do with the role my imagination plays in my photography. Software cannot create what I fail to see.

Let me start with my equipment. I don't like to talk about brand names or models. They are simply tools. Give me any camera brand, any model, and I can create a good image. That said, there are certain features I look for in my equipment.

Cameras. There are certain features I need quickly at my disposal, without losing time searching for them in my menu. Speed is critical in photography, for several reasons. It is not only when the light is changing quickly or when birds are flying that I need to work fast. I like to have the following key features quickly accessible on my camera body.

> **ISO**—I need quick access. I use a higher ISO when I need a lot of depth of field, but also need a fast shutter speed. I use a lower ISO, like 100, when I want to blur rushing waters.

> **White Balance**—seldom used, but there when I need it. It is usually set for daylight, but I adjust as needed. Examples include some street scenes and indoor lighting.

> **Image file formats**--JPEG, TIFF, RAW. I primarily use JPEG, largest file possible, with minimal compression, and convert them to TIFF files before fine tuning.

> **Exposure modes**--aperture priority, shutter priority, manual. I use aperture priority probably 95% of the time, even when shooting subjects in motion.

> **F/stop and shutter speed contols**—I don't need shutter priority.

> **Exposure compensation dial**---the life saver button. See page 92.

> **Metering modes**-evaluative/matrix, center, spot. I use mostly matrix.

> **Self-timer**-for when I want to include myself in the image or I've lost my cable release.

> **Continuous shooting mode**-handy when I want to get several shots off per second.

> **Mirror Up**—I use it when I'm getting 1/60th or slower shutter speeds, to maximize sharpness in my images. Camera vibration is minimized, even when on a tripod. Note of caution: turn your vibration reduction (VR) off when camera is on a tripod.

Lenses. I have alluded to this in my discussion about my photo image creation process. The choices we make should be intentional, unless we like to swing at every marketing curve ball thrown at us. Our choices are based, or should be based, on the type of photography we do. In my case, my focal lengths of choice are from 17mm to 300mm. Today, I have that range in three lenses: a 17mm-50mm, a 24-70mm, and a 70mm-300mm lens. A range from 17mm-24mm meets all of my wide angle needs. A range of 200mm-300mm meets all of my telephoto needs. Although it's hard to say at what focal length I shoot most often, I would say that approximately 75% of my images are shot at focal lengths between 24mm and 200mm.

Filters. I have mentioned polarizers, FLD, and warming filters. On the next page is an example where I doubled up on filters. The scene, and the light I had to work with, was a good scenario for me to combine two filters. I used an FLD filter on the lens, and a warming filter (81B) attached to the FLD filter to give me the unique hues to the overal scene.

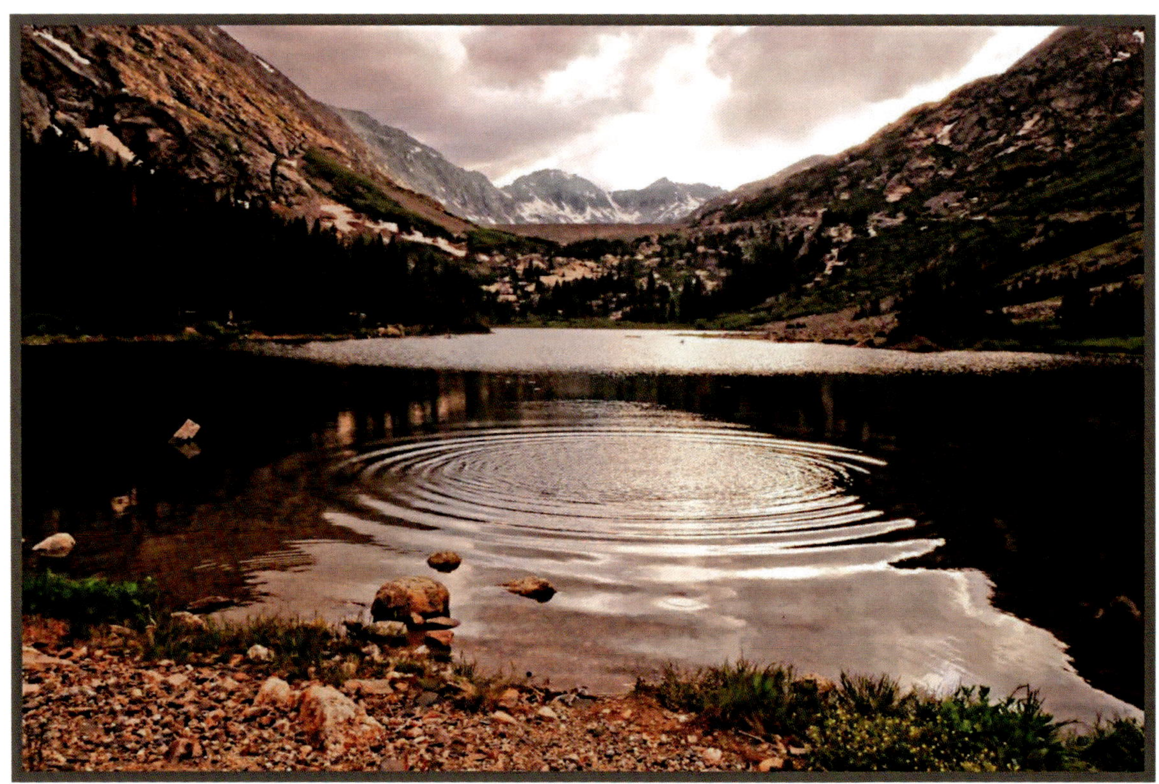

FLD+81B filters combined

Diffuser. I have a 32" diffuser for which I have found several uses. It is not a reflector, but a transluscent white diffuser. I use the diffuser primarily for two purposes: to mimimize or eliminate flare, and also as a backdrop to give me that in-studio look to my images. The next image demonstrates what an improvised "studio" image looks like when shot in the field with a diffuser as a backdrop.

Image created with diffuser as backdrop.

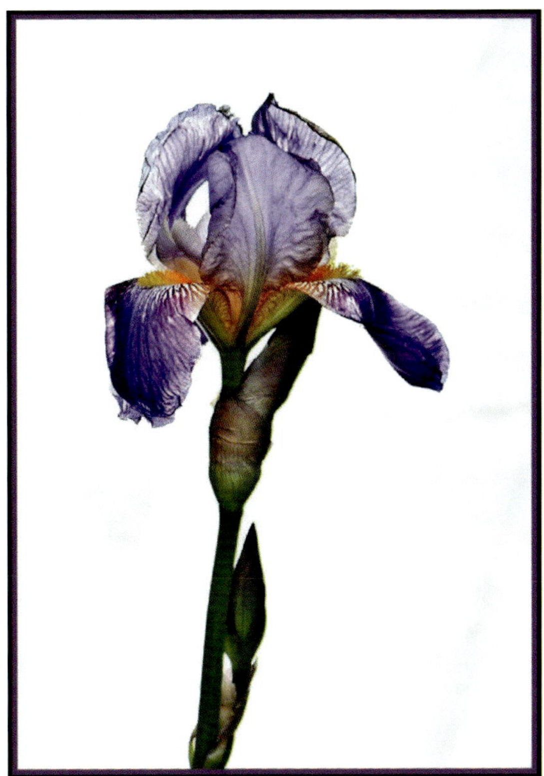

This is how that same, identical image looked like that day. Without the diffuser, the iris had less impact, even with a blurred background. It blended in too much with the background.

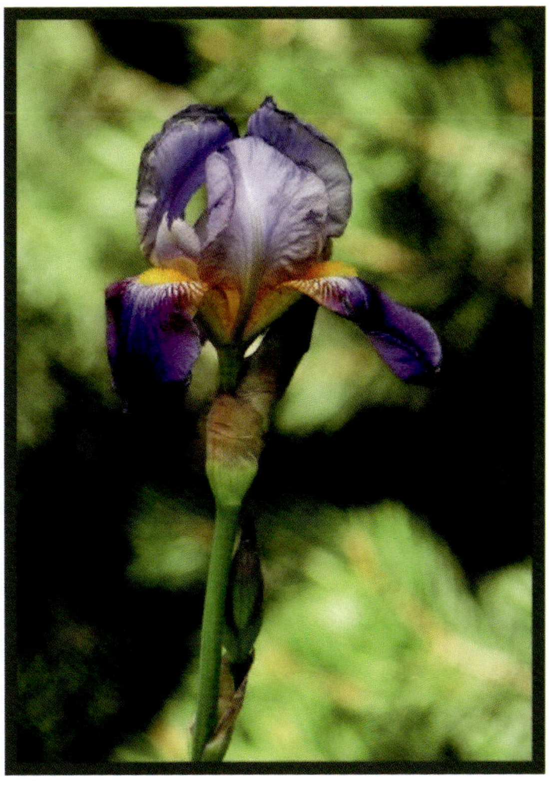

Here are a couple of side-by-side examples that show how I use my diffuser to eliminate flare. The trick is to hold the diffuser, even though it's large, between the light source, in this case the sun, and the lens.

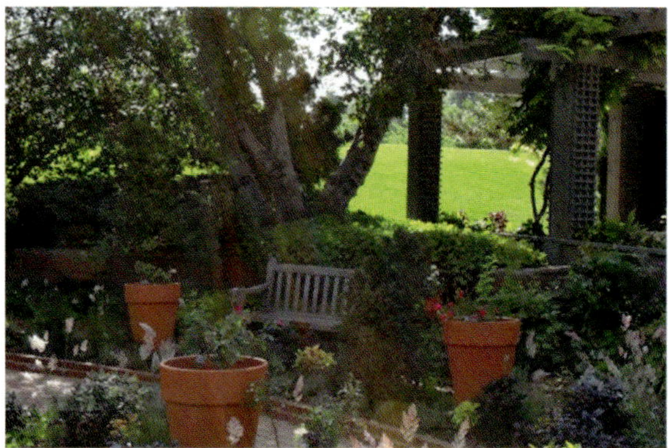

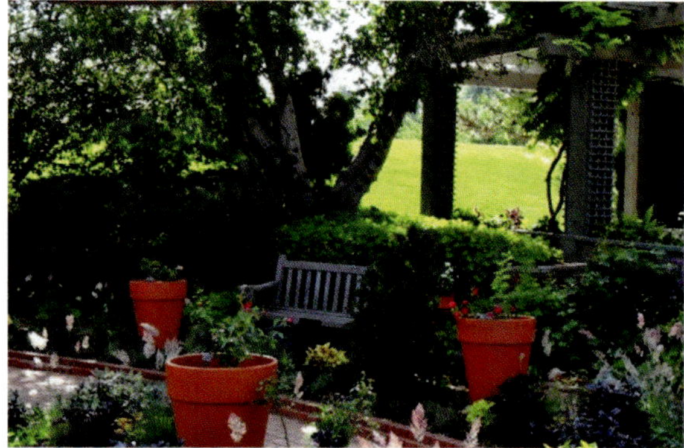

What a difference a simple unconventional tool makes, huh?

Make sure the diffuser cannot be scene in the viewfinder. I also use my diffuser carrying case, with the diffuser in it, in lieu of lens hoods—it gives me more flexibility.

This is yet another way to use a diffuser as a backdrop

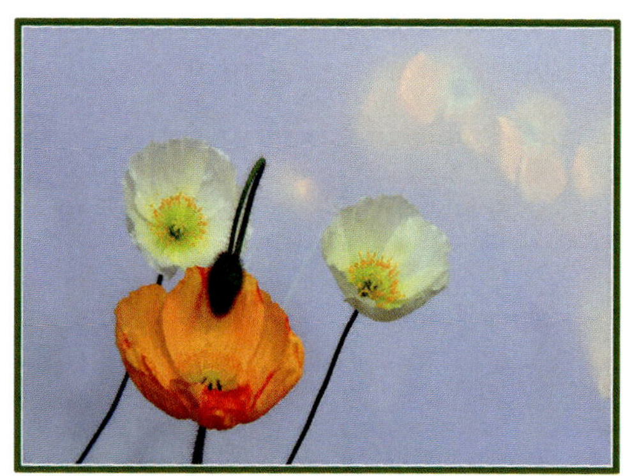

Exhibiting prints Vertical or horizontal? Sometimes I will get my shot horizontally, but know in advance or when I see it on my camera screen that it will look better shown or exhibited vertically. Not everything shot horizontally has to be shown horizontally. Being an artist means knowiing what works best. In the following example, the vertical rendition is more dynamic and powerful in terms of interest and intrigue. The same idea applies to images shot originally as verticals.

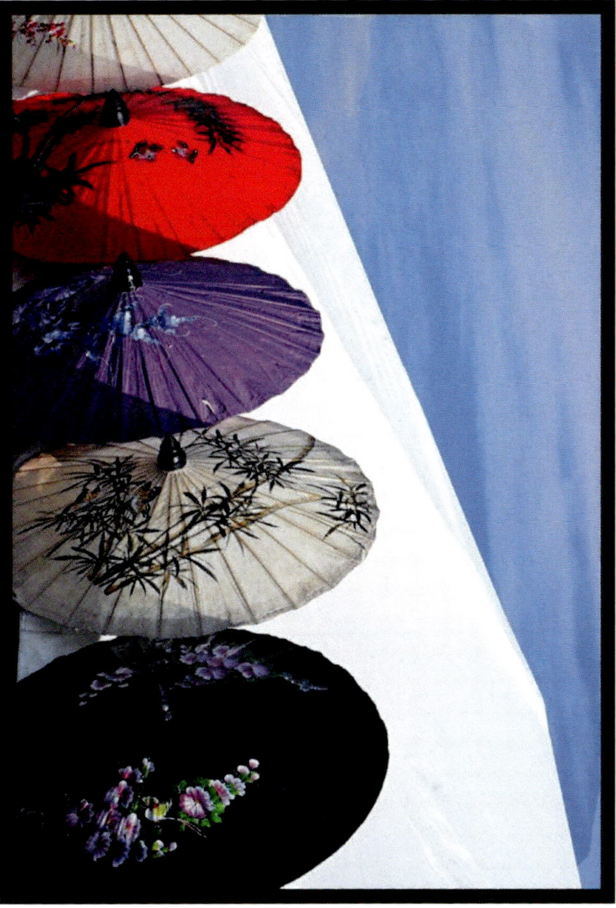

I call this piece “Detachment” because I detached myself from what they really were—just umbrellas hanging from a tent. Detachment also applied to the clouds and the tent, which I saw only as shapes and forms, not subjects.

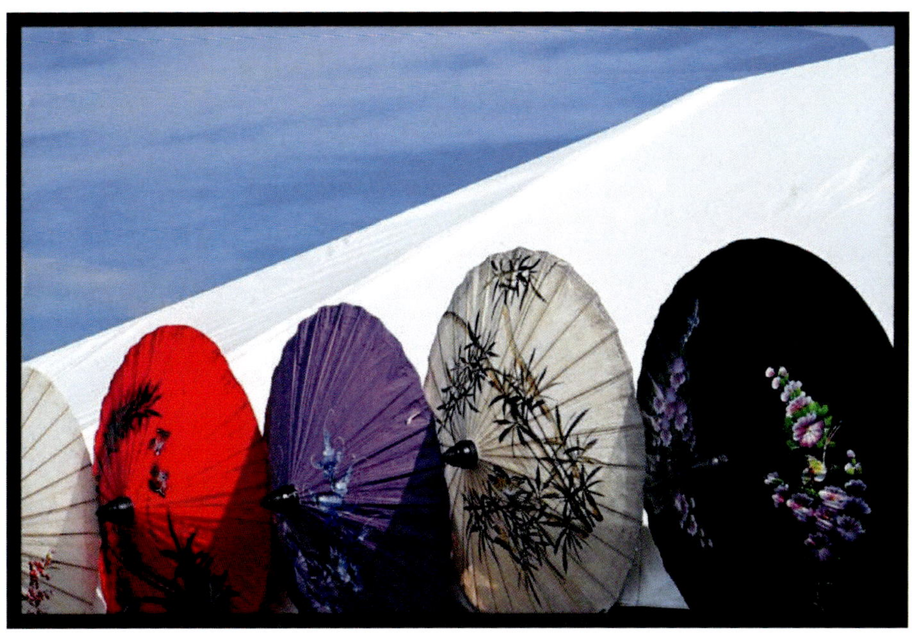

This is the original image, shot horizontally. It was just okay, but too typical.

Improvised backdrops. I mentioned diffusers earlier. I also carry all types of informal, non-manufactured tools to help me create what I want. Among the props I use is a small piece of black non-reflective material. In this next example, the natural background competed with my subject, thistles. They were camouflaged and just blended in with the earthtone background, until I placed the black material behind them as a backdrop. This was in mid morning, on a hiking trail in Boulder, Colorado. The black background made the thistles pop. Notice how simple this image is. We don't always have to include a lot of eye movement. Again, know when to alter the "rules." Sometimes less is more.

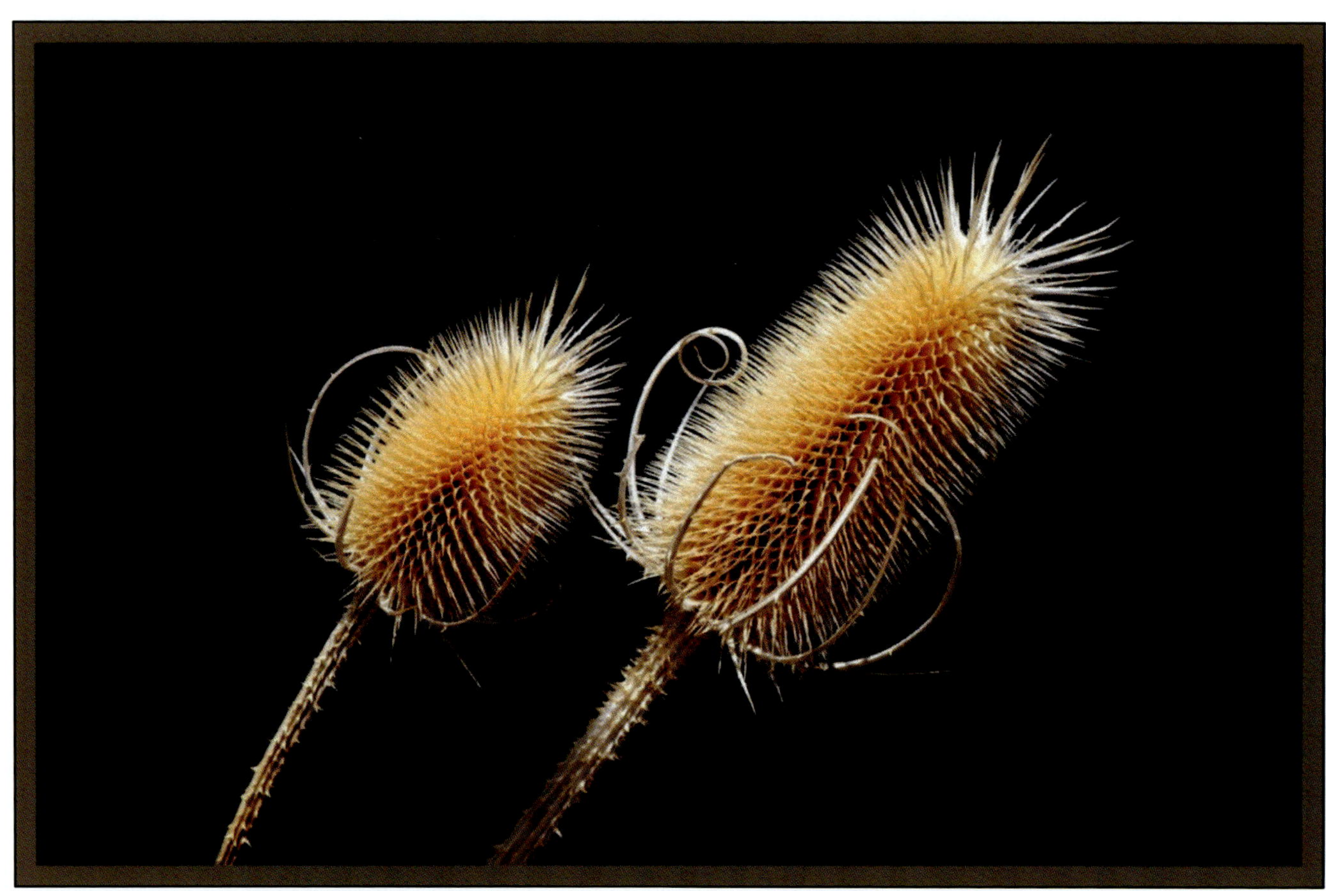

Zooming. This is an in-camera technique I have used for years. There are several variations of this, limited only by imagination. Here is only one example of what you can do.

I mentioned Ron before in my acknowledgements page. After spending a couple of hours photographing several of Ron's beautiful and ornate bass guitars, I was able to create several images, but this next one was one of my favorites. This is an example of yet another paint brush in my photography tool box--the use of black velvet material for backdrops, which I used for this image.

The lighting in Ron's basement was such that I had to change my White Balance to match the temperature of the lighting he had available. We spent some important time carefully setting up his bass guitar so it wouldn't fall off the makeshift stand—Ron appreciated that. After I got a couple of good shots, I looked at them and felt that I hadn't done enough. I had only created some really good images of a bass guitar. You know where I'm going with this, right?

I asked Ron to give me a little more time for this particular shot. He too is a photographer, so he knew that taking more time would pay off. My imagination took over. What would it look like if I....zoomed into it?

Here is the basic idea behind getting a shot like this. Get your exposure down first—make sure the lighting is going to look good. Then, during a several second exposure, click the shutter and wait a few seconds, then zoom in a little and stop, wait a few more seconds then zoom in again and stop, then wait it out until the exposure is done. You might have to do this two or three times, each time checking for what did or didn't work and try it again. This is a form of bracketing. This technique resulted in three separate images, each at different focal lengths, combined into one. It looks like a double exposure. This is right brain photography.

This is the result of my **zoom-n-stop** technique. Just like bracketing, it will take a few tries until you are satisfied with the way you want it to look.

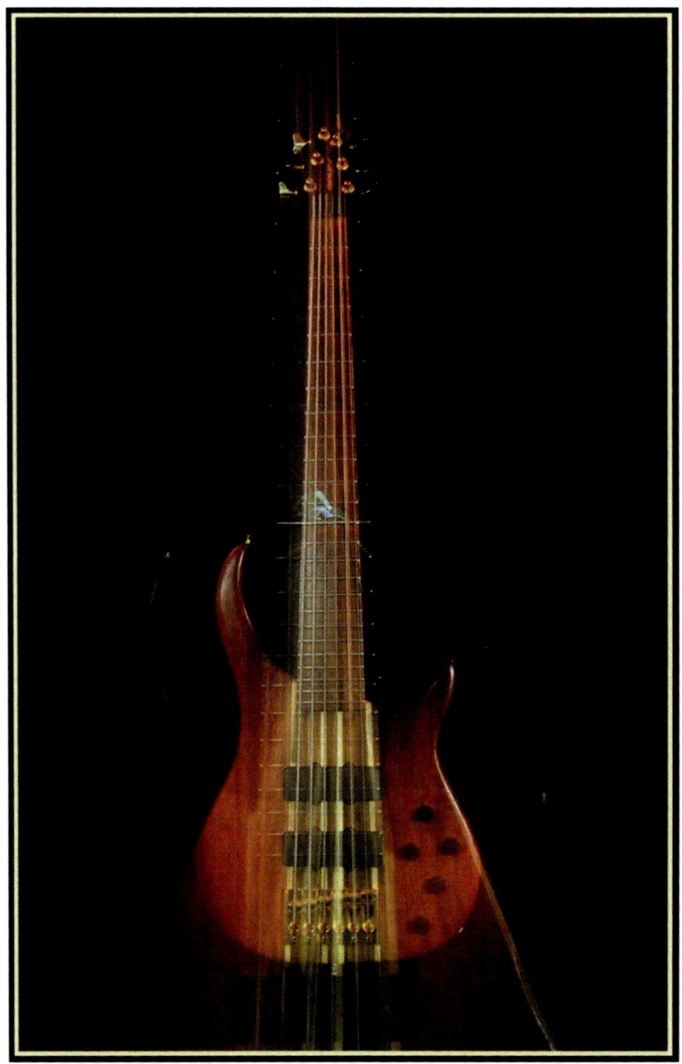

Use of flashlights. I have used flashlights and penlights to "paint with light." There are several techniques, and all are experimental because you don't know exactly how it's going to turn out until you try it. That's what makes it fun!

I used flashlights to create three images included in this book.

For this next example, I applied a technique that piggy-backs on the etymology of the word "photography, " which is "painting with light." This technique works best when there is no light shining on the subject. This red barn is in the countryside east of Eureka Springs, Arkansas. The owner was delighted when I told her I wanted to photograph her barn, but was extremely puzzled when I told her I wanted to photograph it after sunset.

I told my assistant to depress and hold my cable release down until I told him I was done. I then turned on my off-road emergency light and prepared to "paint." I started painting vertically along the backside of the barn first, then slowly worked my way to the front, hightlighting the area around the old exterior lamp at the top. After almost three minutes I had covered both sides of the barn. It took me about four tries to get what I really wanted.

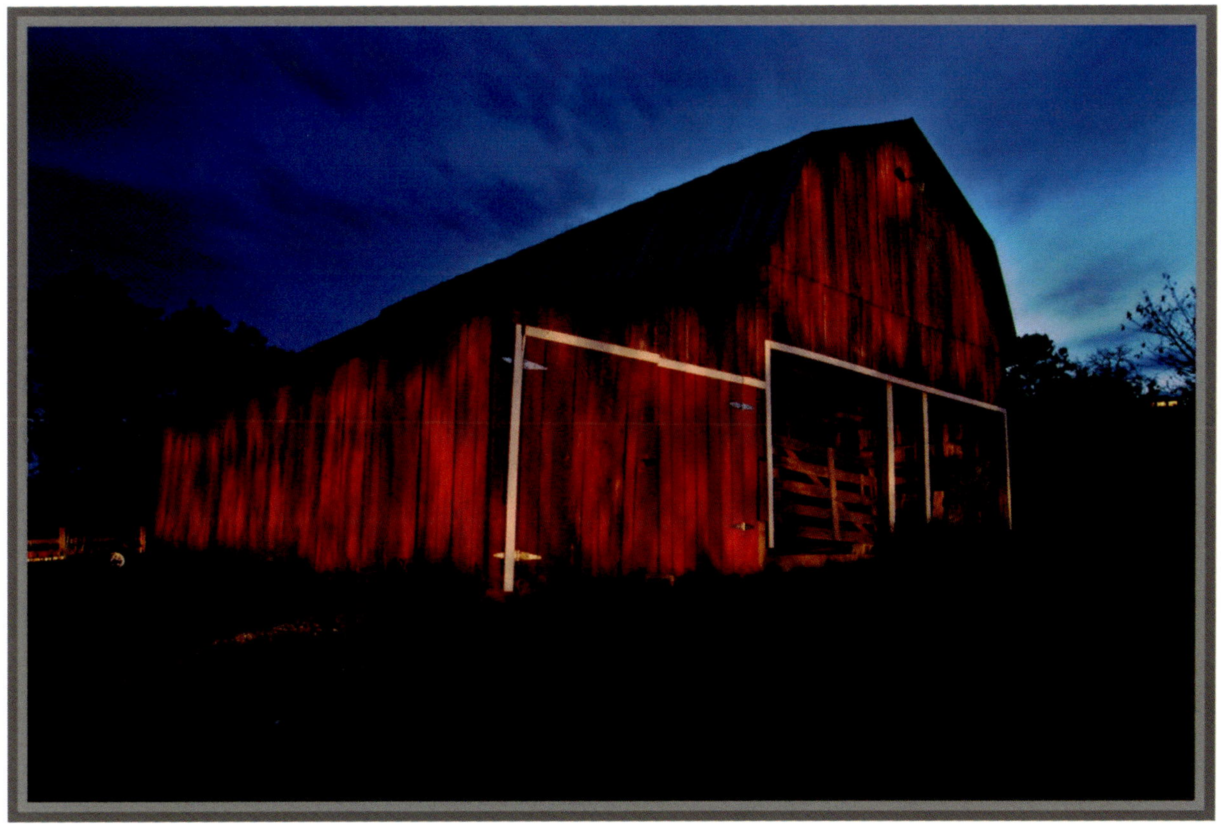

I hope that by taking you behind the camera has given you more insight, ideas, and understanding of the endless possibilities. It's okay not to have total control. Jackson Pollock, the abstract expressionist, once said he liked not always having total control.

SECTION VIII

OUT-TAKES (NO CLUES)

My goal for this last section is to take off your training wheels and test your know-how about everything I have covered in this book. No clues here. I will share several images, but will not explain anything about what I did to create them. You have not seen these images in sections I through VII.

Look at them carefully. Study them. Try to find as many concepts and principles as you can, especially as they pertain to these sections.

> **I.S.E.E. SOMETHING** (pp. 17-35)

> **ELI'S 5-POINT PHOTO ART MODEL** (pp. 38-70)

> **THE PHOTO IMAGE CREATION PROCESS** (pp. 75-114)

> **COMPOSITION** (pp. 122-154)

You can go back and review those four sections before you see the images, or review them as you study each image. Good luck with your scavenger hunt.

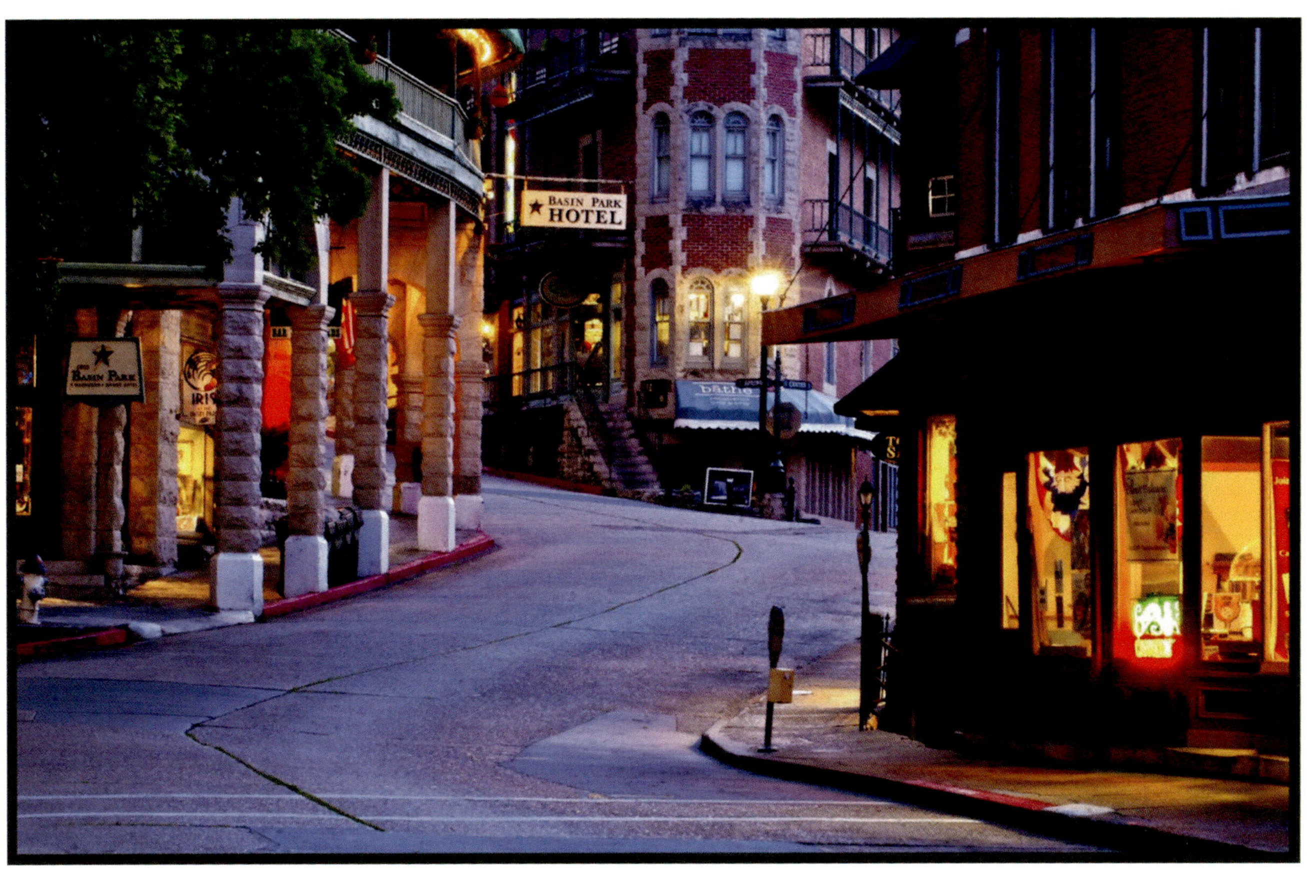

Downtown Eureka Springs, Arkansas

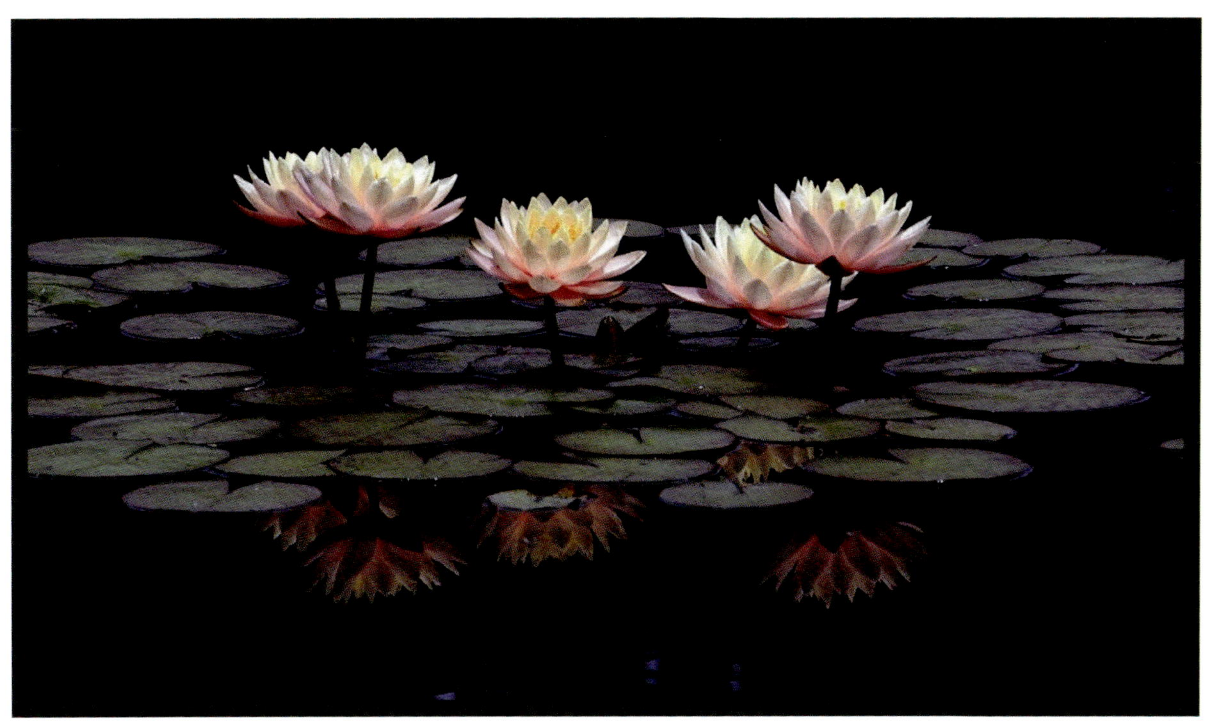

"Unfurled"

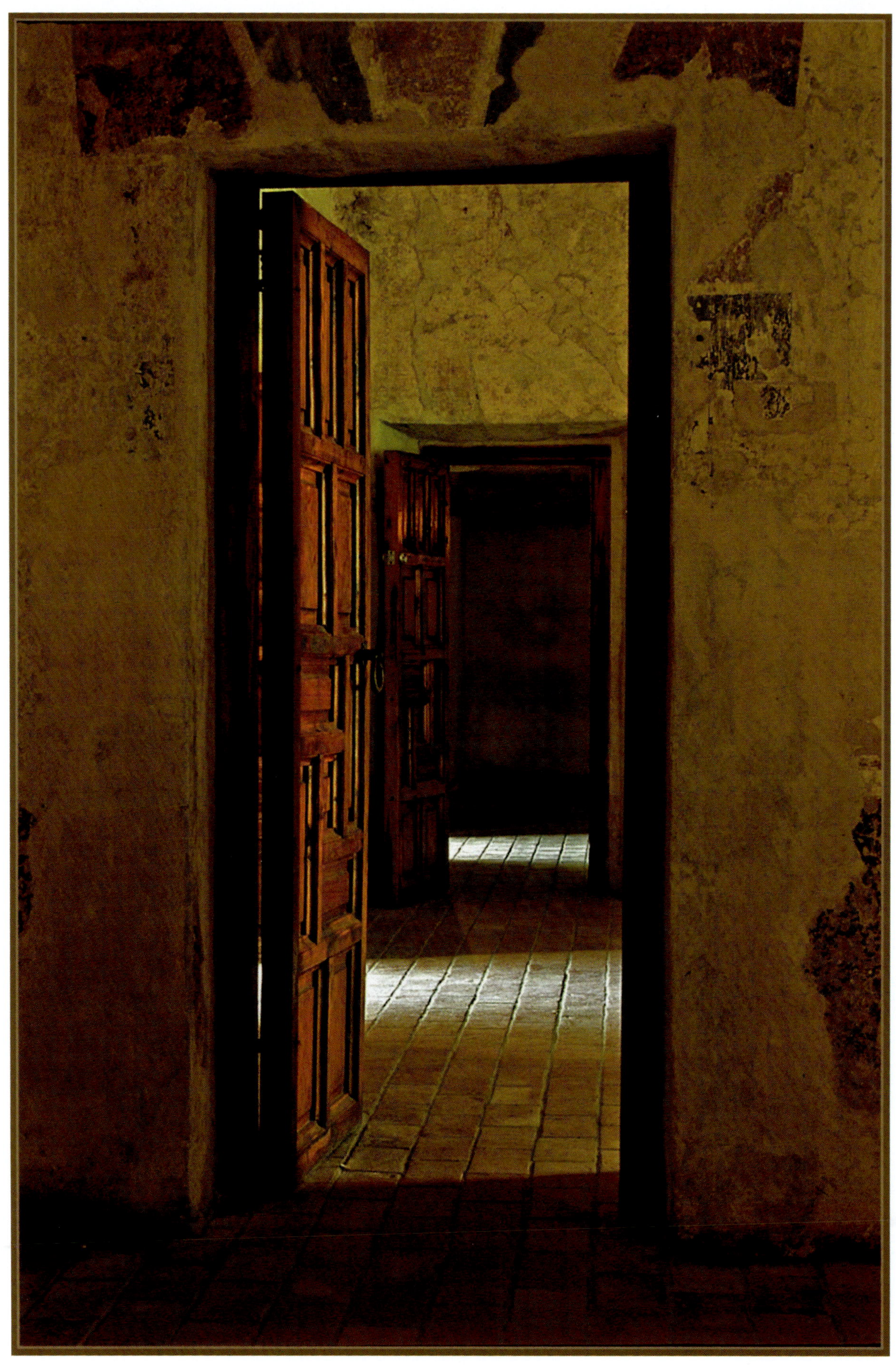

"La Luz de Concepción"

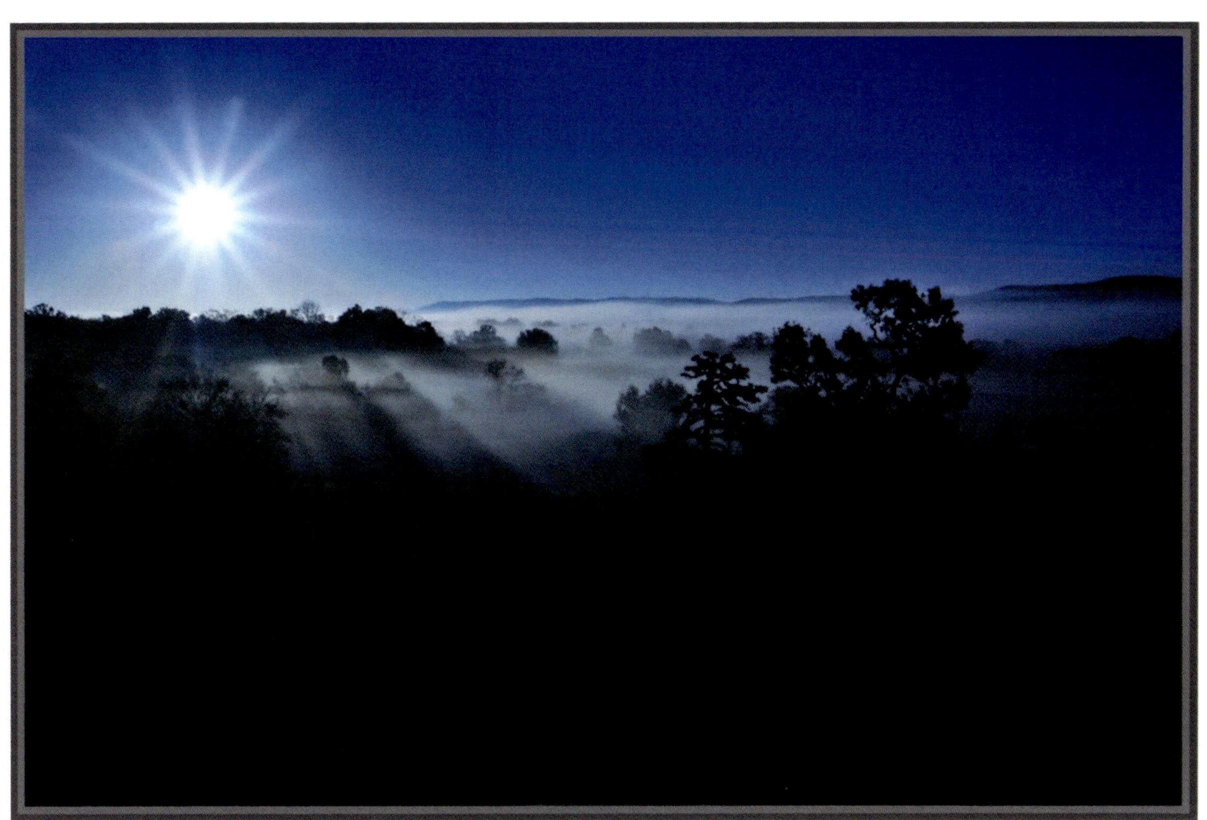

"Sunrise Over The Ozarks"

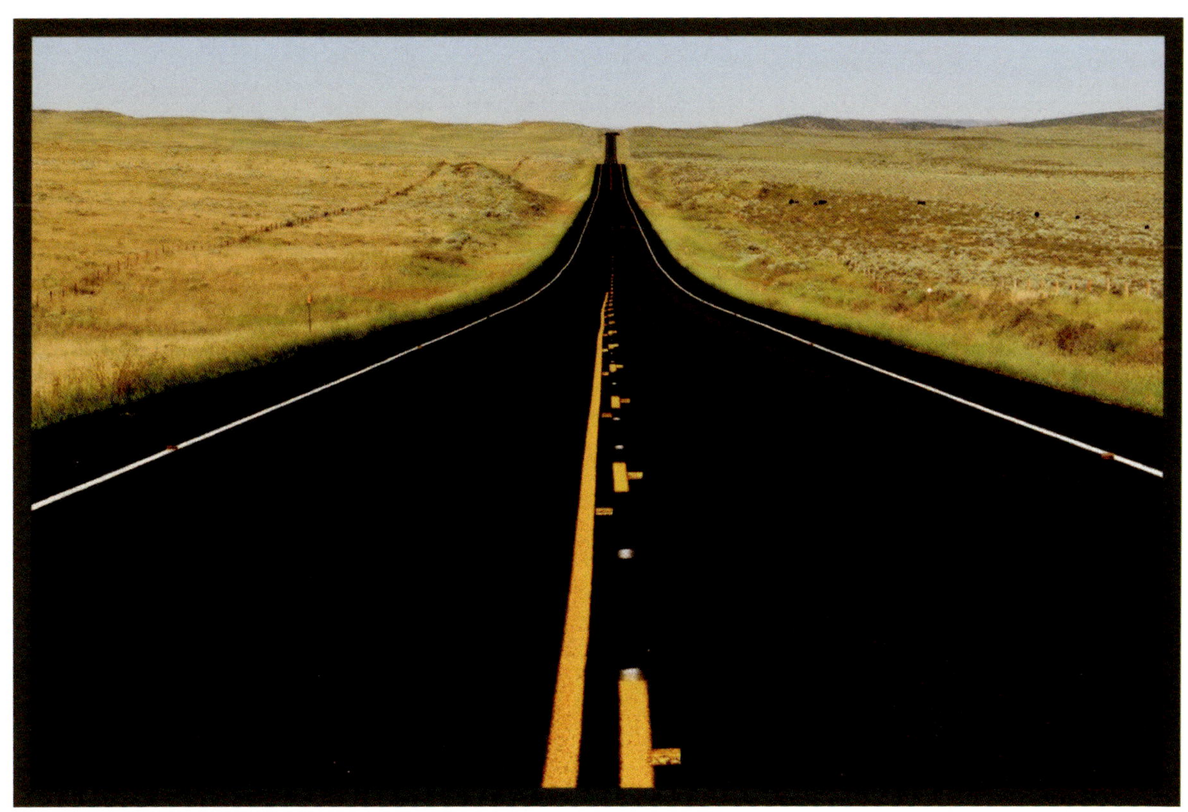

"Road to Somewhere"

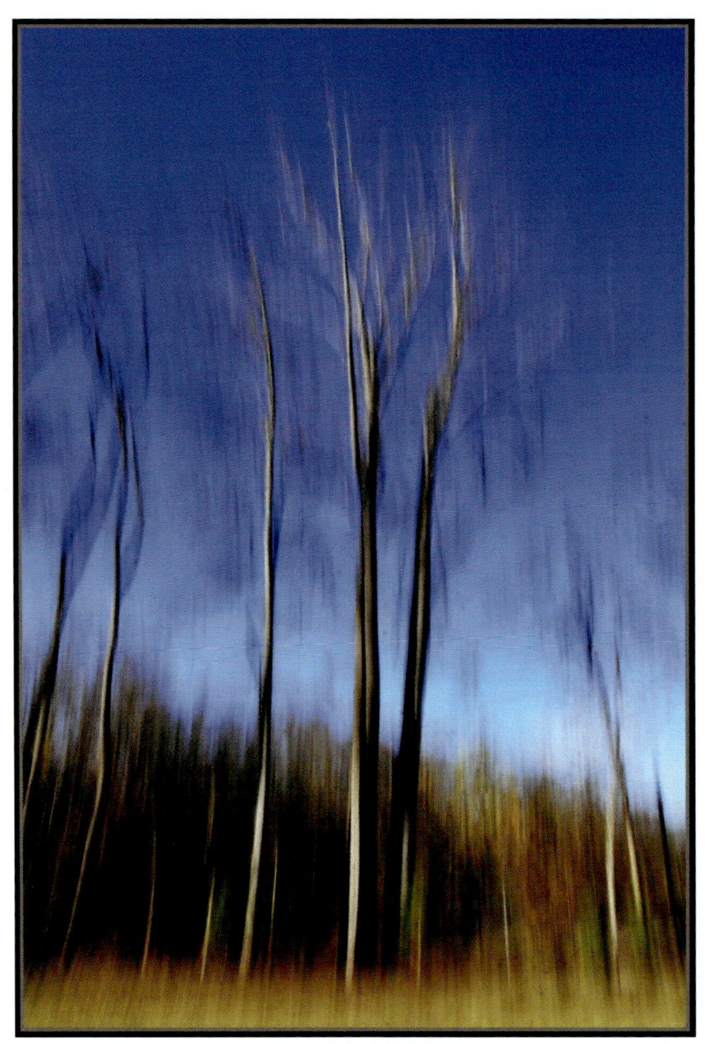

"Crystal Trees"

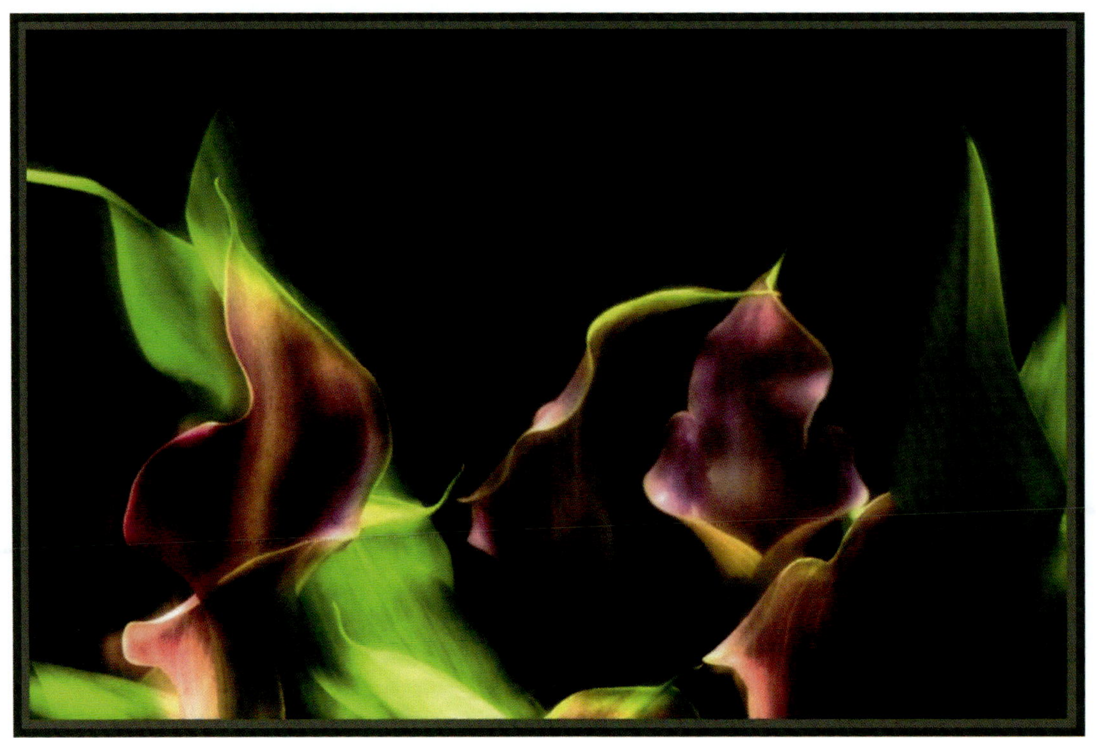

"Halo Beauties"

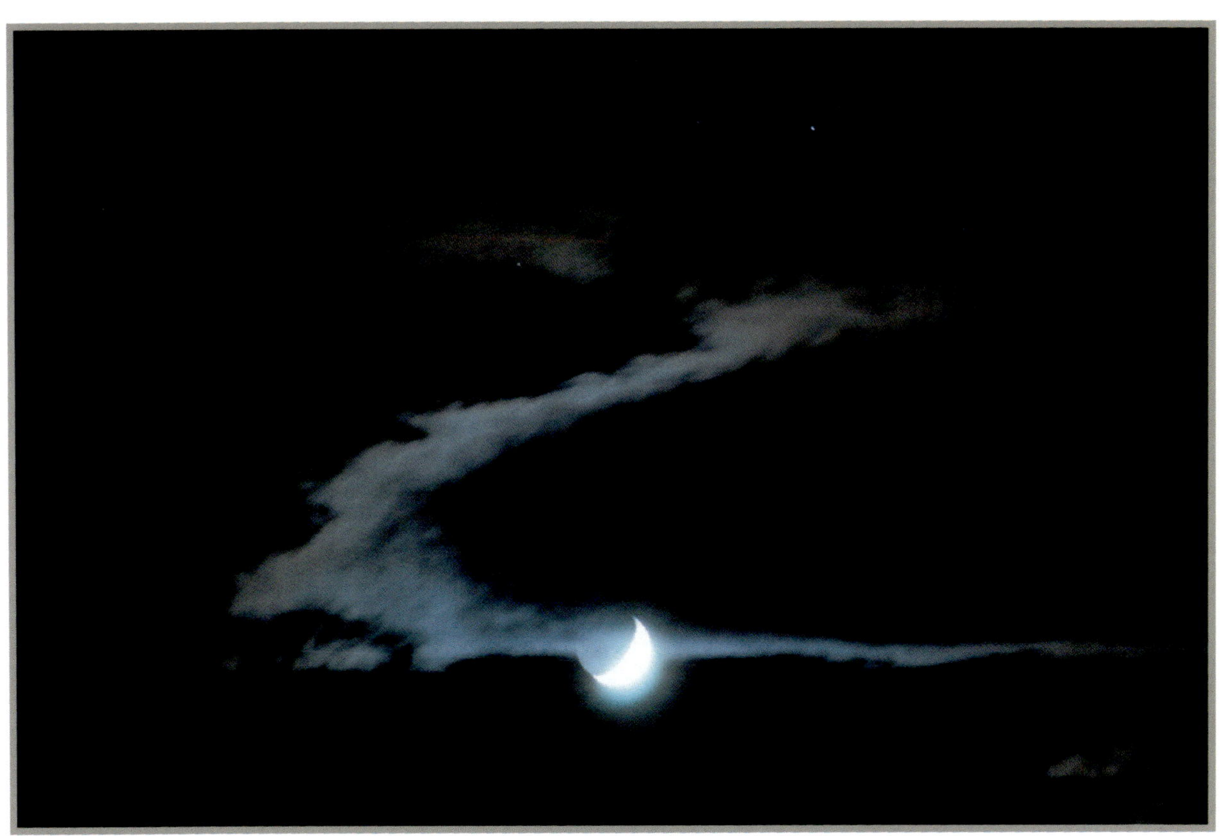

"Zorro Moon"

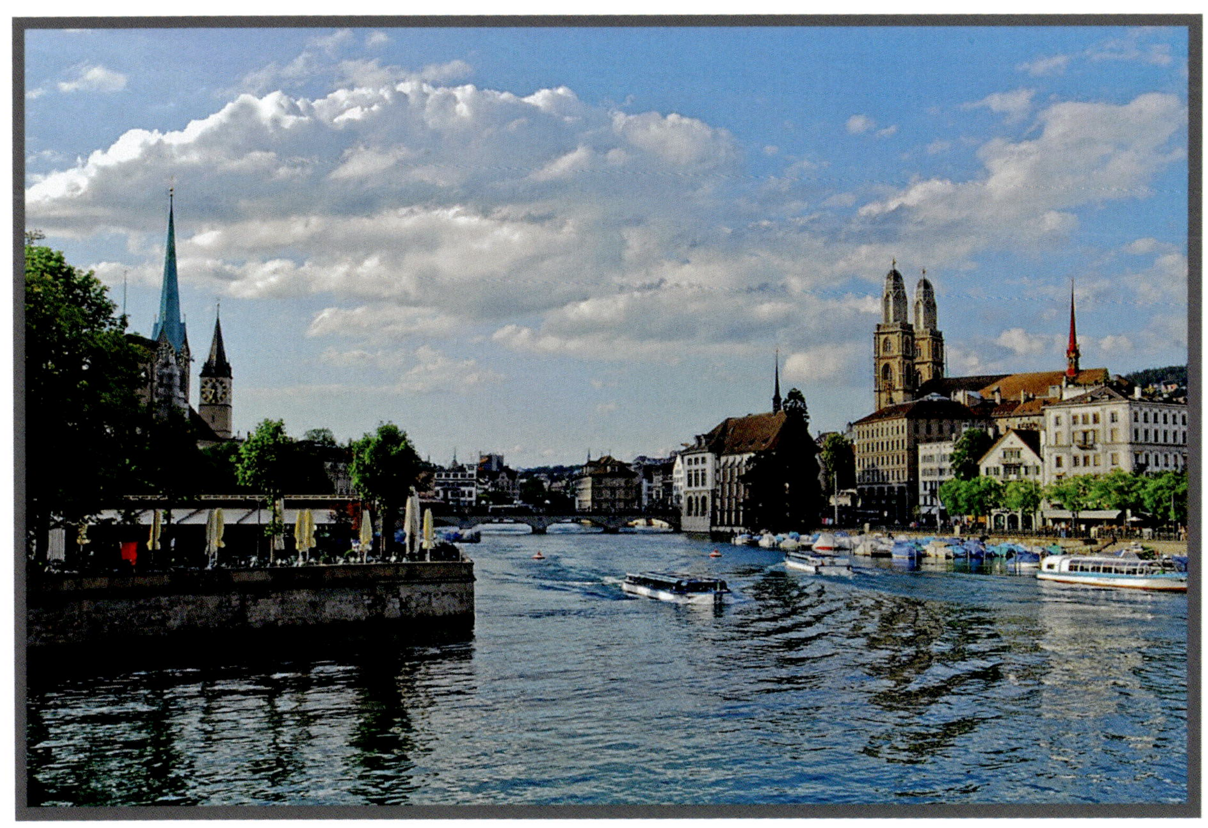

Zurich, Switzerland

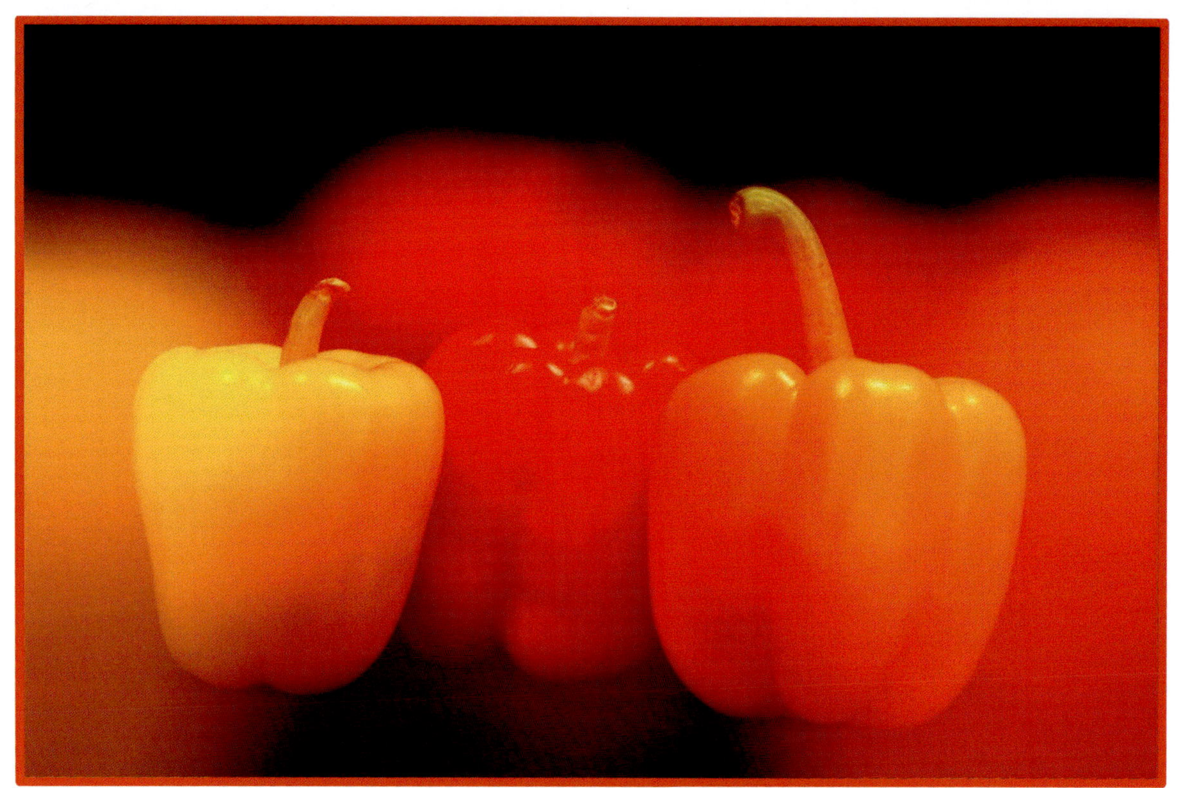

"Peppers"

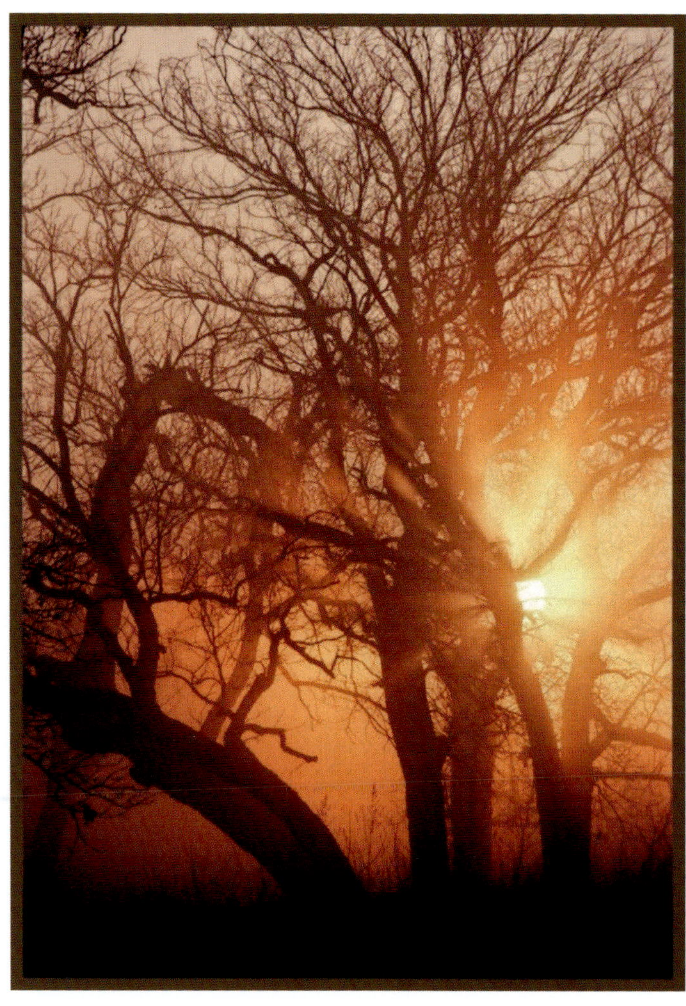

"Morning Has Broken"

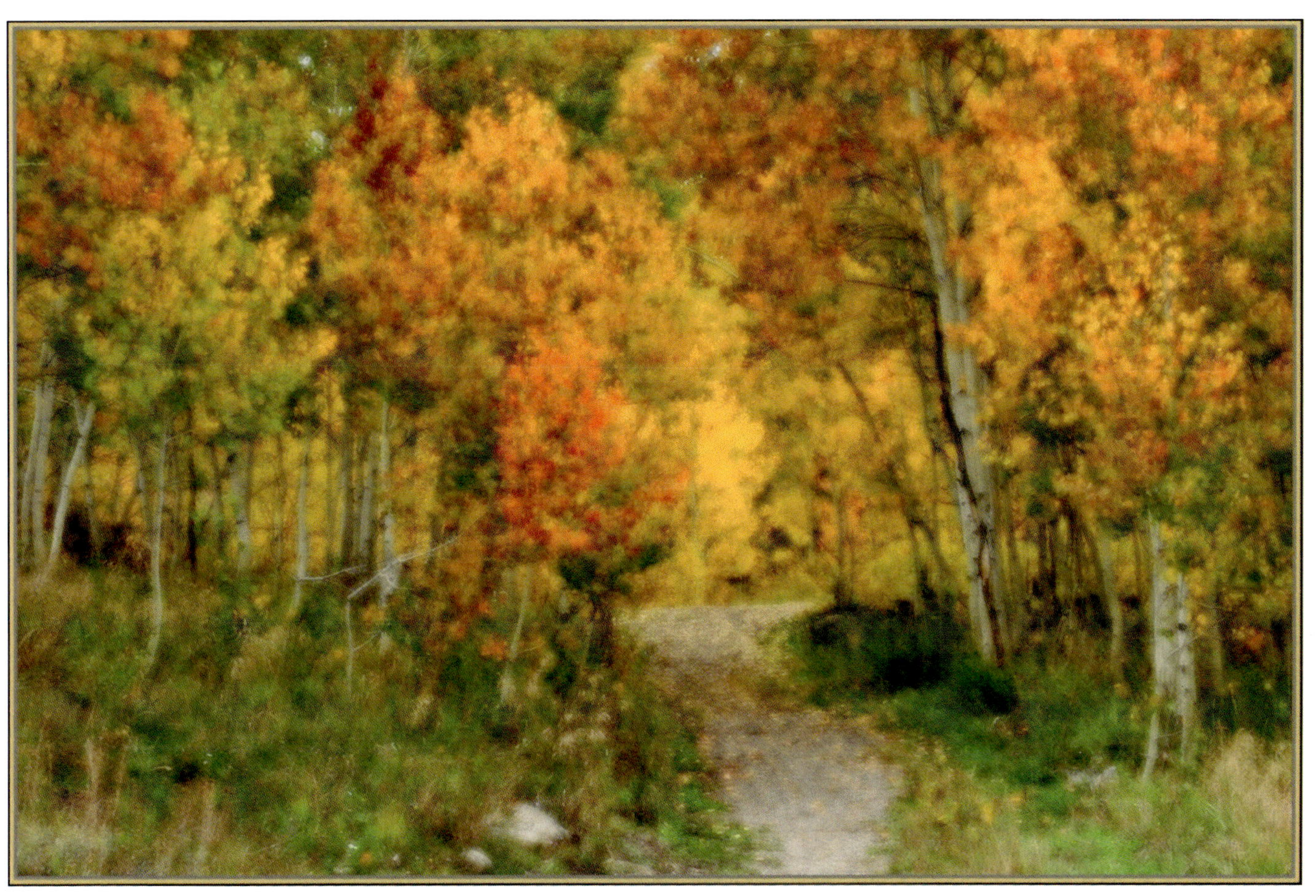

"Autumn Treasure"

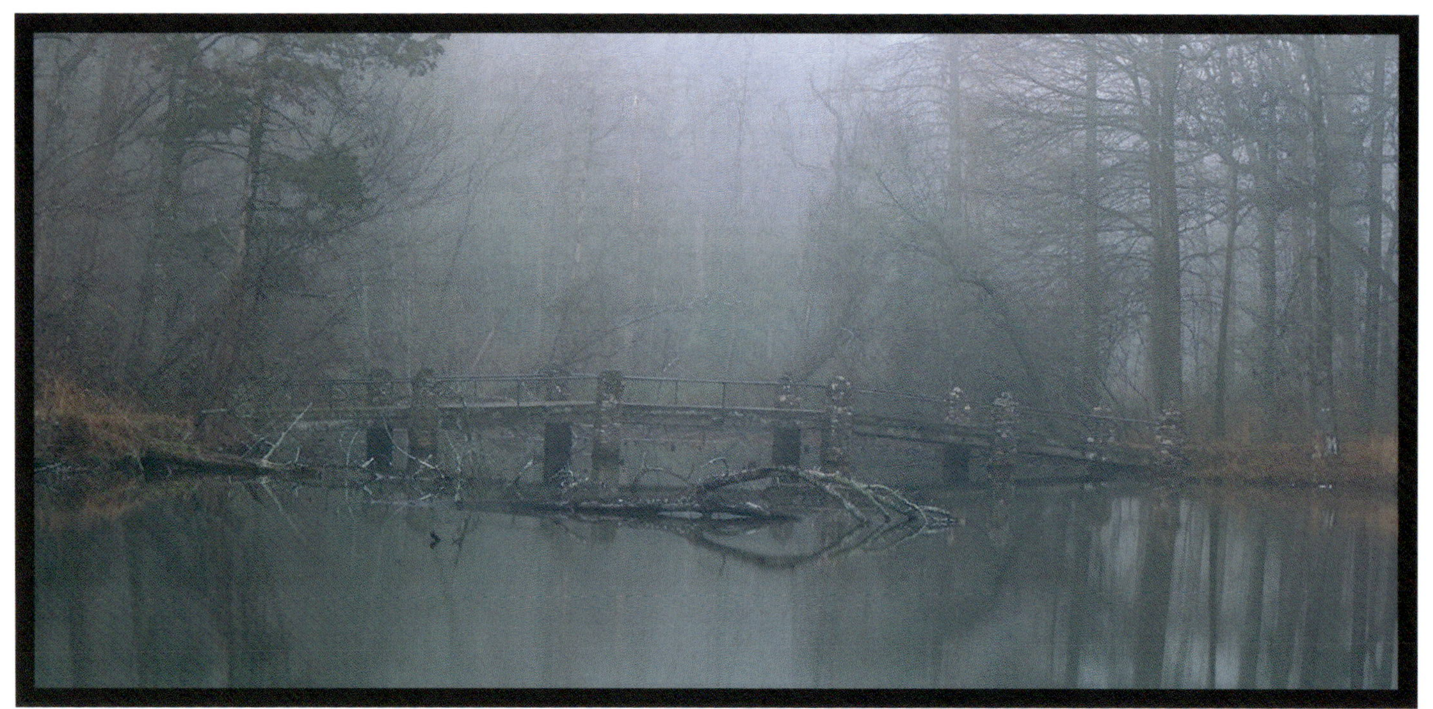

"Mindfulness"

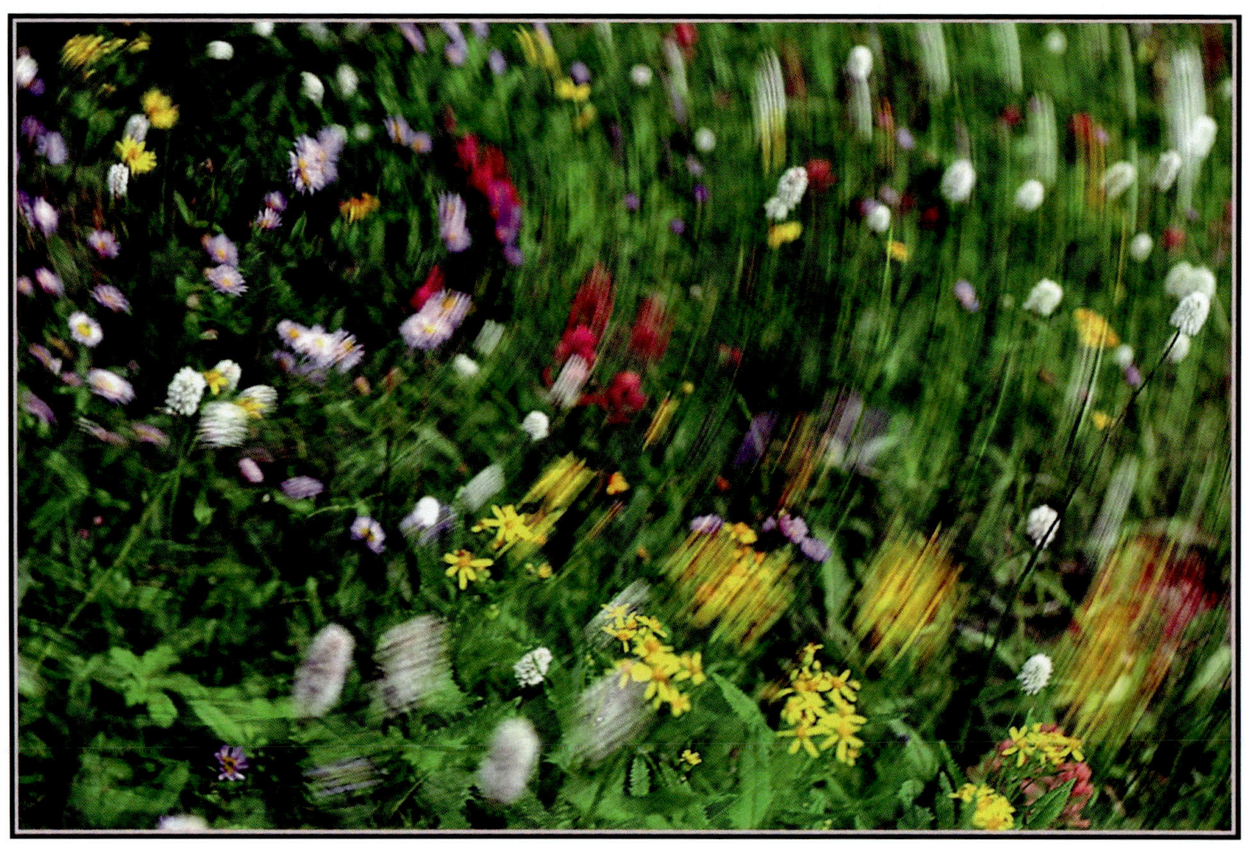

"Wilderness Wildflowers"

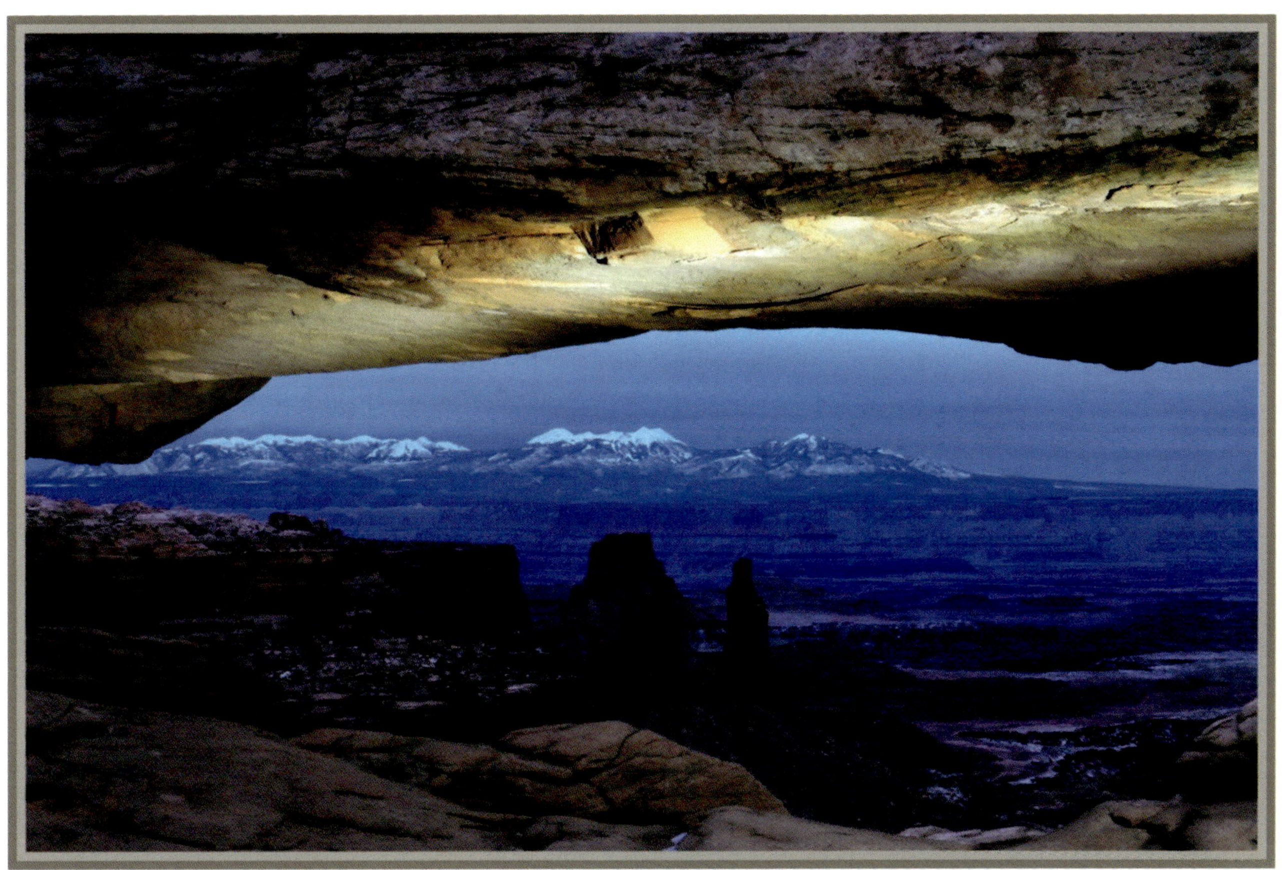

"Mesa Arch at Twilight"

Well? How did you do? I hope this last exercise gave you one more opportunity to review my right brain photography concepts and to connect the dots.

STUDENT EXAMPLES

I included this section to show you that it can be done. The following are examples of how my former students have applied right brain photography. They are not professionals, in terms of career choice, but their work is professionally done. Allow me to introduce their right brain photography. Enjoy.

I thank my former students Chris Roth, Joe Stanley, Theresa Finley, Bob Daugherty, Louis Brad, Ellen Thompson Champion, Cindi Ober, and Donald O'Connor for allowing me to share their art with you. I also applaud them for using their right brains and for using their imaginations while looking at life differently through their cameras. Great work, all of them.

If you are interested in contacting them, I have included a list of contributors at the end of the book.

Let's start with Chris. He calls this image "Lava Tubes."

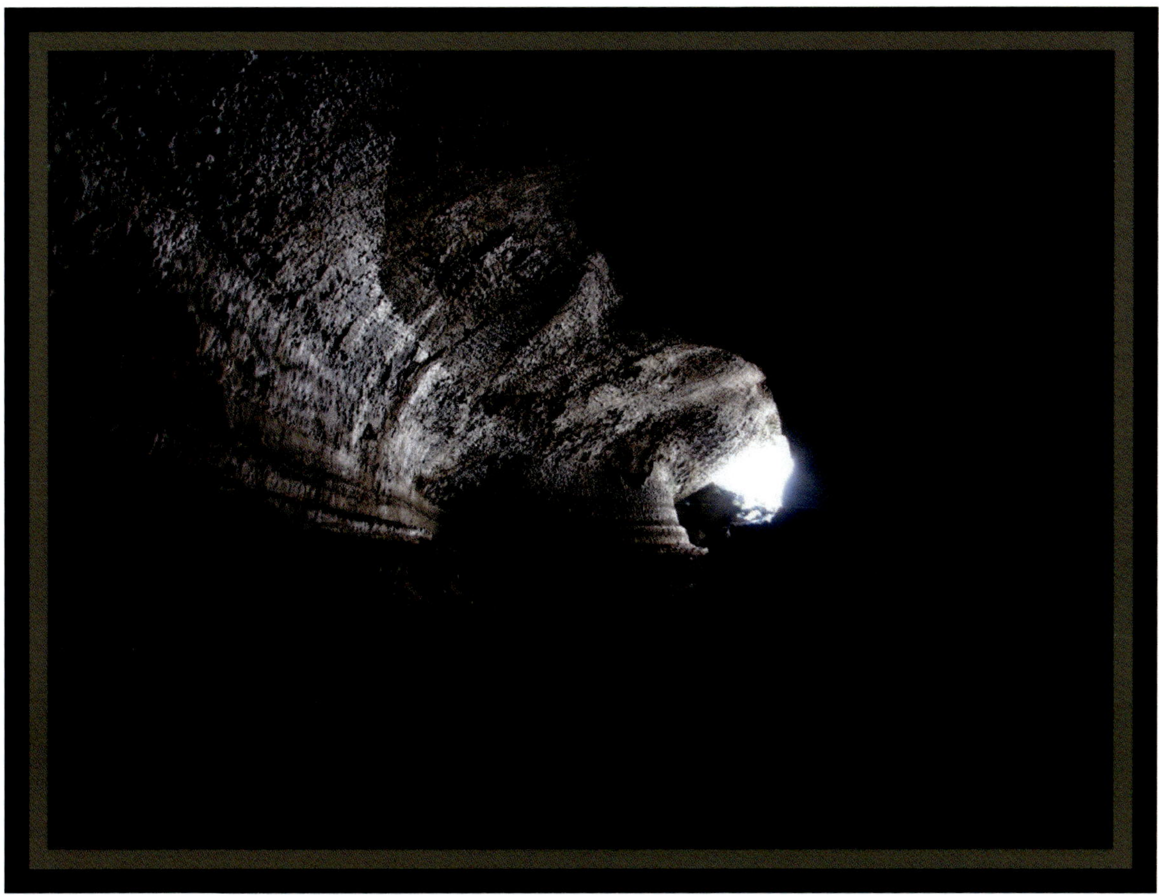

This is what Chris said about this particular piece. "This was taken at Lava Beds National Monument in Northern California, while I was exploring the many lava tubes there. This particular tube was unique in that it had a symmetry about it that was reminiscent of a man-made subway tunnel, with gentle curves, smooth walls, and what looks like a curb poured into the bottom 12 inches along the walls.

I was struck by this unnatural symmetry and the effect of looking from total darkness out into the light, so my intuition told me to get out the tripod and take a shot. The technique used from your class: Intuition – discovering the unexpected."

This image submitted by Chris reminds me that there is always a light at the end of the tunnel. The other connotation is that things might look dark now, but there will be light.

Joe short-circuited my brain when he sent me this mind twisting, surrealistic image. I'll let Joe explain what he did to create his "Lilies of The Night." I'll let you study it first.

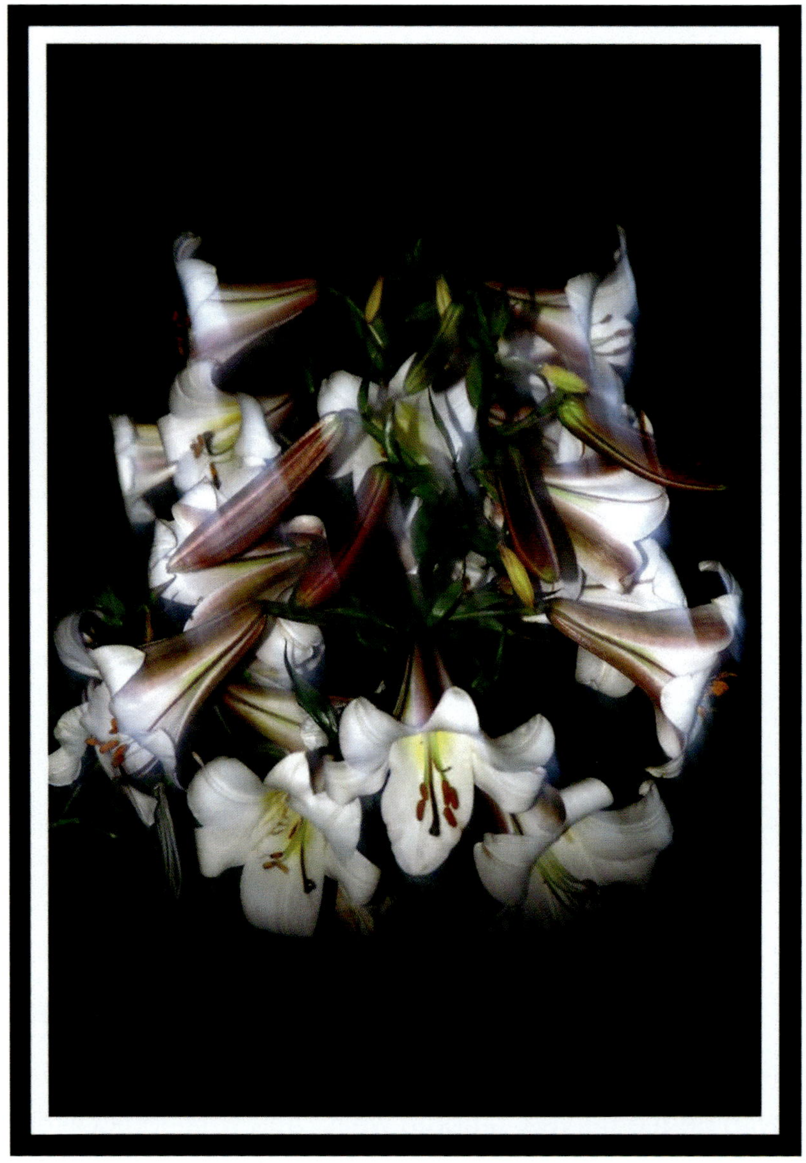

This is Joe's take on his own creation. "I remember two photos of yours that I have tried to emulate. One was Tulip Swirls and the other one was some white daisies that had some movement in it used as the 'tip of the month.' I have been trying several different methods to do something similar. Here is my result. I'm quite pleased with it. I wanted to have clarity, yet also have an effect of movement. It was photographed at night using a flash. I hand held the camera so that I could have slight movement as I shot it. I had a very slight motion of a downward swing as I shot with the movement just as the flash engaged. I have recently been trying to capture eye catching photos with a contrast that has my subject jumping out. I was pleasantly surprised with this result."

Theresa created this while in the middle of one of my right brain photography workshops in Rocky Mountain National Park. We were all awed by her creation. One of the other students told Theresa that it was the kind of image he'd like to hang in his home. I think he and Theresa are still working on that idea.

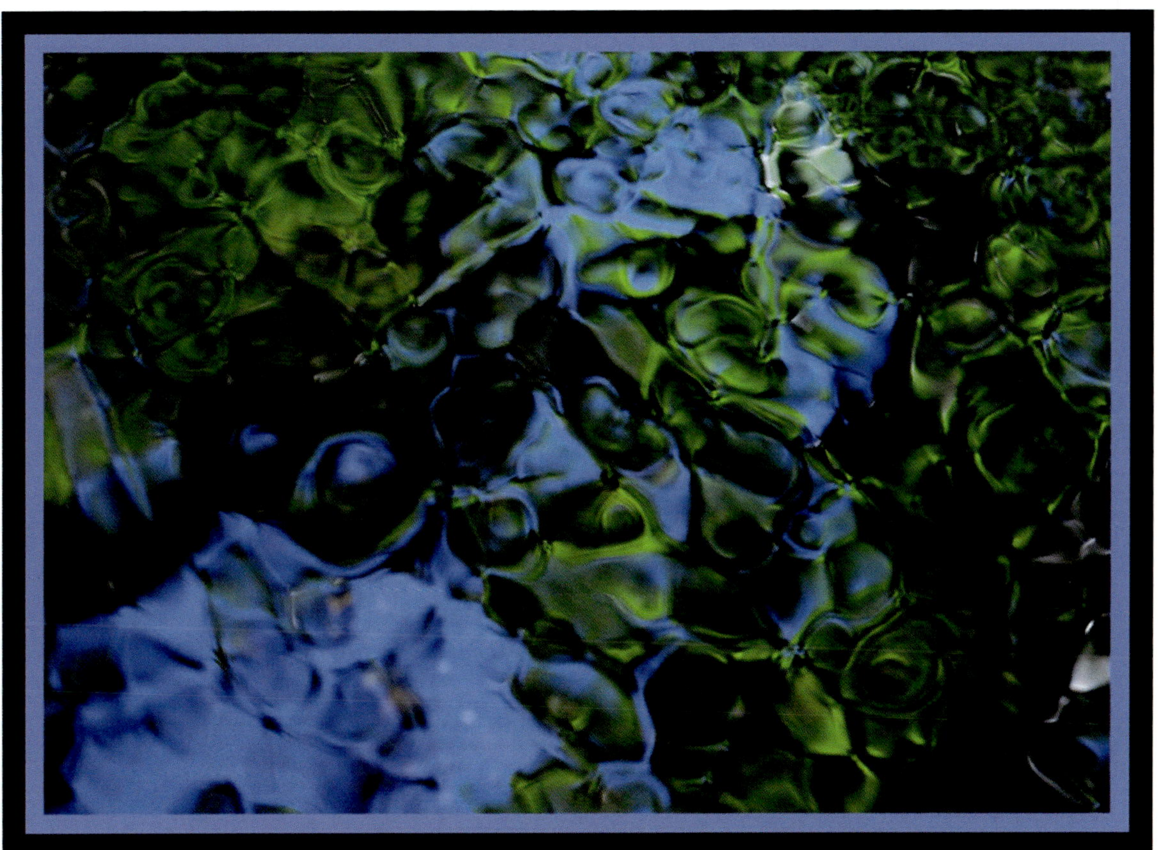

Here is Theresa's explanation of how she created her "Hidden Goblins" image. "This picture was taken while on a class in Rocky Mountain National Park called 'Right Brain Photography' with Eli. We were walking around Bear Lake when I noticed this stream was reflecting these really cool colors so I went to investigate. As I was bending over the pool of water I noticed some unique rippling effects. I thought to myself, I wonder what kind of picture I would get, and this is what I got. This picture is untouched I never applied any kind of post processing program to it."

Ellen was in one of my Rocky Mountain National Park workshops also. As we were shooting around beautiful Sprague Lake, I saw Ellen quietly walk away from the group, just doing her thing. I know from experience that sometimes just creating some space for ourselves can heighten concentration and focus. Well, she was definitely focusing, on this.

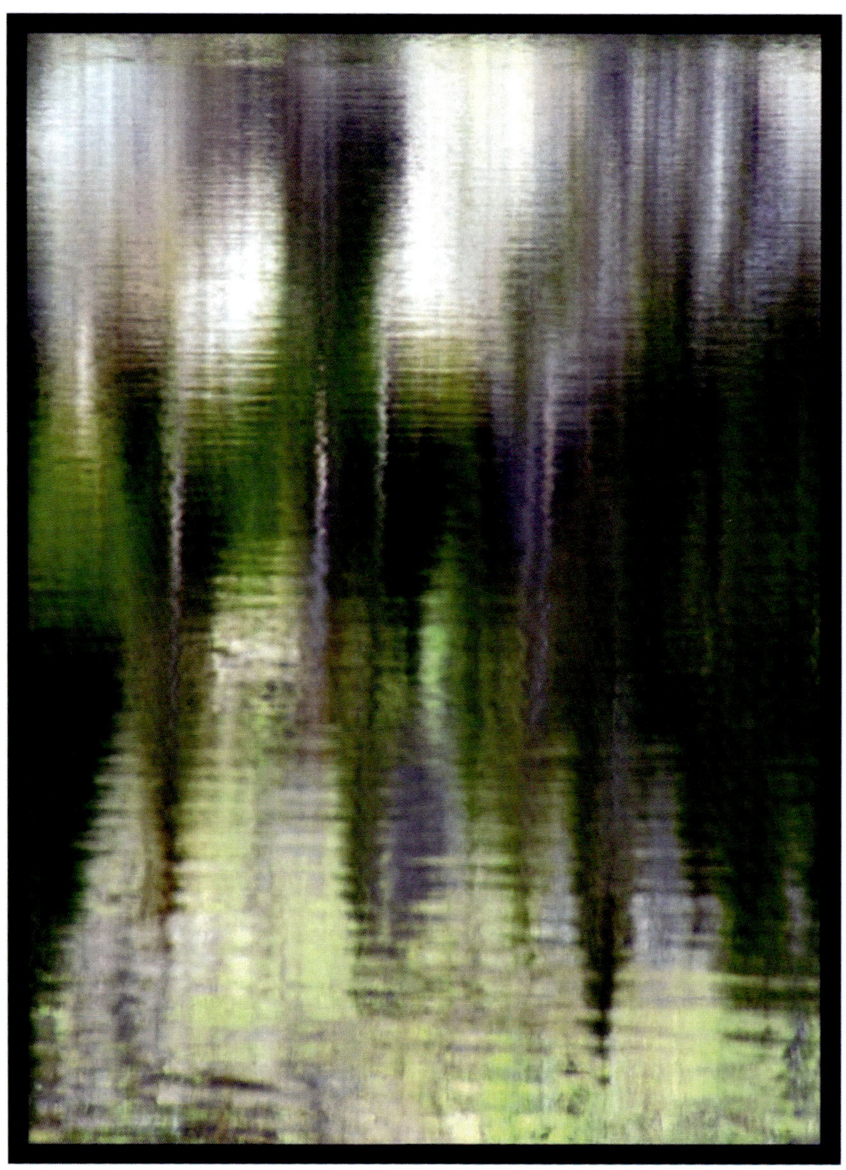

Ellen calls this impressionistic piece “Trees.” It gives you a hint as to what she was concentrating on. This is how Ellen describes the moment. "This image was taken in Rocky Mountain National Park, just after sunrise. The lake had been smooth and quiet, but as the sun came up, it started to have interesting ripples. The trees had such interesting reflections that I just had to capture some of them with my camera!"

Donald, who also attended one of my Rocky Mountain National Park workshops, came up with this nice ethereal image. Donald considers himself a beginner. He says he just started playing with a digital camera this year. At the conclusion of one my Rocky Mountain 3-day workshops, I went around the room, as I like to do during my training, and asked my students what resonated with them, what they learned, what take-aways they had to share. When it was Donald's turn to share, he got notably emotional and said he didn't really expect to get any good results with his photography. He then he added, "But I surprised myself." We all agreed that he had created some great images that weekend.

I want to share an image Donald created a few weeks later during his trip to Peru. It is very impressionistic, with a hint of detachment. I'll let him tell you about it.

You can see Donald's image on the next page. He calls it "Two Suns."

You don't have to try to be perfect, but be perfect at trying.

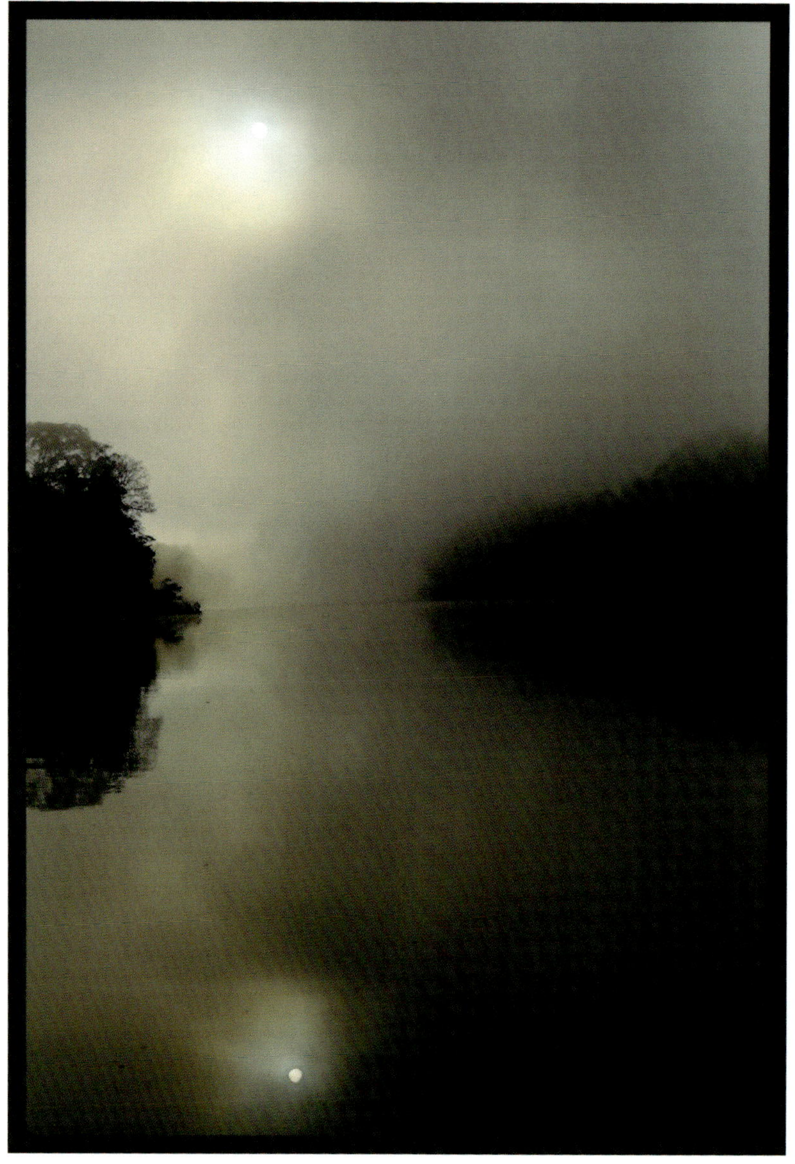

"It does evoke, to me anyway, a kind of other-worldliness which creates a sense of mystery. Interestingly, it looks like a black-and-white photo although it is not. The fog was so thick we could see very little; the objective of photographing wildlife seemed to be in jeopardy. There was no sunrise; it was obscured and I was disappointed that what might have been some beautiful sunrise shots were not to be. As time passed the environment became brighter but still indistinct. Then, the clouds thinned enough that one could determine a spot where the sun was visible. And then, for a brief moment, the clouds thinned enough that the sun was bright enough to create a reflection on the water. I captured only two images before the scene was gone."

I don't think Donald gives himself enough credit. He was dealing with impermanence. Shooting from a boat, he knew he had to think and work fast. He quickly changed his ISO to 800, which gave him a shutter speed of 1/800th of a second. His instincts paid off.

Do you remember one of my earlier stories, on page 53, about one of my students who photographed simple wind chimes? That was Bob. He was in Grand Junction, Colorado. Struggling to find anything worthy of a photograph, he asked himself, "What would Eli see?" He kept looking and thinking until he came up with a creative idea--an idea that came to him as he saw simple wind chimes swaying in the breeze in the backyard. This is what his right brain created. He calls his creation "Wind Chimes In Motion."

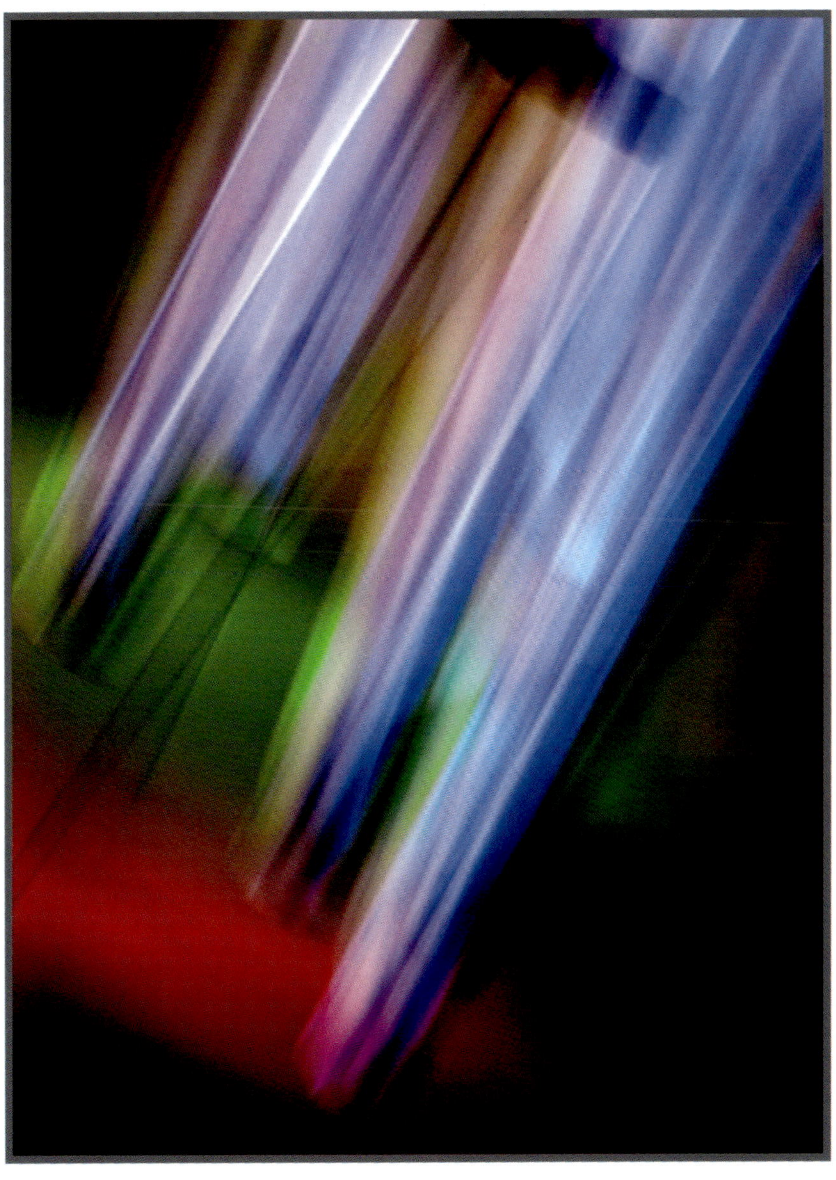

I was watching Cindi during one of my workshops as she tried to get her image. She was applying scanning, extracting, and detachment around Nymph Lake in Rocky Mountain National Park. We were all amazed at her incredible ability to see something. She calls her image "At Peace." This is Cindi's interpretation.

"The wooden man looks like he's had a hard and sad life. He is ready to call it a day, and is saying, Now I'm at peace."

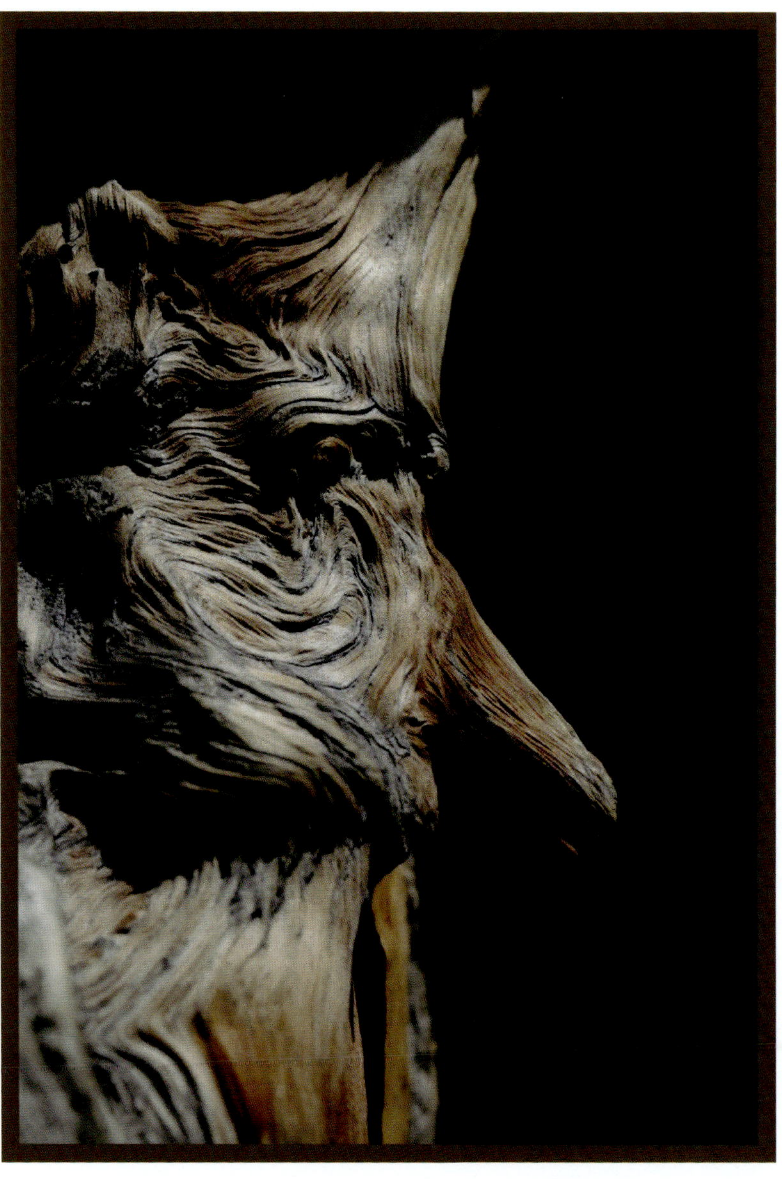

Lastly, we have this psychology quiz from Louis, who realized that having patience and detaching himself from a noun, in this case, a mini iceberg, led to a surreal-like image. The image is in color, but due to the relative lack of color in the scene, it looks like a B&W image. He calls it "One Drop At A Time."

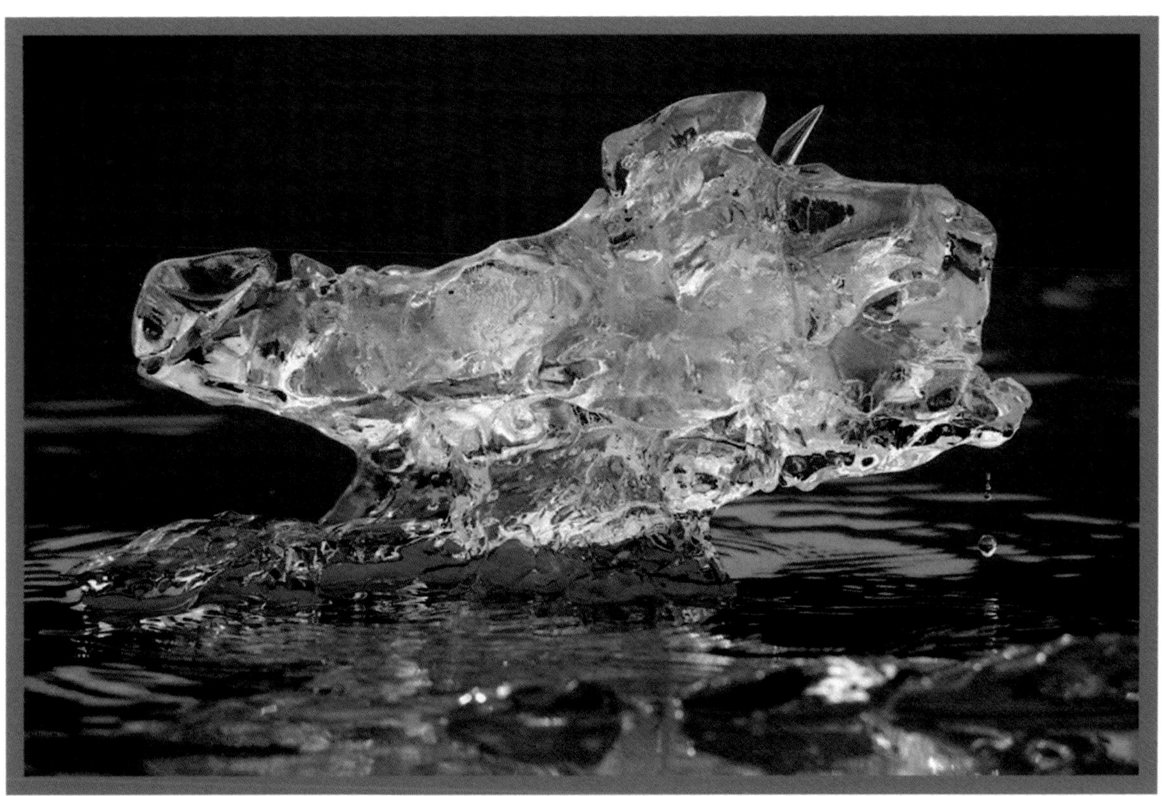

Here is how Louis described his photo experience in creating this image.

"If I had to pick one aspect of Right Brain Photography I had in mind when I was shooting this, it would be impermanence. This image was taken in July at Iceberg Lake in Kachemak Bay State Park in Alaska. It was an overcast day, and not too warm. I became fascinated with the pieces of ice, all different shapes, and with the drops falling off of them. I was seeing different images in the ice (my own personal Rorschach test, I suppose), and loved the drops of water coming off the side of this one particular piece. My goal became to try and get a photograph and catch the drops in mid-air. At first I didn't think it would be too difficult, but it did take a while and many tries to accomplish the task. Once I had the image on the computer I went even further in my mind and began to see all sorts of images in the ice. So this became a favorite image for me because of the challenge, the thought process, the ability to have the final image continue to transform in my eyes long after I've taken it, and just the plain fun of getting it."

I did not include much left brain information about the images created by my students. Every image creation will require a different lens, a different f/stop, a different shutter speed, ISO, and other settings. We need to ask ourselves my trademark question, "What do I want this to look like?" Our right brain will then shake hands with the left brain and say, "This is what I need from you." The right brain is the "what." The left brain is the "how."

Artists who paint on canvasses visualize how they want their final piece to look. They slowly and patiently think about what they need to do in order to create what is in their imagination. Think like an artist. Be an artist first.

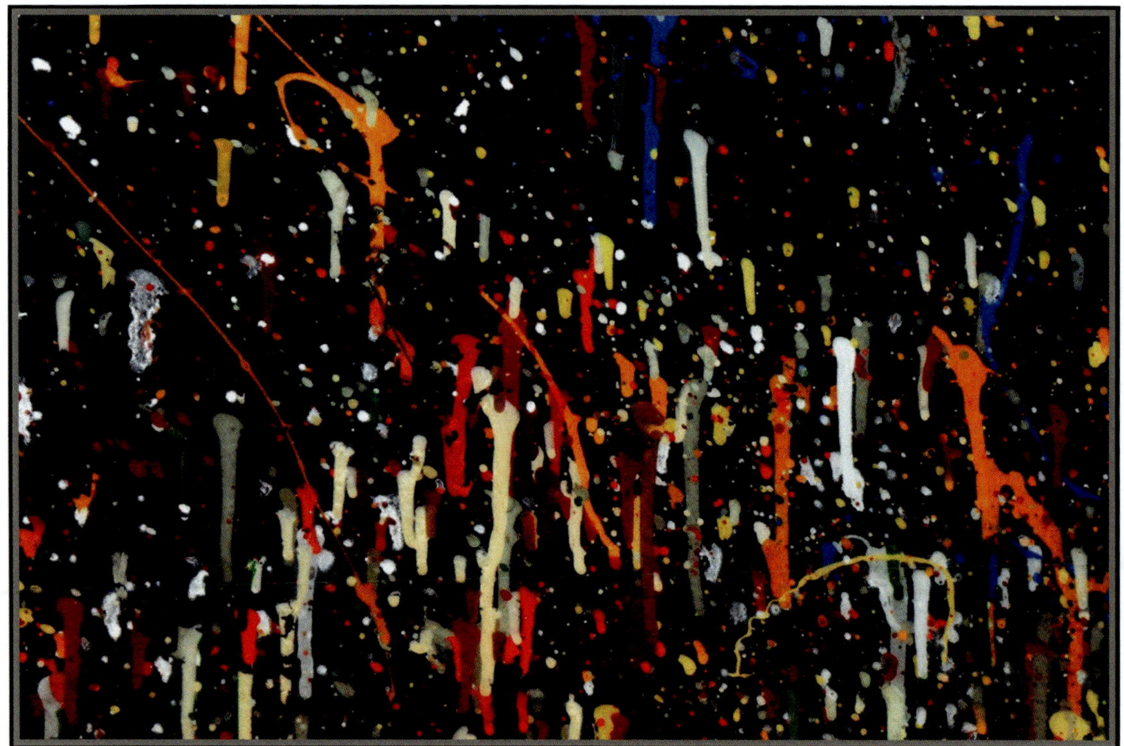

Dried paint on a weathered window

RIGHT BRAIN PHOTOGRAPHY---IN CONCLUSION

I don't "take a picture" and use it as my starting point, from which I create my images. Life and the world around me are my canvas, *my* starting point, from which I create my images.

Use your left brain only to help your right brain with what it needs. Create your personal interpretation; your translation of what you see.

What the eyes see is limited. What the imagination can see is endless.

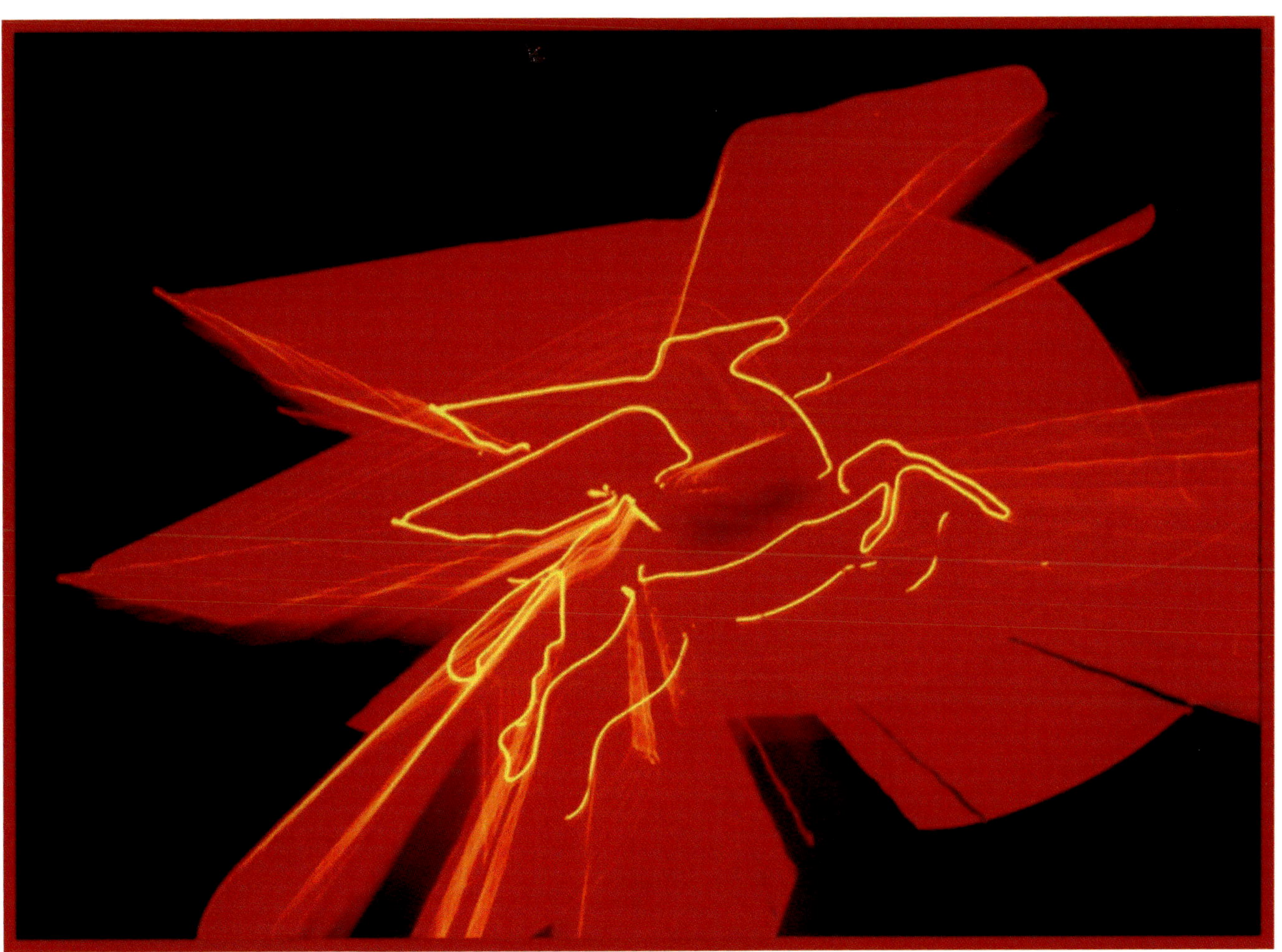

"Pegasus In Flight"

I have given you a lot of food for thought to help you explore all the possibilities for yourself. Now, go out there and exercise your right brain! Have fun with it.

ADDITIONAL REFERENCE NOTES
ON NEXT TWO PAGES

LEFT BRAIN & RIGHT BRAIN CHARACTERISTICS

In which hemisphere do you find yourself?

Circle the words or phrases that best describe *you*. Ask someone who knows you well to do the same, and then compare the two lists. Do both of you see *you* the same? Are you mostly left brain, mostly right brain, or a combination of both?

LEFT BRAIN (Linear thinking)	RIGHT BRAIN (Holistic thinking)
*Methodical *Analytical *Perfectionist *Sequential *Rational *Logical *Scientific *Mathematics *Judging (right/wrong; good/bad) *Strong ego *Stay a path (conventional; security) *Detail oriented	*Artistic *Creative *Intuitive *Instincts *Okay to show emotion *Perceptive *Musically inclined *No artificial boundaries *Open to new possibilities *Right here, right now (in the now) *Sensing *Feeling *Welcome change *Adventurous

How much of each hemisphere do you have?

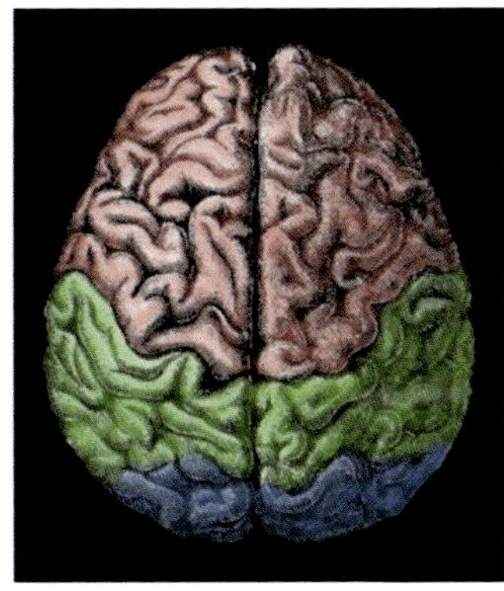

The best photography is found where technical know-how (left brain) and creative aesthetics (right brain) meet.

RELATIONSHIP BETWEEN F/STOPS, SHUTTER SPEEDS AND ISO

There is an inverse relationship between f/stops and shutter speeds, as seen below. These are typical f/stops and shutter speeds. We begin with the assumption that we are shooting at ISO 200, our lens set at 70mm, and we are on Aperture Priority (AV).

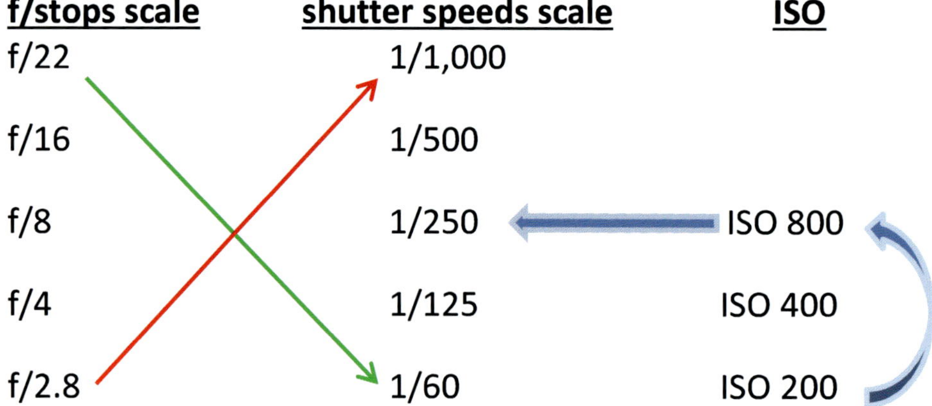

Green line =Our hypothetical starting point. Since we have a very small opening (f/22), it's not letting in much light. Our built-in meter determines that, given the lighting situation, it needs a slow shutter speed of 60, or 1/60th of a second in order to let enough light in to give us a "correct" exposure. Let's assume that "correct" is good enough.

Red line= This is what happens to our shutter speed when we change our f/stop. Since we now have a very large opening (f/2.8) that is letting in a lot of light, our built-in meter determines that it now needs a much faster shutter speed of 1/1,000 of a second in order to give us a good exposure. This is that inverse relationship.

Let's say that we want to keep our f/stop at f/22 to get good depth of field, but we need a shutter speed faster than 1/60th of a second. Enter ISO, or the sensor's sensitivity to light capability. The higher the ISO, the faster the sensitivity to light. In other words, as the ISO increases, our sensor needs *less* time to react to the same light, given the same f/stop. With our hypothetical scenario, if we simply change our ISO to 800 (4x more than 200), our shutter speed also increases approximately 4x, to 1/250th of a second. This is one advantage of digital cameras, especially when many of today's DSLRs can handle ISO 800, or more, extremely well--please check your camera manual to make sure that is the case for your camera.

This scenario shows that we can "have our cake and eat it too."

================ ==

HOW TO CONTACT ELI

Educational roots: Texas Tech University (BA) and the University of Utah (MS).

I Always Wanted To Be Somebody (But, I Settled For Much More: Me), a book about what you do when you don't know what to do. The first half is about Eli's life story, beginning with his birth in a railroad boxcar; the second half is about his life philosophy. Contact Eli to order your signed copy. He is currently its sole distributor.

Eli offers workshops, classes, 1-on-1 lessons, and presentations. He also has an extensive collection of stock photography, and is available for commisioned work—he can meet your communication needs through visual language. If you are a fine art buyer or collector, Eli offers a wide array of images as fine art archival prints.

For more information on Eli's photo services and fine art prints, scan this code.

www.elivega.net

BOOK CONTRIBUTORS

Ron Buckner— Photographer, and Bass player with Buckner Funken Jazz in Littleton, Colorado. bsix@hotmail.com. AKA (B-6) www.buckylove.com

Louis Brad – Contributing photographer from Boulder, Colorado. photovet@comcast.net

Robert (Bob) F. Daugherty-- Contributiing photographer from Longmont, Colorado. rfdaugherty@comcast.net

Theresa Finley-- Contributing photographer from Westminster, Colorado. theresa.f@comcast.net

Bo Jenkins—Artist from Hot Sulphur Springs, Colorado. 970-531-3737. obnone@me.com

Cindi Ober—Contributing photographer, Como, Colorado. einetma7@yahoo.com

Donald O'Connor-- Contributing photographer from Wichita, Kansas. dalor@netzero.net

Chris Roth— Contributing photographer from Littleton, Colorado. rothcp@gmail.com www.flickr.com/photos/104332824@No5/

Joe Stanley-- Contributing photographer from Highlands Ranch, Colorado. joerstanley@yahoo.com

Ellen Thompson Champion-- Contributing photographer from Boulder, Colorado.

Rico Vega—Cover layout design, Lubbock, Texas. www.ricovega.com

Chula Walker-Griffith-- Artist, Steamboat Springs, Colorado. "Rainforest of Gabon" mural in restroom.

INDEX

S

T

U

V

W

Z

TITLED IMAGES

CHALLENGE ASSIGNMENTS & EXERCISES